10/03

THE DESERT READER

THE

DESERT
READER

A LITERARY COMPANION

EDITED BY

GREGORY MCNAMEE

UNIVERSITY OF NEW MEXICO PRESS ■ ALBUQUERQUE

Library of Congress Cataloging-in-Publication Data

Sierra Club desert reader.
    The desert reader : a literary companion / edited by Gregory McNamee
    p. cm.
    Originaly published: The Sierra Club desert reader. San Francisco : Sierra Club
Books, c1995.
    Includes bibliographical references.
    ISBN 0-8263-2984-5
    1. Deserts 2. Deserts—Literary collections. I. McNamee, Gregory. II. Title.
    GB612 .S54 2003
    910'.02154—dc21

                                                            2002035996

*We simply need to see . . . wild country
available to us, even if we never do more than
drive to its edge and look in. It can be a means of
reassuring ourselves of our sanity as creatures,
a part of the geography of hope.*

WALLACE STEGNER

*And yonder all before us lie
Deserts of vast eternity.*

ANDREW MARVELL

ACKNOWLEDGMENTS

"Of the making of many books there is no end," says the poet of Ec-clesiastes. In making this book, I had no end of help from many friends. I want especially to thank William Aylward, my research assistant, for his tireless work; Jim Cohee, my editor at Sierra Club Books, for his encouragement and friendship; and Melissa Mc-Cormick, my wife, who read this manuscript carefully and who otherwise lovingly helped along still another book.

For offering advice and support, I thank: Caroline Alexander, John Bancroft, Adele Barker, Ellen Basso, Steve Bodio, Larry Evers, Tim Finan, W. Eugene Hall, Jane Hirshfield, Hsain Ilahiane, Barbara Kingsolver, Barry Lopez, Susan Lowell, J. Michael Mahar, Tom Miller, Gary Paul Nabhan, John Olsen, José Promis, Marc Rubbo, Herbert Schneidau, Elizabeth Shaw, Gary Snyder, Deanne Stillman, Flo Swann, Scott Thybony, Susan Tweit, Mark Weiss, Peter Wild, and Terry Tempest Williams. I thank as well Linda Purrington, who edited the manuscript.

For permission to use copyright material under their individual ownership, I thank Ray Gonzalez (for "Easter Sunday, 1988, Grand Canyon"), Paul and Sarengowa Maxwell (for "Distances of the Gobi"), and Jerome Rothenberg (for "Rain Songs" and "A Prayer & Invocation to the Prince of Rain").

ACKNOWLEDGMENTS

The following credits for the use of copyright materials constitute an extension of the copyright page of this book.

Excerpt from *The Best of Edward Abbey*, copyright © 1984 by Edward Abbey. Reprinted by permission of Sierra Club Books.

Excerpt from "The South" from *Ficciones* by Jorge Luis Borges, translated by Anthony Kerrigan. Copyright © 1962 by Grove Press, Inc.

Excerpt from *The Gobi Desert* by Mildred Cable, copyright © 1942. Reprinted by permission of Hodder and Stoughton.

Excerpt from *The Crystal Desert*. Copyright © 1992 by David G. Campbell. Reprinted by permission of Houghton Mifflin Co. All rights reserved.

Excerpt from *The Songlines* by Bruce Chatwin. Copyright © 1987 by Bruce Chatwin. Used by permission of Viking Penguin, a division of Penguin Books USA Inc.

Excerpt from *From the Desert to the Book* by Edmond Jabés, published by Station Hill Press. Copyright © 1980 by Edmond Jabés.

Excerpt from *The Desert* by Pierre Loti, published by the University of Utah Press. Translation copyright © 1994 by Jay Paul Minn.

Excerpt from *The Sheltering Desert* by Henno Martin, copyright © 1958 by Thomas Nelson and Sons.

Excerpt from *Confieso que he vivido* by Pablo Neruda, copyright © 1969. Reprinted by permission of Fundación Pablo Neruda, c/o Agencía Literaria Carmen Balcells, Barcelona, Spain. English translation copyright © 1995 by Gregory McNamee.

Excerpt from *Cry of the Kalahari*. Copyright © 1984 by Mark J. and Delia D. Owens. Reprinted by permission of Houghton Mifflin Co. All rights reserved.

Excerpt from "Dzhan," from *The Fierce and Beautiful World* by Andrei Platonov, translated by Joseph Barnes. Translation copyright © 1969, 1970 by E. P. Dutton. Used by permission of Dutton Signet, a division of Penguin Books USA Inc.

Excerpt from *Barren Lives* by Graciliano Ramos, translated by Ralph Edward Dimmick, copyright © 1965. By permission of the University of Texas Press.

Excerpt from *The Long Walk* by Slavomir Rawicz. Copyright © 1956 by Slavomir Rawicz.

ACKNOWLEDGMENTS

Excerpt from *Attending Marvels* by George Gaylord Simpson, copyright ©
1934, 1962. Reprinted by permission of the Trust of George Gaylord
Simpson.

Excerpt from *Singing for Power* by Ruth Underhill, copyright © 1938, 1966
by Ruth Underhill, published by the University of California Press.

CONTENTS

CONTENTS

INTRODUCTION

Study a physical map of the world. As you follow the tropics of Cancer and Capricorn, thirty degrees on either side of the equator, you will see, distributed with suspicious regularity, a brown band of drylands circling the planet, a sere belt warding off greener climes: the deserts of the world. They lie in the so-called horse latitudes, where constant high-pressure systems separate the westerlies and trade winds, driving away the rain clouds, swirling above the earth to the music of global temperature variations and the Coriolis effect produced by the earth's rotation in space.

Some of those drylands, like the Atacama of Chile, the Namib and Kalahari deserts of southern Africa, and the western Australian desert, are the result of cold oceanic currents that divert rain-laden air away from coastlines. Others, like the Mojave and Sonoran deserts of California Arizona, and Mexico and the deserts of central and eastern Australia are caused by the "rainshadow effect," through which coastal mountains milk rain from the air before it passes inland. Still others, like the Gobi and Taklamakan deserts of Mongolia and China, are simply so far away from the ocean that the winds lose any moisture they may hold long before reaching the far-off continental interior, even what little moisture remains in the Indian Ocean–born clouds after they have scraped over the jagged Himalayas.

The world's great desert systems, which make up some 20 percent of the planet's surface, comprise harsh environments: landscapes of burning sands and desiccated vegetation, gravel and dead streambeds, and everywhere a chaos of mountains and dust. They are less single entities than a multifaceted series of microenvironments, which some scientists break down into types like *sicci deserta* (dry desert, like that of the Great Basin), *mobili deserta* (wandering desert, like the great dunefields of the central Sahara), *rupi deserta* (rocky desert, like that of southern Arabia), and *saxi deserta* (stony desert, like that of highland Afghanistan). Indeed, by one measure such microenvironments, punctuated by riparian corridors and mountain-island systems, comprise the largest geographical feature on Earth: the Eurasian Palearctic Desert, which begins at the Atlantic and ends very near the Pacific, embracing the Saharan, Arabian, Iranian, Turkmeni, Indian, Taklamakan, and Gobi deserts.

Desert. The very word conjures up mystery, evokes the windswept fastnesses of *Beau Geste* and *Lawrence of Arabia.* That mystery may be a sign of its imprecision, for the term embraces an improbably vast range of landscapes, from the comparatively lush columnar cactus forests of Arizona and Sonora to the Antarctic, where 90 percent and more of the planet's fresh water lies locked in ice. Even among scientists there is considerable disagreement about just what *desert* means. By most lights it involves, in the biologist Edmund Jaeger's words, a region's receiving "less than ten inches of unevenly distributed rain throughout the year." Attempting a more rigorous definition, in 1918 the Austrian ecologist Wladimir Köppen developed a complex series of climatological and geomorphological indexes that other scientists have gone on to refine. One, the American plant geographer Forrest Shreve, spent years trying to work out a satisfactory explanation of just what constitutes a desert. "It is impossible," he concluded regretfully, "to define desert in terms of a single characteristic, just as truly as it is impossible to differentiate species by such a procedure." He went on to suggest at least a few features that distinguish deserts from other places: irregular and modest rainfall, the low level of moisture in the soil, the swift winds and correspondingly high evaporation rate of surface waters, the land's poorly developed drainage systems, the widely spaced plant life, and rocky or sandy ground. David Quammen, the writer and naturalist, rejoins, "a desert is one of those entities, like virginity and sans serif typefaces, of which the definition must begin with negatives"—no water, that is, no shade, no discernible seasons apart from hot and cold. And finally, the English architectural historian Reyner Banham, who spent the last years of his life bicycling around in the Mojave Desert, reminds us that many deserts are not in fact deserts at all—from the Latin *desertus*, a desolation, a place devoid of people, of life, abandoned by all but scorpions and ghosts.

Absences. Most deserts, in truth, are far from desolate. They swarm with life, albeit life that snarls, hisses, howls, bites, stings, or sticks. True enough, deserts lack water. But they do not lack for one thing: wind, and lots of it. What makes them deserts in the first place is not so much the absence of water as the fact that ever-thirsty winds pull such scant rain as falls from the clouds back skyward before it can reach or penetrate the ground. You can see this in the eerie "virgo" rain phenomenon, where ghostly trails of falling water evaporate thousands of feet above the earth in the thermal-ridden air. In windy Bagdad, California, not a drop of rain fell on the earth for 767 days, from September 3, 1912, to November 8, 1914; yet the sky was full of clouds in their season, water kept from the earth by the constant flow of desiccating wind. A similar arid river blows across West Texas, so strong local legend has it, that if it ever stopped all the cows would fall down.

The mythographer and ethnologist Sir James G. Frazer rightly observed in his landmark study *The Golden Bough*, "Of all natural phenomena, there are, perhaps, none which civilized man feels himself more powerless to influence than the wind." (Let us set aside the adjective "civilized." It has precious little meaning anyway, especially in these thoroughly uncivilized times.) Of the 5,600,000,000,000,000 or so tons of air in the atmosphere, some large part is always whistling down, it seems, on desert rats, for it is the uneven distribution of solar energy that drives the winds—and solar energy is, of course, distributed in an embarrassment of riches across the face of the drylands.

For half the year, most deserts are graced by caressing, soft winds that are nothing less than rejuvenating. In those breezes lies the promise of new life, reverberating through scents, in the case of my neighborhood in the lower Sonoran Desert, like that of the orange blossom—the orange, that marvelous heat-loving berry, having first been introduced to Europeans in the first century by Greek and Roman travelers to the Thar Desert of India, and reintroduced by Moors into the rich gardens of Andalusia, whence most of the Spanish explorers of New Spain arose. On such days the air hangs in the sky like a loose silk gown, so brilliantly clear, so deep blue, that it seems almost as if you could make out each individual molecule.

But were some master of the Chinese necromantic art of *feng shui*—the alignment of buildings to their environment—to design a house for a Sonoran Desert dweller in the normally clement month of February, the plans would have to be scrapped in two months' time. Come late April, when the orange blossoms fade into memory, ever-intensifying winds announce the advent of summer and, not far behind it, the monsoon season—for, as the Akimel O'odham, the "watercourse people" of the Sonoran Desert, say, "The rain is blind and must be led by the wind."

A related wind, the *simoun* (from the Arabic word for poison), shrieks over the Sahara, whipping up sand and dust into fearful, sharp-grained *chevaux de frise*. Herodotus, the great Greek traveler and historian, reports the story of a Libyan army that marched off two and a half millennia ago into the deep Sahara to find and subdue the lord of these storms. The expedition, "disappearing, in battle array, with drums and cymbals beating, into a red cloud of swirling sand," never returned. The Assyrians, it is said, did much the same, sending squads of archers to combat the approaching clouds. And for good reason: a duststorm once buried Ur of the Chaldees, cause enough to seek vengeance.

The *simoun* has many local equivalents: the Moroccan *sirocco*, the Libyan *ghibli*, the Saudi *khamsin*, the Egyptian *zoboa*, the Australian "brickfielder," the Mongolian *karaburan*, the Sudanese *haboob*, the Mauritanian *harmattan*, and the Indian *loo*, which Rudyard Kipling describes in his story "The Man Who Would Be King" as a "red-hot wind from the westward, booming among the tinder-dry trees and pretending that the rain was on its heels." The logic of those winds seems to have prompted evolution to make a few alterations in the master plan; recently, biologists have concluded that camels, strange creatures to begin with, evolved so that, standing, they can clear the sand-laden zone of air, which goes up only to about six feet, slightly lower than the average camel's height. Other creatures, like the antelope-like saiga of Central Asia and certain kinds of desert hares, have filtering tissues surrounding their respiratory tracts that give them the same adaptive advantage.

Closer to my home, the Tohono O'odham, "people of the stony barren," tell of water serpents that dwell in the boiling summer clouds that rage across deserts the world over, bringing rain to the dry earth not in nourishing drops but in great black undulating curtains of water, leaving floods and destruction in their wake. It is no sin to kill such serpents, the O'odham explain, but even their best shamans and archers rarely succeed in doing so. During one such thunderstorm in Arizona in the summer of 1941, a saltwater clam fell from out of the sky on a young boy, who was knocked out cold by the blow. (He fared better than the playwright Aeschylus, on

whose bald head an eagle dropped a tortoise, killing him instantly.)
Scarcely a summer storm goes by when a pelican or albatross is not
blown from the Pacific or the Gulf of California and dropped down
into the heart of the inland desert, there indignantly to await what
has become local tradition: a plane ride back to the coast.

Nothing, the Jesuit missionary Ignaz Pfefferkorn remarked, can
withstand the power of those great storms. Out of them, after all,
have come gods: in the wind-lashed Sinai desert Jehovah, recapitu-
lating his origins as a Semitic storm god like his later rival Baal, first
appeared before Moses as chain lightning; Hercules has his birth as
a Libyan storm god whose cult flourished until very recently in the
Atlas Mountains. You will find in Ezekiel mention of "a storm coming out of the north, a vast cloud with flashes of fire and a brilliant
light about it; and within was a radiance of brass, glowing in the
heart of the flames." Such storms are unique among inorganic phenomena inasmuch as they resist the tendency of all things to slip
away into inertia and entropy; instead, they swell, burst, spawn new
storms, and eventually wander off elsewhere to cause new trouble.
The last one to visit my home behaved less than divinely: it split a
chinaberry tree neatly down the middle, tore up a good section of
prickly-pear fence, and sent a well-rooted agave spinning off into
the street, all within the space of perhaps a minute's time.

Desert tempests have brought down whole governments, like that
of Ur of the Chaldees, like that of the worthy Jimmy Carter, who
never quite recovered from the hostage rescue debacle of 1979,
when nineteen Delta Force elite soldiers maneuvered their helicopters into a funnel of whirling dust over the barren saltpans of Iran.
These "dust devils"—the term comes to us by some unknown
source from the Indian subcontinent—are an astonishment of nature; if you drive from, say, Phoenix to Los Angeles across the sandy
lowlands of the Sonoran and Mojavean deserts, you'll count dozens

of them on most hot, cloudless days of the year, miniature cyclones dancing to their own music alongside the interstate. When I was about six years old, I walked into one as it carved its sinuous course in the gypsum deposits of White Sands, New Mexico, thinking that it would take me off to Oz. I did not retrace Dorothy and Toto's adventures, but Southwestern legend has it that whole flocks of barnyard hens have been swept heavenward through a passing dust devil's fancy. No one has personally seen this occur, of course, but then no one has seen another phenomenon that passes for fact in many parts out this way: it's so hot most days that chickens lay hardboiled eggs.

The tallest dust devil ever recorded was spotted in Utah about thirty years ago. It stood about 2,000 feet tall, lasted for seven hours—an unusually long life span for what is in essence a tornado—and traveled across the alkali desert for more than forty miles. That it came from the comparatively mild desert of Deseret is no surprise, really, for the Great Basin is the source of most of our continental storm systems. Even the fiercest Saharan sandstorm might be preferable to a day's contending with the basin's fierce katabatic winds, which sweep down onto the desert floor from the tall Sierra Nevada and Wasatch mountain fronts, generating howling low-pressure systems like the so-called Washoe winds. Mark Twain wrote of them, "seriously," that they are "by no means a trifling matter." Not so seriously, he described what a Washoe storm hid within its dust clouds:

Hats, chickens and parasols sailing in the remote heavens; blankets, tin signs, sagebrush, and shingles a shade lower; doormats and buffalo robes lower still; shovels and coal scuttles on the next grade; glass doors, cats and little children on the next; disrupted lumber yards, light buggies and wheelbarrows on the next; and down only thirty or forty feet above ground was a scurrying storm of emigrating roofs and vacant lots.

Other falling winds, cousins to the *maloja* of the Swiss Alps, the *yama oroshi* of Japan, and the *reshabar* of the southern Caucasus, are most famously known to Americans as the Santa Anas. The mechanism that drives them works like this: on warm days the air rises uphill from valley floors, and then cools as it ascends, creating an upward–downward (anabatic–katabatic) wind flow. In the case of the Santa Ana winds, high pressure over Utah and Nevada causes air to spill off the Mojave Desert, rushing over the Pacific coastal range and onto the coastal lowlands. The coastal air is robbed of humidity by this thirsty invader and fills with static electricity. As it envelops desert and littoral alike, the Santa Ana creates a weird atmosphere of impending doom. During its season, as Raymond Chandler wrote in his famous short story "Red Wind," "Meek little wives feel the edge of the carving knife and study their husbands' necks. Anything can happen."

Anything can, and it usually does. Most heart attacks and strokes among desert dwellers occur when the wind is blowing at force 4 or 5 on the Beaufort scale, or eleven to twenty-one miles per hour, about the average for a Santa Ana day. And statistics compiled by the Los Angeles Police Department demonstrate that homicide rates, already fantastically high in southern California, double on Santa Ana days. (In the Gobi the winds often blow between fifteen and twenty-five miles an hour for weeks at a time. I wonder why contemporary Mongolians don't massacre each other daily, but understand better why the bloodthirsty Golden Horde exploded from out of the high steppes a millennium ago.) In Pfefferkorn's time, Spanish defendants could cite the wind as an extenuating circumstance in homicide trials. The dust devil, it would seem, made them do it.

Absences of water, abundances of wind. It would seem a strange place, the desert, for humans to settle. But nomads have been wandering into them for millennia, bound by what Frank Herbert called "the bond of water" in his epic novel *Dune*. They did so against all better judgment, for humans did not evolve to live in deserts, unlike the camel and burro, the targa and the packrat. Neither have we adapted to them; exposed to the desert sun, a human will die within a day. With shade and an adequate water supply—at least two gallons of water a day—we can make it a bit longer; with even more water, as the ecologist Bryan Nelson notes, we can exist in biomes where for nine hours of the day the temperature stands at 49°C (119°F) and for the rest stands at 30°C (86°F) and at 15.25 percent humidity, hotter than the world's deserts get for most parts of the year.

A strange place indeed, but humans have long felt an attraction to the drylands. They are holy places: in deserts were born most of the world's great contemporary religions, among them Hinduism, Buddhism, Judaism, Christianity, and Islam. As the French historian Joseph Ernest Rénan remarked, "Le Désert est monothéiste"—the desert is monotheistic, favoring the formation of powerful gods. For his part, Honoré de Balzac elaborated by taking humans out of the equation altogether; "The desert," he wrote, "is where God is and man is not." Ibn Khaldun, the great Moroccan historian, hit the middle ground with his claim that "The Desert People are closer to being good than settled peoples because they are closer to the First State and are more removed from all the evil habits that have infected the hearts of settlers." And John Steinbeck, in his *Log of the Sea of Cortez*, returned to Rénan:

At night in this waterless air the stars come down just out of reach of your fingers. In such a place lived the hermits of the early church piercing to infinity with uninhibited minds. The great concept of oneness and of majestic order seems always to be born in the desert.

In deserts did most of humankind's domesticated plant and animal species evolve and become tamed. In deserts practices of "primitive communism" and elaborate hospitality came about, the stuff of the great anarchist Peter Kropotkin's theory of mutual aid. From deserts arose some of our earliest recognition of environmental problems: the drought-driven collapse of the Sumerian empire and Hohokam civilization brought desert dwellers to the conclusion that smaller is better; the guru Jameshwarji's imprecating the Bisnoi people of the Great Thar Desert of Rajahstan not to cut down trees or kill animals five hundred years ago has as its splendid monuments groves of khejiri (*Prosopis cinerarea*) trees and herds of blackbucks (*Antilope cervicapra*), indexes of the desert's health, and unharmed populations of wolves, jackals, and snakes, all protected within the Bisnoi homeland, all necessary to an ecosystem in balance.

Increasingly, desert ecosystems the world over are under threat. Throughout history the deserts have offered challenges that only a few humans have gladly taken on. Until recent times the mass of humankind has preferred to stay away from them, settling instead in more temperate regions where such luxuries as abundant water and rich soil abound. But with a world human population growing at a disastrous pace and the consequent need both for living space and for food, the deserts are beginning to fill with people and livestock, to be stripped bare of fuelwood, of myriad resources. The deserts now sustain about a sixth of the human population; in the next century, it may be half, and desert ecosystems—fragile for all their seeming fierceness—will suffer accordingly.

We are already seeing the effects of such growth. The Convention on Desertification, ratified in Paris on October 15, 1994, and signed by nearly a hundred nations, recognizes that 75 percent of Africa's arid lands are degraded, while the International Soil Reference and Information Centre of the Netherlands observes that since 1945 *Homo sapiens* has degraded 17 percent of the surface of the globe, large parts of it perhaps irredeemably.

There is hope, however, in both small and large scale. In April 1994 huskies were removed from Antarctica by international law,

ending a wave of canine viruses that spread to native seal populations. Soon afterward, the U.S. Senate passed the Desert Protection
Bill of 1994, which shelters much of the Mojave Desert of California from future development. International aid organizations
have introduced new techniques to halt desertification in places like
Burkina Faso and Chad. The unlikeliest desert of the world, the
five-square-mile Bledowska, nestled at the foot of the Krakow Jura
in Poland, where Erwin Rommel trained his Afrika Korps, has recently been declared off limits to economic activity, with the
thought of setting it aside soon as a national park. All these things
promise a less than calamitous future—if only we act now.

Théodore Monod, the French explorer of the Sahara—who in
1954 crossed a 500-mile wide waterless stretch of Mauretania in
which he discovered dry lakes full of the bones of crocodiles, ibises,
hippopotamuses, and fish—declared that "the desert is probably
the most intensely loved landscape on our earth." Certainly within
it lies the seed of great religions, of great works of the imagination,
and not the least of them books, from the *Mahabharata* to Albert Camus's *The Stranger*, from *The Travels of Marco Polo* to Raymond Chandler's *The Long Goodbye*. The deserts of the world have
spawned a significant body of literature, a corpus well out of proportion to the number of people who actually dwell in them. The work
of the so-called British Orientalists alone is enough to fill a small library, written by men (and a few women) who, as Jonathan Raban
observes, found in the deserts "a perfect theatre for the enactment
of a heroic drama of their own—a drama whose secret was not really
the desert at all but the decadent life of the London drawing-room."

In this anthology, I have tried to gather some of the best of that
body of writing, observing the American poet Ezra Pound's dictum
that literature "is news that stays news." I do not, of course, pretend
to completeness; that is the nature of an anthology, a selection of
texts that reflects its editor's tastes and prejudices. This already

portly volume easily could have tripled in size had I included everything I found newsworthy in the literature of deserts, from indigenous folktales to reportage by such writers as Paul Theroux, Nikos Kazantzakis, V. S. Naipaul, and Colin Thubron. In the main, too, the record of the world's exploration has been kept by European men, who often regarded the inhabitants of other lands as little more than animals. Examples of attitudes we have since, I hope, outgrown pop up here and there in the pages that follow; I have made no attempt to censor them in the interest of modern propriety. All in all, we know too little of the deserts' native voices, many of them already extinct, many of the survivors falling silent as larger cultures expand into the drylands.

The desert—land of djinns, whirlwinds, mirages, and thundering sands, as you will read of in the pages that follow—does not tolerate our inexperience, and it assures us of our many imperfections, tests us, and finds us wanting. We owe the drylands, the home of the gods, greater honor than we seem today to be paying them. It is my hope that this anthology contributes, in some small way, to our moving closer to that "First State," to seeing the desert landscape as a place not of absences but as an embarrassment of riches.

Gregory McNamee
Tucson, Arizona

NORTH
AMERICA

We can try to kill all that is native, string it up by its hind legs
for all to see, but spirit howls and wildness endures.
   Terry Tempest Williams

"I take SPACE to be the central fact to man born in America, from
Folsom cave to now," the poet Charles Olson proclaimed in his
book of criticism *Call Me Ishmael*. "I spell it large because it comes
large here. Large and without mercy." Embracing nearly half a
million square miles, the deserts of North America—the Mojave,
Sonoran, Chihuahuan, and Great Basin—have yielded what is
arguably the strongest body of writing to have emerged from any
of the continent's natural environments, bringing the spirit of
place to the forefront. In the past they have given us such varied
writers as Alvaro Núñez Cabeza de Vaca and Mary Austin, Martha
Summerhayes and Edward Abbey; today new voices, such as those
of Simon Ortiz and Gary Paul Nabhan, Denise Chávez and Luci
Tapahonso, continue to enrich the national literature with the voice
of the western deserts.

The Land of Little Rain

Mary Austin

One of the Anglo Southwest's earliest writers of note, Mary Austin
(1836–1934) brought feminist, ecological, and Native American concerns
to public attention through books set in the Mojave Desert of California
and other parts of the Southwest. Austin, Kenneth Rexroth recalls in
his *Autobiographical Novel*, "was a type I had never known well before,
a thoroughly professionalized and successful woman writer. . . . Talking
about life and letters she helped me to realize that it was possible to adopt
literature as a profession with the same dignity that you adopt medicine,
and in turn demand the same respect from society. . . . She knew people
all over the Southwest, especially off the main lines of travel; people
in remote valleys in central Nevada and east of the mountains on the
California line, around the Four Corners, on the Tonto Rim, and tucked
away in box canyons in Utah, like the one in *Riders of the Purple Sage*."
In this passage from her 1926 book *The Land of Little Rain*, she limns her
territory.

East away from the Sierras, south from Panamint and Amargosa,
east and south many an uncounted mile, is the Country of Lost Borders.

Ute, Paiute, Mojave, and Shoshone inhabit its frontiers, and as far
into the heart of it as a man dare go. Not the law, but the land sets the
limit. Desert is the name it wears upon the maps, but the Indian's is
the better word. Desert is a loose term to indicate land that supports
no man; whether the land can be bitted and broken to that purpose
is not proven. Void of life it never is, however dry the air and villain-
ous the soil.

This is the nature of that country. There are hills, rounded, blunt,
burned, squeezed up out of chaos, chrome and vermilion painted,
aspiring to the snow-line. Between the hills lie high level-looking

plains full of intolerable sun glare, or narrow valleys drowned in a blue haze. The hill surface is streaked with ash drift and black, un-weathered lava flows. After rains water accumulates in the hollows of small closed valleys, and, evaporating, leaves hard dry levels of pure desertness that get the local name of dry lakes. Where the mountains are steep and the rains heavy, the pool is never quite dry, but dark and bitter, rimmed about with the efflorescence of alkaline deposits. A thin crust of it lies along the marsh over the vegetating area, which has neither beauty nor freshness in the broad wastes open to the wind the sand drifts in hummocks about the stubby shrubs, and be-tween them the soil shows saline traces. The sculpture of the hills here is more wind than water work, though the quick storms do sometimes scar them past many a year's redeeming. In all the West-ern desert edges there are essays in miniature of the famed, terrible Grand Cañon, to which, if you keep on long enough in this country, you will come at last.

Since this is a hill country one expects to find springs, but not to depend upon them; for when found they are often brackish and un-wholesome, or maddening, slow dribbles in a thirsty soil. Here you find the hot sink of Death Valley, or high rolling districts where the air has always a tang of frost. Here are the long heavy winds and breathless calms on the tilted mesas where dust devils dance, whirl-ing up into a wide, pale sky. Here you have no rain when all the earth cries for it, or quick downpours called cloud-bursts for violence. A land of lost rivers with little in it to love; yet a land that once visited must be come back to inevitably. If it were not so there would be little told of it.

This is the country of three seasons. From June on to November it lies hot, still, and unbearable, sick with violent unrelieving storms, then on until April, chill, quiescent, drinking its scant rain and scanter snows, from April to the hot season again, blossoming, ra-diant, and seductive. These months are only approximate; later or earlier the rain-laden wind may drift up the water gate of the Colorado from the Gulf, and the land sets its seasons by the rain.

The desert floras shame us with their cheerful adaptations to the seasonal limitations. Their whole duty is to flower and fruit, and they do it hardly, or with tropical luxuriance, as the rain admits. It is recorded in the report of the Death Valley expedition that after a year of abundant rains, on the Colorado desert was found a specimen of Amaranthus ten feet high. A year later the same species in the same place matured in the drought at four inches. One hopes the land may breed like qualities in her human offspring, not tritely to "try," but to do. Seldom does the desert herb attain the full stature of the type. Extreme aridity and extreme altitude have the same dwarfing effect, so that we find in the high Sierras and in Death Valley related species in miniature that reach a comely growth in mean temperatures. Very fertile are the desert plants in expedients to prevent evaporation, turning their foliage edgewise toward the sun, growing silky hairs, exuding viscid gum. The wind, which has a long sweep, harries and helps them. It rolls up dunes about the stocky stems, encompassing and protective, and above the dunes, which may be, as with the mesquite, three times as high as a man, the blossoming twigs flourish and bear fruit.

There are many areas in the desert where drinkable water lies within a few feet of the surface, indicated by the mesquite and the bunch grass (*Sporobolus airoides*). It is this nearness of unimagined help that makes the tragedy of desert deaths. It is related that the final breakdown of that hapless party that gave Death Valley its forbidding name occurred in a locality where shallow wells would have saved them. But how were they to know that? Properly equipped it is possible to go safely across that ghastly sink, yet every year it takes its toll of death, and yet men find there sun-dried mummies, of whom no trace or recollection is preserved. To underestimate one's thirst, to pass a given landmark to the right or left, to find a dry spring where one looked for running water—there is no help for any of these things.

Along springs and sunken watercourses one is surprised to find such water-loving plants as grow widely in moist ground, but the true desert breeds its own kind, each in its particular habitat. The angle of the slope, the frontage of a hill, the structure of the soil determines the plant. South-looking hills are nearly bare, and the lower tree-line higher here by a thousand feet. Cañons running east and west will have one wall naked and one clothed. Around dry lakes and marshes the herbage preserves a set and orderly arrangement. Most species have well-defined areas of growth, the best index the voiceless land can give the traveler of his whereabouts.

If you have any doubt about it, know that the desert begins with the creosote. This immortal shrub spreads down into Death Valley and up to the lower timberline, odorous and medicinal as you might guess from the name, wandlike, with shining fretted foliage. Its vivid green is grateful to the eye in a wilderness of gray and greenish white shrubs. In the spring it exudes a resinous gum which the Indians of those parts know how to use with pulverized rock for cementing arrow points to shafts. Trust Indians not to miss any virtues of the plant world!

Nothing the desert produces expresses it better than the unhappy growth of the tree yuccas. Tormented, thin forests of it stalk drearily in the high mesas, particularly in that triangular slip that fans out eastward from the meeting of the Sierras and coastwise hills where the first swings across the southern end of the San Joaquin Valley. The yucca bristles with bayonet-pointed leaves, dull green, growing shaggy with age, tipped with panicles of fetid, greenish bloom. After death, which is slow, the ghostly hollow network of its woody skeleton, with hardly power to rot, makes the moonlight fearful. Before the yucca has come to flower, while yet its bloom is a creamy cone-shaped bud of the size of a small cabbage, full of sugary sap, the Indians twist it deftly out of its fence of daggers and roast it for their own delectation so it is that in those parts where man inhabits one sees young plants of *Yucca arborensis* infrequently. Other yuccas, cacti, low herbs, a thousand sorts, one finds journeying east from the coastwise hills. There is neither poverty of soil nor species to account for the sparseness of desert growth, but simply that each plant requires more room. So much earth must be preëmpted to extract so much moisture. The real struggle for existence, the real brain of the plant, is underground; above there is room for a rounded perfect growth. In Death Valley, reputed the very core of desolation, are nearly two hundred identified species.

Above the lower tree-line, which is also the snow-line, mapped out abruptly by the sun, one finds spreading growth of piñon, juniper, branched nearly to the ground, lilac and sage, and scattering white pines.

There is no special preponderance of self-fertilized or wind-fertilized plants, but everywhere the demand for and evidence of insect life. Now where there are seeds and insects there will be birds and small mammals and where these are, will come the slinking, sharp-toothed kind that prey on them. Go as far as you dare in the heart of a lonely land, you cannot go so far that life and death are not before you. Painted lizards slip in and out of rock crevices, and pant on the white hot sands. Birds, hummingbirds even, nest in the cactus scrub; woodpeckers befriend the demoniac yuccas, out of the stark, treeless waste rings the music of the night-singing mockingbird. If it be summer and the sun well down, there will be a burrowing owl to call. Strange, furry, tricksy things dart across the open places, or sit motionless in the conning towers of the creosote. The poet may have "named all the birds without a gun," but not the fairy-footed, ground-inhabiting, furtive, small folk of the rainless regions. They are too many and too swift; how many you would not believe without seeing the footprint tracings in the sand. They are nearly all night workers, finding the days too hot and white. In mid-desert where there are no cattle, there are no birds of carrion, but if you go far in that direction the chances are that you will find yourself shadowed by their tilted wings. Nothing so large as a man can move unspied upon in that country, and they know well how the land deals with strangers. There are hints to be had here of the way in which a land forces new habits on its dwellers. The quick increase of sun at the end of spring sometimes overtakes birds in their nesting and effects a reversal of the ordinary manner of incubation. It becomes necessary to keep eggs cool rather than warm. One hot, stifling spring in the Little Antelope I had occasion to pass and repass frequently the nest of a pair of meadowlarks, located unhappily in the shelter of a very slender weed. I never caught them sitting except near night, but at midday they stood, or drooped above it, half fainting with pitifully parted bills, between their treasure and the sun. Sometimes both of them together with wings spread and half lifted continued a spot of shade in a temperature that constrained me at last in a fellow feeling to spare them a bit of canvas for permanent shelter. There was a fence in that country shutting in a cattle range, and along its fifteen miles of posts one could be sure of finding a bird or two in every strip of shadow; sometimes the sparrow and the hawk, with wings trailed and beaks parted, drooping in the white truce of noon.

If one is inclined to wonder at first how so many dwellers came to be in the loneliest land that ever came out of God's hands, what they do there and why stay, one does not wonder so much after having lived there. None other than this long brown land lays such a hold on the affections. The rainbow hills, the tender bluish mists, the luminous radiance of the spring, have the lotus charm. They trick the sense of time, so that once inhabiting there you always mean to go away without quite realizing that you have not done it. Men who have lived there, miners and cattle-men, will tell you this, not so fluently, but emphatically, cursing the land and going back to it. For one thing there is the divinest, cleanest air to be breathed anywhere in God's world. Some day the world will understand that, and the little oases on the windy tops of hills will harbor for healing its ailing, house-weary broods. There is promise there of great wealth in ores and earths, which is no wealth by reason of being so far removed from water and workable conditions, but men are bewitched by it and tempted to try the impossible.

You should hear Salty Williams tell how he used to drive eighteen- and twenty-mule teams from the borax marsh to Mojave, ninety miles, with the trail wagon full of water barrels. Hot days the mules would go so mad for drink that the clank of the water bucket set them into an uproar of hideous, maimed noises, and a tangle of harness chains, while Salty would sit on the high seat with the sun glare heavy in his eyes, dealing out curses of pacification in a level, uninterested voice until the clamor fell off from sheer exhaustion. There was a line of shallow graves along that road; they used to count on dropping a man or two of every new gang of coolies brought out in the hot season. But when he lost his swamper, smitten without warning at the noon halt, Salty quit his job; he said it was "too durn hot." The swamper he buried by the way with stones upon him to keep the coyotes from digging him up, and seven years later I read the penciled lines on the pine headboard, still bright and unweath-ered.

But before that, driving up on the Mojave stage, I met Salty again crossing Indian Wells, his face from the high seat, tanned and ruddy as a harvest moon, looming through the golden dust above his eigh-teen mules. The land had called him.

The palpable sense of mystery in the desert air breeds fables, chiefly of lost treasure. Somewhere within its stark borders, if one believes report, is a hill strewn with nuggets, one seamed with virgin silver; an old clayey water-bed where Indians scooped up earth to make cooking pots and shaped them reeking with grains of pure gold. Old miners drifting about the desert edges, weathered into the semblance of the tawny hills, will tell you tales like these convincingly. After a little sojourn in that land you will believe them on their own account. It is a question whether it is not better to be bitten by the little horned snake of the desert that goes sidewise and strikes without coiling, than by the tradition of a lost mine.

And yet—and yet—is it not perhaps to satisfy expectation that one falls into the tragic key in writing of desertness? The more you wish of it the more you get, and in the mean time lose much of pleasantness. In that country which begins at the foot of the east slope of the Sierras and spreads out by less and less lofty hill ranges toward the Great Basin, it is possible to live with great zest, to have red blood and delicate joys, to pass and repass about one's daily performance an area that would make an Atlantic seaboard State, and that with no peril, and, according to our way of thought, no particular difficulty. At any rate, it was not people who went into the desert merely to write it up who invented the fabled Hassayampa, of whose waters, if any drink, they can no more see fact as naked fact, but all radiant with the color of romance. I, who must have drunk of it in my twice seven years' wanderings, am assured that it is worth while.

For all the toll the desert takes of a man it gives compensations, deep breaths, deep sleep, and the communion of the stars. It comes upon one with new force in the pauses of the night that the Chaldeans were a desert-bred people. It is hard to escape the sense of mastery as the stars move in the wide clear heavens to risings and settings unobscured. They look large and near and palpitant; as if they moved on some stately service not needful to declare. Wheeling to their stations in the sky, they make the poor world-fret of no account. Of no account you who lie out there watching, nor the lean coyote that stands off in the scrub from you and howls and howls.

Why the Desert Is Hot

Yuma Folktale

Pedro Font, a seventeenth-century Spanish priest attached to
Juan de Anza's expedition into northern New Spain, recorded
this Yuma etiological folktale that accounts for the origins of the
desert's blasting heat.

A long time ago there came to that country a man who was called
The Bitter Man because of his ill nature and his harsh rule. This
man was old, but he had a young daughter. And there came in his
company a young man who was not a relative of his or of anybody
else, and married the daughter, who was very pretty as he was
handsome. And this old man brought as servants the Wind and the
Clouds.

When the old man began to build that great house he ordered his
son-in-law to go and look for timber with which to roof it. The young
man went a long distance, but since he had no ax or anything with
which to cut the trees, he was gone many days, and he finally returned without bringing any timbers. Now the old man was very angry, and he said that son-in-law was good-for-nothing, and he
would show him how he would bring the timbers. And so the old
man went away to a sierra where there are many pines, and, calling
on God to aid him, he cut many pines and brought many timbers for
the roof of the house.

When this Bitter Man came, there were no trees in the country,
nor any plants, but he brought seeds of all kinds and reaped very
large harvests, with the aid of his two servants, the Wind and the
Clouds, who served him. But because of his ill nature he became
angry with the two servants, and discharged them, and they went a
long way off. And then, for lack of servants, he was not able to reap

the harvests, so he ate all that he had raised, for he was now dying of hunger. He then sent his son-in-law to call the two servants and bring them back, but he could not find them no matter how much he looked for them. Then the old man went to look for them, and having found them he took them again into his service, and with their aid he again reaped great harvests. And so they continued to live for many years in that country, but after a long time they went away, and they have heard nothing more about them.

He said also that after the old man there came to that country a man called The Drinker. He became angry with the people there and sent so much water that all the land was covered with it. Then he went to a very high sierra, which is seen from there and is called the Sierra de la Espuma, taking with him a little dog and a coyote. They call it Sierra de la Espuma because at the end of it, which is cut off with a cliff like the corner of a tower, one sees high up near the top a white ledge-like rock, which continues the same all along the sierra for a long distance. And the Indians say that this mark was made by the foam of the water which reached up to there. Well, The Drinker went up there and left the dog below so that he might tell when the water reached this ledge of the foam, and when it reached there the dog told The Drinker, for then the animals talked; and then he too went up. After several days The Drinker sent to the Humming Birds and to the Coyote to have them bring him some mud. They brought it, and from it he made several men, some of whom turned out to be good and others bad. These men scattered out through the country, upstream and downstream, and after a while he sent some of his own people to see if the men upstream talked. They went and returned saying that although they talked they did not understand what they said. And so The Drinker became very angry because these men talked without his having given them permission. Afterward he sent other men downstream to see those who were there, and they returned saying that they had given them a friendly welcome and that they talked another language, but that they had understood them. Then The Drinker said to them that the men who lived down the stream were the good men, these being the ones as far as the Opas, with whom they are friendly. And those who lived upstream he said were the bad men, these being the Apaches, toward whom they are hostile.

He said also that once The Drinker became angry with the people, and killed many of them and changed them into saguaros, and this is why there are so many saguaros in that country. The saguaro has a green trunk, is watery, very tall and equally round, and straight from the bottom to the top, with rows of thick spines all the way up, and it usually has two or three branches of the same form, which look like arms.

Besides this he said that The Drinker at another time became very angry with the men, and made the sun come down to burn them, and so he finished them. The men begged him earnestly not to burn them, so he ordered the sun to go up, but not so high as it had been before, and told them that he was leaving it lower in order to burn them with it if they made him angry again; and this is why it is so hot in that country in the summer.

Nevada's Dead Towns

John Muir

The great naturalist and outdoorsman John Muir (1836–1914), who founded the Sierra Club, spent many happy years roaming through odd corners of the desert and mountain West. In this essay for the *San Francisco Evening Bulletin* of January 15, 1879, he tellingly writes of a desert constant: the boom-and-bust movements of humans.

Nevada is one of the very youngest and wildest of the States; nevertheless it is already strewn with ruins that seem as gray and silent and time-worn as if the civilization to which they belonged had perished centuries ago. Yet, strange to say, all these ruins are results of mining efforts made within the last few years. Wander where you may throughout the length and breadth of this mountain-barred wilderness, you everywhere come upon these dead mining towns, with their tall chimney-stacks, standing forlorn amid broken walls and furnaces, and machinery half buried in sand, the very names of many of them already forgotten amid the excitements of later discoveries, and now known only through tradition—tradition ten years old.

While exploring the mountain-ranges of the State during a considerable portion of three summers, I think that I have seen at least five of these deserted towns and villages for every one in ordinary life. Some of them were probably only camps built by bands of prospectors, and inhabited for a few months or years, while some specially interesting cañon was being explored, and then carelessly abandoned for more promising fields. But many were real towns, regularly laid out and incorporated, containing well-built hotels, churches, school-houses, post-offices, and jails, as well as the mills on which they all depended; and whose well-graded streets were filled with lawyers, doctors, brokers, hangmen, real-estate agents, etc., the whole population numbering several thousand.

A few years ago the population of Hamilton is said to have been nearly eight thousand; that of Treasure Hill, six thousand; of Shermantown, seven thousand; of Swansea, three thousand. All of these were incorporated towns with mayors, councils, fire departments, and daily newspapers. Hamilton has now about one hundred inhabitants, most of whom are merely waiting in dreary inaction for something to turn up. Treasure Hill has about half as many, Shermantown one family, and Swansea none, while on the other hand the graveyards are far too full.

In one cañon of the Toyabe Range, near Austin, I found no less than five dead towns without a single inhabitant. The streets and blocks of "real estate" graded on the hillsides are rapidly falling back into the wilderness. Sage-brushes are growing up around the forges of the blacksmith shops, and lizards bask on the crumbling walls.

While traveling southward from Austin down Big Smoky Valley, I noticed a remarkably tall and imposing column, rising like a lone pine out of the sage-brush on the edge of a dry gulch. This proved to be a smokestack of solid masonry. It seemed strangely out of place in the desert, as if it had been transported entire from the heart of some noisy manufacturing town and left here by mistake. I learned afterwards that it belonged to a set of furnaces that were built by a New York company to smelt ore that never was found. The tools of the workmen are still lying in place beside the furnaces, as if dropped in some sudden Indian or earthquake panic and never afterwards handled. These imposing ruins, together with the desolate town, lying a quarter of a mile to the northward, present a most vivid picture of wasted effort. Coyotes now wander unmolested through the brushy streets, and of all the busy throng that so lavishly spent their time and money here only one man remains—a lone bachelor with one suspender.

Mining discoveries and progress, retrogression and decay, seem to have been crowded more closely against each other here than on any other portion of the globe. Some one of the band of adventurous prospectors who came from the exhausted placers of California would discover some rich ore—how much or little mattered not at first. These specimens fell among excited seekers after wealth like sparks in gunpowder, and in a few days the wilderness was disturbed with the noisy clang of miners and builders. A little town would then spring up, and before anything like a careful survey of any particular lode would be made, a company would be formed, and expensive mills built. Then, after all the machinery was ready for the ore, perhaps little, or none at all, was to be found. Meanwhile another discovery was reported, and the young town was abandoned as completely as a camp made for a single night; and so on, until some really valuable lode was found, such as those of Eureka, Austin, Virginia, etc., which formed the substantial groundwork for a thousand other excitements.

Passing through the dead town of Schellbourne last month, I asked one of the few lingering inhabitants why the town was built. "For the mines," he replied. "And where are the mines?" "On the mountains back here." "And why were they abandoned?" I asked. "Are they exhausted?" "Oh, no," he replied, "they are not exhausted; on the contrary, they have never been worked at all, for unfortunately, just as we were about ready to open them, the Cherry Creek mines were discovered across the valley in the Egan Range, and everybody rushed off there, taking what they could with them— houses, machinery, and all. But we are hoping that somebody with money and speculation will come and revive us yet."

The dead mining excitements of Nevada were far more intense and destructive in their action than those of California, because the prizes at stake were greater, while more skill was required to gain them. The long trains of gold-seekers making their way to California had ample time and means to recover from their first attacks of mining fever while crawling laboriously across the plains, and on their arrival on any portion of the Sierra gold belt, they at once began to make money. No matter in what gulch or cañon they worked, some measure of success was sure, however unskillful they might be. And though while making ten dollars a day they might be agitated by hopes of making twenty, or of striking their picks against hundred- or thousand-dollar nuggets, men of ordinary nerve could still work on with comparative steadiness, and remain rational.

But in the case of the Nevada miner, he too often spent himself in years of weary search without gaining a dollar, traveling hundreds of miles from mountain to mountain, burdened with wasting hopes of discovering some hidden vein worth millions, enduring hardships of the most destructive kind, driving innumerable tunnels into the hillsides, while his assayed specimens again and again proved worthless. Perhaps one in a hundred of these brave prospectors would "strike it rich," while ninety-nine died alone in the mountains or sank out of sight in the corners of saloons, in a haze of whiskey and tobacco smoke.

The healthful ministry of wealth is blessed; and surely it is a fine thing that so many are eager to find the gold and silver that lie hid in the veins of the mountains. But in the search the seekers too often become insane, and strike about blindly in the dark like raving madmen. Seven hundred and fifty tons of ore from the original Eberhardt mine on Treasure Hill yielded a million and a half dollars, the whole of this immense sum having been obtained within two hundred and fifty feet of the surface, the greater portion within one hundred and forty feet. Other ore-masses were scarcely less marvelously rich, giving rise to one of the most violent excitements that ever occurred in the history of mining. All kinds of people—shoemakers, tailors, farmers, etc., as well as miners—left their own right work and fell in a perfect storm of energy upon the White Pine Hills, covering the ground like grasshoppers, and seeming determined by the very violence of their efforts to turn every stone to silver. But with few exceptions, these mining storms pass away about as suddenly as they rise, leaving only ruins to tell of the tremendous energy expended, as heaps of giant boulders in the valley tell of the spent power of the mountain floods.

In marked contrast with this destructive unrest is the orderly deliberation into which miners settle in developing a truly valuable mine. At Eureka we were kindly led through the treasure chambers of the Richmond and Eureka Consolidated, our guides leisurely leading the way from level to level, calling attention to the precious ore-masses which the workmen were slowly breaking to pieces with their picks, like navvies wearing away the day in a railroad cutting; while down at the smelting works the bars of bullion were handled with less eager haste than the farmer shows in gathering his sheaves.

The wealth Nevada has already given to the world is indeed wonderful, but the only grand marvel is the energy expended in its development. The amount of prospecting done in the face of so many dangers and sacrifices, the innumerable tunnels and shafts bored into the mountains, the mills that have been built—these would seem to require a race of giants. But, in full view of the substantial results achieved, the pure waste manifest in the ruins one meets never fails to produce a saddening effect.

The dim old ruins of Europe, so eagerly sought after by travelers, have something pleasing about them, whatever their historical associations; for they at least lend some beauty to the landscape. Their picturesque towers and arches seem to be kindly adopted by nature, and planted with wild flowers and wreathed with ivy; while their rugged angles are soothed and freshened and embossed with green mosses, fresh life and decay mingling in pleasing measures, and the whole vanishing softly like a ripe, tranquil day fading into night. So, also, among the older ruins of the East there is a fitness felt. They have served their time, and like the weather-beaten mountains are wasting harmoniously. The same is in some degree true of the dead mining towns of California. But those lying to the eastward of the

Sierra throughout the ranges of the Great Basin waste in the dry wilderness like the bones of cattle that have died of thirst. Many of them do not represent any good accomplishment, and have no right to be. They are monuments of fraud and ignorance—sins against science. The drifts and tunnels in the rocks may perhaps be regarded as the prayers of the prospector, offered for the wealth he so earnestly craves; but, like prayers of any kind not in harmony with nature, they are unanswered. But, after all, effort, however misapplied, is better than stagnation. Better toil blindly, beating every stone in turn for grains of gold, whether they contain any or not, than lie down in apathetic decay.

The fever period is fortunately passing away. The prospector is no longer the raving, wandering ghoul of ten years ago, rushing in random lawlessness among the hills, hungry and footsore; but cool and skillful, well supplied with every necessary, and clad in his right mind. Capitalists, too, and the public in general, have become wiser, and do not take fire so readily from mining sparks; while at the same time a vast amount of real work is being done, and the ratio between growth and decay is constantly becoming better.

The Climate of Sonora

Ignaz Pfefferkorn

Ignaz Pfefferkorn (1725–1793) spent seven years in Sonora, a province of New Spain that included most of present-day Arizona, and later a Mexican state. There he served as a Jesuit priest among the Eudeve, Opata, and Tohono O'odham peoples. The ruins of the church built for him by the last group may still be seen at Guevavi, near present-day Nogales, Arizona. Pfefferkorn had little admiration for peaceful agriculturalists under his charge:

> Their natural stupidity, their complete neglect of themselves, the baseness of their spirits; these are the main sources of the hardness of their minds and, as it were, of their insensitivity. Would that the indifference with which they view everything transitory did not extend to the eternal and to the care of their souls.

The farmers took small revenge by serving Pfefferkorn a bowl of chile-laden meat as his first meal in the Pimería, which he remembered for years: "The constant use of this hot sauce is at first an unbelievable hardship for the Europeans. . . . After the first mouthful the tears started to come. I could not say a word and believed I had hellfire in my mouth."

In this passage from his book *Beschreibung der Landschaft Sonora* (*Sonora: A Description of the Province*), Pfefferkorn gives an account of the region's climate.

Although Sonora is situated outside the torrid zone, beginning in the twenty-seventh degree of north latitude, it is nevertheless, on the whole, a very warm country. By February one is bothered by the sun, though the heat is not continual in this month. For one or two days it is almost as warm as Germany in the hot summer-time, but immediately thereafter it is cold again. On a given day the weather may be so changeable that one feels great heat and severe cold, and not infrequently this change takes place in the space of two or three hours. The reason for this change is the inconstancy of the winds, which blow from all points of the compass. In March the heat rises, although this month also is often subject to changes. By May the heat is already as intense as it usually is in Germany toward the end of June. It rises until the end of July and continues so to the end of September. October and thence to about the end of December is really the most comfortable time, this period being comparable to the mild spring months in Germany. The sun is so moderately warm that it is not vexatious, nor does it become cold. Only the morning

19

and evening hours and the nights are cool, though so moderately that a single bedcover provides enough warmth for the night.

Toward the end of December, winter and low temperatures commence. This condition lasts through January to the beginning of February, and is very similar to that which one is accustomed to experience along the Rhine River in March during years of average winter. When north winds blow they cover the fields with frost, but never with snow, and it is considered an astonishing occurrence and a sign of severe cold if snow falls on the plains. In the eleven years which I spent in Sonora, this happened only once, in the year 1761. However, the snow disappeared after it had remained on the ground only a few minutes. It is often seen, indeed, on high mountain peaks, but there also the sun does not allow it to remain for long. Now and then ice forms on the edges of brooks, and thin sheets of it will cover little pools also; but in houses water never freezes. Moreover, the cold is so tolerable that one can well do without having a stove in the room. A German needs nothing more than a good mantle to protect himself sufficiently against the cold, but a Sonora-born Spaniard, on the other hand, who cannot endure any cold, is somewhat more sensitive and must at times take refuge at a fire, which he builds under the open sky. The Indians, who have no clothes or covers . . . tend a small fire throughout the night to warm themselves in their lowly and tightly closed huts.

The summer heat begins in May, as already stated, and lasts until the end of September. One would think that the heat would be greatest in Sonora, as it is here in Germany, in the second half of the summer; however, experience proves the opposite. May, June, and July are noticeably hotter than the months which follow, since no winds blow in those three months, and, if there is a stray breeze, it is so weak that it cannot cool the atmosphere. Besides, as a rule, not a drop of rain falls from the beginning of January to the end of June.

Consequently the earth as well as the air is greatly parched by the sun's burning rays, augmented by the so-called *quemazones*, or conflagrations. . . .

Since the heat in May, June, and July is already so intense, it would necessarily be quite unbearable during the hot season in August and September were the heat not moderated, in Sonora as in New Spain in general, by daily rains. Consequently, this season is called *tiempo de aguas*, or the rainy period. It begins in July and ends in September. The rain is not continuous, but passes off in two or three hours. However, the precipitation is so heavy that brooks and rivers are extraordinarily swollen and are very dangerous to those who, because of pressing need or audacity, would cross them on horseback, for there are no bridges in this country. When the storm has ended, the rivers fall again as rapidly as they have risen, and the sky assumes its former brightness. These rain showers are not general; at times they affect a stretch of but a few miles, over which the rain-cloud empties itself, while the surrounding regions remain completely dry. Where rain does not occur for some days, field products, especially maize or Indian corn, stand in danger of drying up, because it is not everywhere possible to irrigate the country from ditches. However, such a misfortune is not very often to be feared. After the first heavy shower the heat is indescribable, so that at night as well as in the day-time one nearly suffocates. After some days, though, the air becomes cooled by repeated rains and the heat so moderated that it is quite bearable.

Sonora, through these daily rains, receives a pleasant relief from the heat, and at the same time its products are increased. Hence, these rains would surely be considered as priceless blessings of nature were they not always accompanied by the most horrible thunder-storms, which not infrequently do great damage to men and animals in the villages and in the fields. One cannot listen to the continuous crashing of the thunder without shuddering. At times such thunder-storms bring with them a damaging hail, which destroys all growing things in the field and garden; or there may occur a ruinous cloudburst, in Sonora called *culebra de agua*, or water snake, which will flood over country and villages, devastating them. Sometimes the thunder-storms are accompanied by violent wind-storms and whirlwinds, which lift the sand in a very thick, twisted column almost to the clouds. Nothing these whirlwinds seize can withstand their power. Even the strongest trees are often uprooted, roofs are uncovered, and houses upset, if they are not very solid. It is noteworthy that these thunder-storms and heavy showers never occur in the morning but always in the afternoon. Mornings the sky is entirely clear, but afternoons clouds form and two or three hours thereafter there breaks out the fearful thunder-storm, which sometimes returns at night and rages again. Hence, during these months everyone avoids traveling in the afternoon if possible, because of the constant danger of being caught in such a storm. Therefore, wherever one reaches a shelter around noon, or even a little before, the day's journey is ended.

This three-month rainy season ends, indeed, as has already been stated, in September. However, this is true only of the daily showers accompanied by terrific thunder-storms, for quiet, gentle rains occur intermittently in the three months following. These are general rains which last from one to three days. It even happens, although very seldom, that they continue eight, nine, or ten days. Twice in eleven years I experienced this; the one time it rained ten, the other twelve days and nights, practically without ceasing. At this time the rivers rose over their banks, flooded the surrounding regions, made the roads impassable, and cut off communications with the neighboring villages. Even in the houses, one was afforded little protection. In Sonora the roofs are in very poor condition, since they

consist only of twigs with earth thrown upon them. When the water
has penetrated them, they drip continuously. Consequently, in such
a protracted rain there remained hardly a spot where one could find
shelter.

The Great Salt Lake

Jedediah Smith

The noted explorer Jedediah Smith (1799–1831) traveled throughout the
West during the course of his short life, bestowing his name to rivers and
valleys in Colorado, Idaho, California, and Oregon. It was he who located
Wyoming's South Pass thus opening up the Oregon Trail, and who
mapped much of the interior of Utah, knowledge that Brigham Young
would put to advantage during the Mormon migration that soon followed.
Smith seems to have shown contempt for the Indians he encountered,
as these pages from his journals show. In 1831 a party of Comanches
returned the favor, killing Smith as he traveled eastward along the Santa Fe
Trail.

JUNE 20, 1827. N E 20 miles along a valley sandy as usual and
just at night found water. In this part of the plain almost all the high
hills have snow on their tops. But for these snowy Peaks the country
would be utterly impassible as they furnish almost the only grass or
water of this unhospitable land They are to this place like the islands of the Oceans. Rising but a short distance from the sandy base
the snowy region commences which is an evidence of the great ele-
vation of this plain.

There after encamping some indians came to me. They appeared verry friendly. These as well as those last mentioned I supposed were somewhat acquainted with whites as I saw among them some iron arrow points and some beads. They gave me some squirrels and in return I gave them presents of such little things as I had after which they went to their camp and we our rest.

21ST. 25 MILES NORTH. Early this morning the indians that were at the camp last night returned and with them several others. They seemed to have come out of mere curiosity and as I was ready for starting they accompanied me a short distance. Some of them I presume had never before seen a white man and as they were handling and examining almost every thing I fired off my gun as one of them was fingering about the double triggers. At the sound some fell flat on the ground and some sought safety in flight. The indian who had hold of the gun alone stood still although he appeared at first thunder struck yet on finding that he was not hurt he called out to his companions to return. I endeavored to learn from those indians by signs something in relation to the distance and course to the Salt Lake. But from them I could get no satisfaction whatever for instead of answering my signs they would imitate them as nearly as possible. After vexing myself for some time with those children of nature I left them and continued on my way. All the indians I had seen since leaving the Lake had been the same unintelligent kind of beings. Nearly naked having at most a scanty robe formed from the skin of the hare peculiar to this place which is cut into narrow strips and interwoven with a kind of twine or cord made apparently from wild flax or hemp. They form a connecting link between the animal and intellectual creation and quite in keeping with the country in which they are located. In the course of the day I passed water several times. It came out from a range of hills on the west on the top of which was some snow. I encamped on the bank of a Salt Lake. The water was very salt and a good deal of salt was formed along the beach. In crossing a mirey place just before encamping one of my horses was mired. After some considerable exertion I found it impossible to get him out I therefore killed him and took a quarter of his flesh which was a seasonable replenishment for our stock of provision as the little I took of the horse I killed last was at that time exhausted.

22ND JUNE 1827. NORTH 25 MILES. My course was parallel with a chain of hills on the west on the top of which was some snow and from which ran a creek to the north east. On this creek I encamped. The Country in the vicinity so much resembled that on the south side of the Salt Lake that for a while I was induced to believe that I was near that place. During the day I saw a good many Antelope but could not kill any. I however killed 2 hares which when cooked at night we found much better than horse meat.

JUNE 23D. N E 35 MILES. Moving on in the morning I kept down the creek on which we had encamped until it was lost in a small Lake. We then filled our horns and continued on our course passing some brackish as well as some verry salt springs and leaving on the north of the latter part of the days travel a considerable Salt Plain. Just before night I found water that was drinkable but continued on in hopes of find better and was obliged to encamp without any.

JUNE 24TH. N E 40 MILES. I started verry early in hopes of soon finding water. But ascending a high point of a hill I could discover nothing but sandy plains or dry Rocky hills with the Exception of a snowy mountain off to the NE at the distance of 50 or 60 Miles. When I came down I durst not tell my men of the desolate prospect ahead but framed my story so as to discourage them as little as possible. I told them I saw something black at a distance near which no doubt we would find water. While I had been up one of the horses gave out and had been left a short distance behind. I sent the men back to take the best of his flesh for our supply was again nearly exhausted whilst I would push forward in search of water. I went on a short distance and waited until they came up. They were much discouraged with the gloomy prospect but I said all I could to enliven their hopes and told them in all probability we would soon find water. But the view ahead was almost hopeless. With our best exertion we pushed forward walking as we had been for a long time over the soft sand. That kind of traveling is verry tiresome to men in good health who can eat when and what they choose and drink as often as they desire, and to us worn down with hunger and fatigue and burning with thirst increased by the blazing sands it was almost insupportable. At about 4 O clock we were obliged to stop on the side of a sand hill under the shade of a small Cedar. We dug holes in the sand and laid down in them for the purpose of cooling our heated bodies. After resting about an hour we resumed our wearysome journey and traveled until 10 O clock at night when we laid down to take a little repose. Previous to this and a short time after sun down I saw several turtle doves and as I did not recollect of ever having seen them more than 2 or 3 miles from water I spent more than an hour in looking for water but it was in vain. Our sleep was not repose for tormented nature made us dream of things we had not and for the want of which it then seemed possible and even probable we might perish in the desert unheard of and unpitied. In those moments how trifling were all those things that hold such an absolute sway over the busy and the prosperous world. My dreams were not of Gold or ambitious honors but of my distant quiet home of murmuring brooks, of cooling cascades. After a short rest we continued our march and traveled all night. The murmur of falling waters still sounding in our ears and the apprehension that we might never live to hear that sound in reality weighed heavily uppon us.

JUNE 25TH. When morning came it saw us in the same unhappy situation pursuing our journey over the desolate waste now gleaming in the sun and more insupportably tormenting than it had been during the night. At 10 O Clock Robert Evans laid down in the plain under the shade of a small cedar being able to proceed no further. The Mountain of which I have before spoken was apparently not far off and we left him and proceeded onward in the hope of finding water in time to return with some in season to save his life. After traveling about three Miles we came to the foot of the Mt and then to our inexpressible joy we found water. Goble plunged into it at once and I could hardly wait to bath my burning forehead before I was pouring it down regardless of the consequences. Just before we arrived at the spring I saw two indians traveling in the direction in which Evans was left and soon after the report of two guns was heard in quick succession. This considerably increased our apprehension for his safety but shortly after a smoke was seen back on the trail and I took a small kettle of water and some meat and going back found him safe. He had not seen the indians and had discharged his gun to direct me where he lay and for the same purpose had raised a smoke. He was indeed far gone being scarcely able to speak. When I came the first question he asked me was have you any water! I told him I had plenty and handed the kettle which would hold 6 or 7 quarts in which there was some meat mixed with the water. O says he why did you bring the meat and putting the kettle to his mouth he did not take it away until he had drank all the water of which there was at least 4 or 5 quarts and then asked me why I had not brought more. This however revived him so much that he was able to go on to the spring. I cut the horse meat and spread it out to dry and determined to remain for the rest of the day that we might repose our wearied and emaciated bodies. I have at different times suffered all the extremes of hunger and thirst. Hard as it is to bear for successive days the knawings of hunger yet it is light in comparison to the agony of burning thirst, and on the other hand I have observed that a man reduced by hunger is some days in recovering his strength. A man equally reduced by thirst seems renovated almost instantaneously. Hunger can be endured more than twice as long as thirst. To some it may appear surprising that a man who has been for several days without eating has a most incessant desire to drink and although he can drink but a little at a time yet he wants it much oftener than in ordinary circumstances. In the course of the day several indians showed themselves on the high points of the hills but would not come to my camp.

Canyonlands

Ray Gonzalez

In his poem "Easter Sunday, 1988, The Grand Canyon, Arizona," poet Ray Gonzalez offers a contemplation of mortality in the face of an immortal landscape.

Bodies are resurrected
as the whole earth opens
to show how far we must fall
to keep falling,
how deeply we must fear
the savage god
that tears the distance
into red miles of a planet
we will never reach,
the other side of fear
we will never climb because
the trail to the bottom
leads to the tomb of the river
where the earth continues
to eat itself,
feeding upon the river

that devours the river
until bodies rise
in their own space
to float miles across a canyon
that is not a landscape,
but remains of a great prayer
whose chant cut hundreds of miles
of rock into one big tomb
where bodies suddenly
start falling again,
descending to the bottom
of the inner atmospheres
where gravity grabs us
off the rim,
the river rising to meet us
the last thing we ever see.

Death Valley

Edward Abbey

Edward Abbey (1927–1989) defined the modern desert rat. A fierce
champion of wilderness, he worked for sixteen years as a park ranger and
fire lookout at places like Organ Pipe Cactus National Monument, Aztec
Peak in the Mazatzal Mountains Wilderness, and the North Rim of the
Grand Canyon, all the while crafting a series of novels and books of essays,
among them *Black Sun*, *Abbey's Road*, and *The Monkey Wrench Gang*, and
his most famous paean to the arid lands, *Desert Solitaire*. This passage is
taken from his 1977 book *The Journey Home*.

FURNACE CREEK, DECEMBER 10. The oasis. We stand near the edge of a grove of date palms looking eastward at the soft melting mud hills above Texas Spring. The hills are lemon yellow with dark brown crusts on top, like the frosting on a cake. Beyond the hills rise the elaborate, dark, wine-red mountains. In the foreground, close by, irrigation water plunges into a pool, from which it is diverted into ditches that run between the rows of palms.

The springs of Furnace Creek supply not only the palms but also the water needs of the hotel, the motel (both with swimming pools), Park Service headquarters and visitor center, an Indian village, and two large campgrounds. I do not know the output of these springs as measured in gallons per minute. But I do know that during the Christmas and Easter holidays there is enough water available to serve the needs of 10,000 people. Where does it come from? From a natural reservoir in the base of the bleak, fatally arid Funeral Mountains. A reservoir that may be joined to the larger underground aquifers beneath the Amargosa and Pahrump valleys to the east. This does not mean that the Furnace Creek portion of Death Valley could support a permanent population of 10,000 drinking, back-scrubbing, hard-flushing suburbanites. For the water used here comes from a supply that may have required years to charge; it is not sustained by rainfall—not in a county where precipitation averages two inches per year.

That's the mistake they made in central Arizona—Tucson and Phoenix—and are now making in Las Vegas and Albuquerque. Out of greed and stupidity, but mostly greed, the gentry of those cities overexpanded their investment in development and kept going by mining the underground water supply. Now that the supply is dwindling they set up an unholy clamor in Congress to have the rest of the nation save them from the consequences of their own folly. Phoenix might rise again from ashes—but not, I think, from the sea of sand that is its likely destiny.

There are about 200 springs, all told, within the boundaries of Death Valley National Monument, counting each and every tiny seep that produces any flow at all. None except those in the northeast corner of the park are comparable to the springs at Furnace Creek. In addition to the springs there are the heavily saline, undrinkable waters of Salt Creek, Badwater, and the valley floor itself.

All this water is found in what meteorologists believe to be the hottest place on earth, year in and year out hotter than the Sahara, the Great Karroo, the Negev, the Atacama, the Rub'-al-Khali ("Empty Quarter") of Arabia, or the far-out-back-of-beyond in central Australia. The world's record is held by Libya, where a temperature of 136 degrees Fahrenheit was once recorded at a weather station called Azizia. Death Valley's high so far is a reading of 134 degrees at Furnace Creek. But Azizia has been unable to come near repeating its record, while temperatures at Furnace Creek consistently exceed the mean maximums for Azizia by ten percent. And Badwater, only twenty miles south of Furnace Creek, is on the average always four degrees hotter. It follows that on the historic day when the thermometer reached 134 at Furnace Creek, it was probably 138 at Badwater. But there was nobody around at Badwater that day (July 10, 1913).

Official weather readings are made from instruments housed in a louvered wooden box set five feet above the ground. In Death Valley the temperature on the surface of the ground is ordinarily fifty percent higher than in the box five feet above. On a normal summer's day in Death Valley, with the thermometer reading 120 degrees Fahrenheit, the temperature at ground surface is 180.

Curiosities: There are fish in the briny pools of Salt Creek, far out on the hottest, bleakest, saltiest part of the valley floor—the inch-long cyprinodon or pupfish. There is a species of softbodied snail living in the Epsom salts, Glauber's salt, and rock salts of Badwater. There are fairy shrimp in the *tinajas* or natural cisterns of Butte Valley in the southwest corner of the park; estivating beneath the clay most of the year, they wriggle forth to swim, rejoice, and reproduce after that rarest and most wonderful of Death Valley events, a fall of rain.

More curiosities: Blue herons enter the valley in winter, also trumpeter swans; grebes, coots, and mallards can be seen in the blue ponds of Saratoga Springs; and for a few weeks in the fall of one year (1966) a real flamingo made its home among the reeds that line the shore of the sewage lagoon below Park Village. Where this flamingo came from no one could say; where it went the coyotes most likely could testify. Or perhaps the lion.

A lean and hungry mountain lion was observed several times that year during the Christmas season investigating the garbage cans in the campgrounds. An old lion, no doubt—aging, possibly ill, probably retired. In short, a tourist. But a lion even so.

But these are mere oddities. All the instruments agree that Death Valley remains the hottest place on earth, the driest in North America, the lowest in the Western Hemisphere. Of all deathly places the most deadly—and the most beautiful.

BADWATER, JANUARY 19. Standing among the salt pinnacles of what is called the Devil's Golf Course, I heard a constant tinkling and crackling noise—the salt crust expanding in the morning sun. No sign of life out there. Experimentally I ventured to walk upon, over, among the pinnacles. Difficult, but not impossible. The formations are knee-high, white within but stained yellow by the dusty winds, studded on top with sharp teeth. Like walking on a jumble of broken and refrozen slabs of ice: At every other step part of the salt collapses under foot and you drop into a hole. The jagged edges cut like knives into the leather of my boots. After a few minutes of this I was glad to return to the security of the road. Even in January the sun felt uncomfortably hot, and I was sweating a little.

Where the salt flats come closest to the base of the easterly mountairs, at 278 feet below sea level, lies the clear and sparkling pool known as Badwater. A shallow body of water, surrounded by beds of snow-white alkali. According to Death Valley legend the water is poisonous, containing traces of arsenic. I scooped up a handful and sampled it in my mouth, since the testing of desert waterholes has always been one of my chores. I found Badwater lukewarm, salty on the tongue, sickening. I spat it out and rinsed my mouth with fresh water from my canteen.

From here, the lowest point in all the Americas, I gazed across the pale lenses of the valley floor to the brown outwash fan of Hanaupah Canyon opposite, ten miles away, and from the canyon's mouth up and up and up to the crest of Telescope Peak with its cornices of frozen snow 11,049 feet above sea level. One would like to climb or descend that interval someday, the better to comprehend what it means. Whatever it means.

I have been part of the way already, hiking far into Hanaupah Canyon to Shorty Borden's abandoned camp, up to that loveliest of desert graces, a spring-fed stream. Lively, bubbling, with pools big enough and cold enough, it seemed then, for trout. But there are none. Along the stream grow tangles of wild grapevine and willow; the spring is choked with watercress. The stream runs for less than a mile before disappearing into the sand and gravel of the wash. Beyond the spring, up-canyon, all is dry as death again until you reach the place where the canyon forks. Explore either fork and you find water once more—on the right a little waterfall, on the left in a grottolike glen cascades sliding down through chutes in the dark blue andesite. Moss, ferns, and flowers cling to the damp walls—the only life in this arid wilderness. Almost no one ever goes there. It is necessary to walk for many miles.

The Alkali Desert

Mark Twain

Samuel Langhorne Clemens (1835–1910), better known by his pen name Mark Twain, was renowned in his time as an intrepid adventurer, and he spent his share of time in the deserts of North Africa and the Near East while writing *The Innocents Abroad*. Those deserts he found comparatively tame next to the Great Salt Lake Desert of western Utah, an imposing alkali flat that sees little more than the occasional drag race or military bombing (and, on the Nevada side of the line, the odd casino). In this excerpt from *Roughing It* (1872), an account of his "variegated vagabonding" throughout the West in the late 1860s, Twain recalls what was then a harrowing passage through this forbidding region.

At eight in the morning we reached the remnant and ruin of what had been the important military station of "Camp Floyd," some forty-five or fifty miles from Salt Lake City. At four P.M. we had doubled our distance and were ninety or a hundred miles from Salt Lake. And now we entered upon one of that species of deserts whose concentrated hideousness shames the diffused and diluted horrors of Sahara—an "*alkali*" desert. For sixty-eight miles there was but one break in it. I do not remember that this was really a break; indeed it seems to me that it was nothing but a watering depot *in the midst* of the stretch of sixty-eight miles. If my memory serves me, there was no well or spring at this place, but the water was hauled there by mule and ox teams from the further side of the desert. There was a stage station there. It was forty-five miles from the beginning of the desert, and twenty-three from the end of it.

We plowed and dragged and groped along, the whole livelong night, and at the end of this uncomfortable twelve hours we finished the forty-five-mile part of the desert and got to the stage station where the imported water was. The sun was just rising. It was easy enough to cross a desert in the night while we were asleep; and it was pleasant to reflect, in the morning, that we in actual person *had* encountered an absolute desert and could always speak knowingly of deserts in presence of the ignorant thenceforward. And it was pleasant also to reflect that this was not an obscure, back country desert, but a very celebrated one, the metropolis itself, as you may say. All this was very well and very comfortable and satisfactory—but now we were to cross a desert in *daylight*. This was fine—novel—romantic—dramatically adventurous—this, indeed, was worth living for, worth traveling for! We would write home all about it.

This enthusiasm, this stern thirst for adventure, wilted under the sultry August sun and did not last above one hour. One poor little hour—and then we were ashamed that we had "gushed" so. The poetry was all in the anticipation—there is none in the reality. Imagine a vast, waveless ocean stricken dead and turned to ashes; imagine this solemn waste tufted with ash-dusted sage-bushes; imagine the lifeless silence and solitude that belong to such a place; imagine a coach, creeping like a bug through the midst of this shoreless level, and sending up tumbled volumes of dust as if it were a bug that went by steam; imagine this aching monotony of toiling and plowing kept up hour after hour, and the shore still as far away as ever, apparently; imagine team, driver, coach and passengers so deeply coated with ashes that they are all one colorless color; imagine ash-drifts roosting above moustaches and eyebrows like snow accumulations on boughs and bushes. This is the reality of it.

The sun beats down with dead, blistering, relentless malignity; the perspiration is welling from every pore in man and beast, but scarcely a sign of it finds its way to the surface—it is absorbed before it gets there; there is not the faintest breath of air stirring; there is not a merciful shred of cloud in all the brilliant firmament; there is not a living creature visible in any direction whither one searches the blank level that stretches its monotonous miles on every hand; there is not a sound—not a sigh—not a whisper—not a buzz or a whir of wings, or distant pipe of bird—not even a sob from the lost souls that doubtless people that dead air. And so the occasional sneezing of the resting mules, and the champing of the bits, grate harshly on the grim stillness, not dissipating the spell but accenting it and making one feel more lonesome and forsaken than before.

The mules, under violent swearing, coaxing and whipcracking, would make at stated intervals a "spurt," and drag the coach a hundred or may be two hundred yards, stirring up a billowy cloud of dust that rolled back, enveloping the vehicle to the wheel-tops or higher, and making it seem afloat in a fog. Then a rest followed, with the usual sneezing and bit-champing. Then another "spurt" of a hundred yards and another rest at the end of it. All day long we kept this up without water for the mules and without ever changing the team. At least we kept it up ten hours, which, I take it, is a day, and a pretty honest one, in an alkali desert. It was from four in the morning till two in the afternoon. And it was so hot! and so close! and our water-canteens went dry in the middle of the day and we got so thirsty! It was so stupid and tiresome and dull! and the tedious hours did lag and drag and limp along with such a cruel deliberation! It was so trying to give one's watch a good long undisturbed spell and then take it out and find that it had been fooling away the time and not trying to get ahead any! The alkali dust cut through our lips, it persecuted our eyes, it ate through the delicate membranes and made our noses bleed and *kept* them bleeding—and truly and seriously the romance all faded far away and disappeared, and left the desert trip nothing but a harsh reality—a thirsty, sweltering, longing, hateful reality!

Two miles and a quarter an hour for ten hours—that was what we accomplished. It was hard to bring the comprehension away down to such a snail-pace as that, when we had been used to making eight and ten miles an hour. When we reached the station on the farther verge of the desert, we were glad, for the first time, that the dictionary was along, because we never could have found language to tell how glad we were, in any sort of dictionary but an unabridged one with pictures in it. But there could not have been found in a whole library of dictionaries language sufficient to tell how tired those mules were after their twenty-three mile pull. To try to give the reader an idea of how *thirsty* they were, would be to "gild refined gold or paint the lily."

Somehow, now that it is there, the quotation does not seem to fit—but no matter, let it stay, anyhow. I think it is a graceful and attractive thing, and therefore have tried time and time again to work it in where it *would* fit, but could not succeed. These efforts have kept my mind distracted and ill at ease, and made my narrative seem broken and disjointed, in places. Under these circumstances it seems to me best to leave it in, as above, since this will afford at least a temporary respite from the wear and tear of trying to "lead up" to this really apt and beautiful quotation.

The Pinacate

Carl Lumholtz

Born at Lillehammer, Norway, Carl Lumholtz (1851–1922) first traveled abroad to Australia in 1880 to collect zoological specimens for European museums and zoos. There he fell in love with the desert and resolved to see the arid lands of the world. He traveled throughout Mexico in the 1890s, and in 1909 and 1910 he journeyed across the Sonoran Desert on horseback, making the notes on which his 1912 book *New Trails in Mexico* is based. During World War I he lived in Borneo, and he died at Saranac

Lake, New York, while writing a book about his adventures in the jungle. This passage describes the Pinacate region of the Sonoran Desert, graduate school to the rest of the desert's romper room.

We camped on the sand for the night. Although there was considerable galleta grass growing here and there, all the mules, donkeys, and horses gathered at once around a lone but very large palo fierro tree to eat its dark green juicy leaves, which they much preferred. They stretched their necks like giraffes in eager competition and, paying no heed to its numerous thorns, they pulled away mouthfuls of leaves. We usually cut down large branches, Mexican fashion, from which they could feed more comfortably. The palo fierro (*olneya tesota*) is to one who travels in the desert the most useful of all trees; whenever it is to be found, his animals are sure to get something good to eat, and the man who gathers wood for the camp first of all directs his steps toward it. Usually some of its branches are dry, and they furnish the very best camp-fire, especially for cooking purposes. In the cold winter, when a warm fire is needed, the traveller should look for a dry log of this kind. As the wood is extremely hard—hence its name, iron-wood—the easiest way to fell a dry tree is to make a fire round the base. It ignites easily and burns the whole night through without any further attention. During many months of travel in the desert, I was always thankful when I caught sight of this tree which harbors so much comfort for man and beast. In the spring, before the leaves come out, it has beautiful flowers of the pea family.

There was, of course, no water here, but at this time of the year animals that are being worked do not suffer from going a couple of days without drinking. In the winter at Sonoita the horses running loose in the neighborhood come in to drink only every fourth day, and in the summer every third day. For our own consumption we had our generous barrels which we refilled when occasion offered. The

sand was temptingly clean and made a soft bed, all the men delight-
ing in it. The next day I remained behind with the guide in order to
examine the sand dunes. That part of the sand-dune belt where we
were, south of Pinacate, starts only twenty to twenty-five miles east
of there. The height of a sand-hill that we ascended was one hundred and eighty-five feet, both my aneroids giving the same result. I
calculated the length of its base, which was measured by the steps of
our horses, to be at least two thousand eight hundred feet. There
were others equally high or higher. Farther west, toward Laguna
Prieta, are found the highest sand-hills, but they would probably not
be much above two hundred feet, if measured. On top of the one we
climbed, an absolute calm reigned. Toward the west as far as the eye
could detect the dunes extended, like the sea when exposed to a
strong gale in appearance, though with waves much more irregular.
The large ones forming the extreme northern part of the belt, were
fewer than I expected. Southward from our hill the waves first became considerably smaller, then grew somewhat higher again before
reaching the coast, where they ended in more or less irregular sand
flats or low hills The sea did not seem more than eight or nine miles
away.

The Mexicans use the euphonious name médanos for the sand
dunes, great and small; in fact, the whole region along the upper part
of the Gulf east of the Colorado River is thus designated. The name
has an almost mystic sound, suggesting in the summer aridity and
danger, fierce heat, rattlesnakes, and other reptiles—in the winter
cold wind, fog, and occasional drizzling rain.

Most Mexicans are afraid of los médanos, as they themselves
have told me, on account of the risk of losing animals and of the
troubles in general connected with travel there. As is the case with
all regions about which little or nothing is known, the sand region is
reputed to harbor fabulous wealth of gold and silver in its hill-tops
and mountain ranges, and a lonely prospector with a couple of don-

keys sometimes attempts in the winter an exploration for these precious metals. His expectations may lead him farther than is prudent, and his canteens may give out too soon for him to have time to return for water. There is nothing depressing, however, about the sand dunes. In the late afternoon sun, when seen from the north, they look especially picturesque, running one after the other in long, majestic, though somewhat uneven, waves of light roseate hue.

A curious feature of the dunes south of Pinacate was a remarkable display of tracks made by the big beetle from which the whole region derived its Mexican name. These insects (*eleodes*), of which the body may be over an inch in length, were numerous at that time of the year in the northern part of the sand dunes. In certain localities they are the principal means of subsistence for the coyote. They wander far and wide on the sand, leaving surprisingly large tracks, most of which are fairly straight. The weather had been calm for twenty-four hours at least, and the tracks were even more distinct than those seen on cold, hard snow. The long lines ran almost parallel to each other across the great fans of sand that stretched down from the tops of the dunes. Some of them ran upward, for these beetles wander to the very summit. One of them in coming down the slope of a drift had amused himself in going in a spiral line for many yards and then continuing in his ordinary fashion. The beetle to which this pictograph was due was undoubtedly a different species, because its tracks were somewhat lighter and the straight line less pronounced. Another one had for many yards followed the ridge of a sand drift, but progressing all the while from one side to the other, and leaving low, hanging festoons from the top of the ridge in regular serpentine figure. Only one, making his way very straight and quite fast up the slope toward the ridge on which we stood, was actually seen. I was puzzled as to why these insects should go up there on the sand dunes, but, whatever their reasons were, they certainly left in their wake beautiful decorative marks hundreds of feet long.

The pool called Tinaja de los Chivos was reached on a slowly rising lava flow ten miles north of the sand dunes. There is no grass within a mile or two of this camp, which derives its Mexican name from the vulgar designation of mountain-sheep as *chivos*, goats. Fuel is also scarce here. It is the largest of all the natural water tanks of the Pinacate and lasts longer than the rest. It is situated at the junction of two arroyos, and at one of them, a mile away, is found another reservoir, called Tinaja del Tule. The following morning the sky was overcast with stratus and light nimbus clouds, and the long even range of Lower California looked quite impressive in the hazy atmosphere. Before sunrise we had a beautiful tanager-red glow which extended over the western horizon before it assumed a blue hue.

In order to reach the next place where water is found, Tinaja de los Papagos, a circuitous route has to be followed. In descending to the dunes again, we found a very good track which led to the headquarters, four miles away, of the former sand-dune people. The trail was worn a foot deep in places, and stones had been removed to smooth the path for the busy feet of the women who had to go this distance every day to fill their jars. We discovered two old camps at the edge of the dunes, each on a low sand ridge. There were the usual features of rude corrals of stones, but the sand inside of them had been scooped out, leaving a hollow. Sometimes pits were noticed without any stones around them. On a plain near by feasts and ceremonies had in former times been performed, and among them the great annual festival which is now given at Quitovac.

The afternoon turned out to be moderately warm and calm, the sun appearing now and then, and the weather, for the middle of January, was very enjoyable. I ascended a small ridge at one side of the track to get a better view of a crumbling and much serrated sierra which appeared in front of us, and near which we were going to camp. It showed two formations, most of it the usual gray, weather-worn granite, but at the southeastern end an intrusion of a reddish rock had taken place, which proved afterward to consist of rhyolite with all oxydized rim of red. South of it at a short distance stretched a low, jagged range, half buried in the sand. To the north-east, south of the Gila Range and far away at the end of a large llano, a single mountain was seen. It looked deep blue and, having no name, we called it Cerro Pinto, because its color is different from the rest of the mountains. The distant country westward, directly in front of us, presented a sea of sand dunes that seemed to stretch on indefinitely offering a fascinating vista. Just as the sun, breaking through the clouds, covered them with a brilliant white light, I turned around to secure my camera, and in doing so was delayed scarcely a minute, but when I looked again westward, while adjusting my kodak, all the magic of the scene was gone—the sun was hidden from view and all chance of photography over, though I waited half an hour for another. An opportunity to take such a picture never did return as long as the expedition lasted.

Salt Gathering

Tohono O'odham song

The Tohono O'odham ("stony ground people") of the Sonoran Desert have developed a substantial body of ritual song over the centuries, with a musical complement to nearly every aspect of daily life. This song, translated by the anthropologist Ruth Underhill in her book *Singing for Power*, is traditionally sung before the annual salt-gathering journey to the Gulf of California, some five days' walk from the Tohono homeland.

Food she cooked for me,
I did not eat.

Water she poured for me,
I did not drink.
Then thus to me she said:
"What is it? You did not eat the food which I have cooked;
The water which I fetched you did not drink."
Then thus I said:
"It is a thing I feel."

I rose and across the bare spaces did go walking,
Did peep through the openings in the scrub,
Looking about me, seeking something.
Thus I went on and on.
Where there was a tree that suited me,
Beneath it prone and solitary I lay,
My forehead upon my folded arms I lay.

There was an ancient woman.
Some lore she had somehow learned
And quietly she went about telling it.
To me she spoke, telling it.
Then did I raise myself upon my hands;
I put them to my face and wiped away the dust,
I put them to my hair and shook out rubbish.

I rose. I reached the shade before my house.
There did I try to sit: not like itself it seemed.
Then did I make myself small and squeeze through
    my narrow door.
On my bed I tried to lie: not like itself it seemed.
About me with my hand I felt.
About the withes that bound the walls I felt
Seeking my jointed reed [cigarette].

Then thus I did.
Within my hut I tried to feel about with my fingers.
At the base of my hut, in the dirt,
I tried to feel about with my fingers
Seeking my jointed reed.
I could not find it.
To the center of the house did I go crawling
    [the roof being low].
And the center post
Seemed a white prayer stick,
So like it was.
At its base did I go feeling in the dirt
Seeking my jointed reed.
I could not find it.

There did I seize my flat stick [for hoeing];
I leaned upon it. I made myself small and squeezed out the door.
Lo, I saw my ashes in many piles.
Already were they all hardened and all cracked. I sat
down and with the hoe I went to breaking
    them.
Among them, somehow, did I find my reed joint.

Then did I scratch it.
Lo, there still tobacco lay.
There beside me then I saw
Near me, lying, a shaman ember charred.

Long ago had it grown moldy and full of holes.
I took it up and four times hard did shake it. Within,
a spark burst out and brightly burned.

Then the reed point did I light and to my lips I
    put it,
And somehow tried to move toward my desire.

[The speaker begins "throwing words"]

In what direction shall I first breathe out?
To eastward did I breathe.
It was my reed smoke in white filaments stretching.
I followed it and I went on and on.
Four times I stopped, and then I reached
The rain house standing in the east.
Wonderful things were done there.

All kinds of white clouds thatch it.
All kinds of rainbows form the binding withes.
The winds upon its roof fourfold are tied.
Powerless was I there.
It was my reed smoke.
Therewith did I go untying them.
Quietly I peeped in.
Lo, there I saw
Him [the rain-maker], my guardian.
Yonder, far back in the house, facing away from
    me he sat.
My reed smoke toward him did circling go.
Toward the door it caused him to turn his eyes,
And set him there.

Then did I say:
"What will you do, my guardian?
Yonder see!

The earth which you have spread thus wretched
  seems.
The mountains which you placed erect now
  crumbling stand.
The trees you planted have no leaves,
The birds you threw into the air
Wretchedly flit therein and do not sing.
The beasts that run upon the earth
At the tree roots go digging holes
And make no sound.
The wretched people
See nothing fit to eat."
Thus did I say.

Then did the bowels within him crack with pity.
"Verily, nephew, for so I name you,
Do you enter my house and do you tell me
  something?
The people are afraid, none dares to enter;
But you have entered and have told me,
And something indeed I will cause you to see."

"But let me reach my house, then let it happen."

Then in his breast he put his hand and brought forth seed:
White seeds blue seed, red seed, smooth seed.
Then did I fold it tight and grasp it and rush forth.
I saw the land did sloping lie.
Before I had gone far, the wind did follow and
  breathe upon me.
Then down at the foot of the east there moved
  the clouds

And from their breasts the lightning did go roaring.
Though the earth seemed very wide,
Straight across it fell the rain
And stabbed the north with its needles.
Straight across it fell the rain
And stabbed the south with its needles.
The flood channels, lying side by side,
Seemed many,
But the water from all directions went filling
    them to the brim.
The ditches, lying side by side,
Seemed many,
But the water along them went bubbling.
The magicians on the near-by mountains
Went rushing out, gathering themselves together;
The storm went on and on.
It reached the foot of the west, it turned and faced about.
It saw the earth spongy with moisture.

Thus beautifully did my desire end.
Thus perchance will you also feel, my kinsmen.

SOUTH
AMERICA

Now surrounded by light
I am serene.
   César Vallejo

The South American continent embraces two narrow but extensive
deserts: the Patagonian of Argentina (260,000 square miles),
produced by the rainshadow effect of the Andes cordillera, and the
smaller Atacama of Chile (140,000 square miles), which runs up
the northern coast of Chile alongside a cold ocean current that
keeps precipitation from falling inland. Neither has been
thoroughly explored, and both present continued challenges to
latter-day travelers and geographers. Some geographers also
consider parts of the northeastern Brazilian state of Ceará, an area
called the Sertão, to be true desert; certainly it has produced some
of the most powerful writing to depict the hard lives of those who
make their homes in the drylands.

The Four Winds

Ona folktale

The Ona Indians are among the few indigenous peoples of southernmost Patagonia, a harsh land of blasting winds and subzero temperatures. They tell a story of the winds' struggle for supremacy.

The four winds were once human beings and, like humans, argued among themselves over who was strongest. They decided to wrestle. A crowd gathered to watch as they paired off and began their combat.

Wintekhaiyin, East Wind, blew too gently and was easily defeated by the other three. He put on his alpaca robe and conceded defeat. Orroknnhaiyin, South Wind, was much stronger, but not strong enough. He, too, left the contest.

Hechuknhaiyin, North Wind, was evil-tempered and fierce. But Kenenikhaiyin, West Wind, who comes down from the mountains, was just as mean and strong, and much more persistent. Kenenikhaiyin won.

A Giant of Patagonia

Antonio Pigafetta

In 1519, the Portuguese sailor Ferdinand Magellan (1479–1521) set out under the flag of Spain to find a westward passage to the Spice Islands. He never arrived; having survived scurvy, mutiny, and hunger, he was killed by Filipino tribesmen while taking on supplies. En route, his scribe Antonio Pigafetta, who made his way home to Spain in 1522, kept a careful logbook. It includes this remarkable sighting in Patagonia.

One day, without anyone expecting it, we saw a giant, who was on the shore of the sea, quite naked, and was dancing and leaping, and singing, and while singing he put sand and dust on his head. He was so tall that the tallest of us came up only to his waist, and he was strongly built. He had a broad face, painted red, and his eyes were ringed by yellow paint as well. He had two little hearts painted on his cheeks; he did not have much hair on his head, and what little he had was painted white. When he came before the captain he was clothed with the skin of an animal that had the head and ears of a mule, but the neck and body of a camel, a deer's legs, and a horse's tail. Many such animals live in this place.

The captain ordered that this giant be given food and water; then he showed him a few things, among them a metal mirror. When the giant saw himself in it he was terrified. He jumped away and knocked down three or four of our men.

One of the giant's brethren, who never came to the ship, saw him come aboard with our crew. He ran to the camp of the other giants. They came out, naked, and began to jump and sing, pointing one finger to heaven. They showed us a white powder made of roots, which they stored in clay pots, and gave us to understand that they live on it alone. Their women came after them loaded like donkeys with their household goods. They were not as tall as the men, but they were large all the same. When we saw them we were amazed, because their breasts were huge. Their faces were painted, too, and they wore animal skins like the men. They also wore a small loin-cloth to cover themselves. They brought along four of the little animals whose skins they wear, leashed together like dogs.

The Plains of Patagonia

W. H. Hudson

William Henry Hudson (1841–1922) was born to English parents in Quilmes, Argentina, and lived in Patagonia for the next thirty-three years, after which he moved to London. Among his many books are the classics *Green Mansions* (1904), *The Purple Land* (1885), and a memoir completed late in life, *Idle Days in Patagonia* (1917), from which the following excerpt is drawn.

We know that the more deeply our feelings are moved by any scene the more vivid and lasting will its image be in memory—a fact which accounts for the comparatively unfading character of the images that date back to the period of childhood, when we are most emotional. Judging from my own case, I believe that we have here the secret of the persistence of Patagonian images, and their frequent recurrence in the minds of many who have visited that gray, monotonous, and in one sense, eminently uninteresting region. It is not the effect of the unknown, it is not imagination; it is that nature in these desolate scenes, for a reason to be guessed at by-and-by, moves us more deeply than in others. In describing his rambles in one of the most desolate spots in Patagonia, Darwin remarks: "Yet, in passing over these scenes, without one bright object near, an ill-defined but strong sense of pleasure is vividly excited." When I recall a Patagonian scene, it comes before me so complete in all its vast extent, with all its details so clearly outlined, that, if I were actually gazing on it, I could scarcely see it more distinctly; yet other scenes, even those that were beautiful and sublime, with forest, and ocean, and mountain, and over all the deep blue sky and brilliant sunshine of the tropics, appear no longer distinct and entire in memory, and

only become more broken and clouded if any attempt is made to regard them attentively. Here and there I see a wooded mountain,
a grove of palms, a flowery tree, green waves dashing on a rocky
shore—nothing but isolated patches of bright color, the parts of
the picture that have not faded on a great blurred canvas, or series
of canvases. These last are images of scenes which were looked on
with wonder and admiration—feelings which the Patagonian wastes
could not inspire—but the gray, monotonous solitude woke other
and deeper feelings, and in that mental state the scene was indelibly
impressed on my mind.

I spent the greater part of one winter at a point on the Rio Negro,
seventy or eighty miles from the sea, where the valley on my side of
the water was about five miles wide. The valley alone was habitable,
where there was water for man and beast, and a thin soil producing
grass and grain; it is perfectly level, and ends abruptly at the foot of
the bank or terrace-like formation of the higher barren plateau. It
was my custom to go out every morning on horseback with my gun,
and, followed by one dog, to ride away from the valley; and no sooner
would I climb the terrace and plunge into the gray universal thicket,
than I would find myself as completely alone and cut off from all sight
and sound of human occupancy as if five hundred instead of only
five miles separated me from the hidden green valley and river. So
wild and solitary and remote seemed that gray waste, stretching
away into infinitude, a waste untrodden by man, and where the wild
animals are so few that they have made no discoverable path in the
wilderness of thorns. There I might have dropped down and died,
and my flesh been devoured by birds, and my bones bleached white
in sun and wind, and no person would have found them, and it would
have been forgotten that one had ridden forth in the morning and
had not returned. Or if, like the few wild animals there—puma,
huanaco, and harelike colichotis, or Darwin's rhea and the crested

tinamou among the birds—I had been able to exist, and dwelt there until I had grown gray as the stones and trees around me, and no human foot would have stumbled on my hiding-place.

Not once, nor twice, nor thrice, but day after day I returned to this solitude, going to it in the morning as if to attend a festival, and leaving it only when hunger and thirst and the westering sun compelled me. And yet I had no object in going—no motive which could be put into words; for although I carried a gun, there was nothing to shoot—the shooting was all left behind in the valley. Sometimes a dolichotis, starting up at my approach, flashed for one moment on my sight, to vanish the next moment in the continuous thicket; or a covey of tinamous sprang rocket-like into the air, and fled away with long wailing notes and loud whir of wings; or on some distant hillside a bright patch of yellow, or a deer that was watching me, appeared and remained motionless for two or three minutes. But the animals were few, and sometimes I would pass an entire day without seeing one mammal, and perhaps not more than a dozen birds of any size. The weather at that time was cheerless, generally with a gray film of cloud spread over the sky, and a bleak wind, often cold enough to make my bridle hand feel quite numb. Moreover, it was not possible to enjoy a canter; the bushes grew so close together that it was as much as one could do to pass through at a walk without brushing against them; and at this slow pace, which would have seemed intolerable in other circumstances, I would ride about for hours at a stretch. In the scene itself there was nothing to delight the eye. Everywhere through the light, gray mold, gray as ashes and formed by the ashes of myriads of generations of dead trees, where the wind had blown on it, or the rain had washed it away, the underlying yellow sand appeared, and the old ocean-polished pebbles, dull red, and gray, and green, and yellow. On arriving at a hill, I would slowly ride to its summit, and stand there to survey the prospect. On every side it stretched away in great undulations; but the undulations were wild

and irregular; the hills were rounded and cone-shaped; they were
solitary and in groups and ranges; some sloped gently, others were
ridge-like and stretched away in league-long terraces, with other
terraces beyond; and all alike were clothed in the gray everlasting
thorny vegetation. How gray it all was! hardly less so near at hand
than on the haze-wrapped horizon, where the hills were dim and the
outline blurred by distance. Sometimes I would see the large eagle-
like white-breasted buzzard, *Buteo erythronotus*, perched on the summit of a bush half a mile away; and so long as it would continue stationed motionless before me my eyes would remain involuntarily
fixed on it, just as one keeps his eyes on a bright light shining in the
gloom; for the whiteness of the hawk seemed to exercise a fascina-
tion power on the vision, so surpassingly bright was it by contrast in
the midst of that universal unrelieved grayness. Descending from
my look-out, I would take up my aimless wanderings again, and visit
other elevations to gaze on the same landscape from another point;
and so on for hours, and at noon I would dismount and sit or lie on
my folded poncho for an hour or longer. One day, in these rambles, I
discovered a small grove composed of twenty to thirty trees, about
eighteen feet high, and taller than the surrounding trees. They were
growing at a convenient distance apart, and had evidently been re-
sorted to by a herd of deer or other wild animals for a very long time,
for the boles were polished to a glassy smoothness with much rubbing, and the ground beneath was trodden to a floor of clean, loose
yellow sand. This grove was on a hill differing in shape from other
hills in its neighborhood, so that it was easy for me to find it on other
occasions; and after a time I made a point of finding and using it as a
resting-place every day at noon. I did not ask myself why I made
choice of that one spot, sometimes going miles out of my way to sit
there, instead of sitting down under any one of the millions of trees
and bushes covering the country, on any other hillside. I thought
nothing at all about it but acted unconsciously; only afterwards,

when revolving the subject, it seemed to me that after having rested there once, each time I wished to rest again the wish came associated with the image of that particular clump of trees, with polished stems and clean bed of sand beneath; and in a short time I formed a habit of returning, animal-like, to repose at that same spot.

It was perhaps a mistake to say that I would sit down and rest, since I was never tired: and yet without being tired, that noonday pause, during which I sat for an hour without moving, was strangely grateful. All day the silence seemed grateful, it was very perfect, very profound. There were no insects, and the only bird sound—a feeble chirp of alarm emitted by a small skulking wren-like species—was not heard oftener than two or three times an hour. The only sounds as I rode were the muffled hoof-strokes of my horse, scratching of twigs against my boot or saddle-flap, and the low panting of the dog. And it seemed to be relief to escape even from these sounds when I dismounted and sat down: for in a few moments the dog would stretch his head out on his paws and go to sleep, and then there would be no sound, not even the rustle of a leaf. For unless the wind blows strong there is no fluttering motion and no whisper in the small still undeciduous leaves; and the bushes stand unmoving as if carved out of stone. One day while *listening* to the silence, it occurred to my mind to wonder what the effect would be if I were to shout aloud. This seemed at the time a horrible suggestion of fancy, a "lawless and uncertain thought" which almost made me shudder, and I was anxious to dismiss it quickly from my mind. But during those solitary days it was a rare thing for any thought to cross my mind; animal forms did not cross my vision or bird-voices assail my hearing more rarely. In that novel state of mind I was in, thought had become impossible. Elsewhere I had always been able to think most freely on horseback; and on the pampas, even in the most lively places, my mind was always most active when I traveled at a swinging gallop. This was doubtless habit; but now, with a horse under me, I had become incapable of reflection: my mind had suddenly transformed itself from a thinking machine into a machine for some other unknown purpose. To think was like setting in motion a noisy engine in my brain; and there was something there which bade me be still, and I was forced to obey. My state was one of *suspense* and *watchfulness*: yet I had no expectation of meeting with an adventure, and felt as free from apprehension as I feel now when sitting in a room in London. The change in me was just as great and wonderful as if I had changed my identity for that of another man or animal; but at the time I was powerless to wonder at or speculate about it; the state seemed familiar rather than strange, and although accompanied by a strong feeling of elation, I did not know it—did not know that something had come between me and my intellect—until I lost it and returned to my former self—to thinking, and the old insipid existence.

The South

Jorge Luis Borges

Long considered the premier Spanish-language writer of his time, the Argentine poet and fabulist Jorge Luis Borges (1899–1986) devoted most of his attention to cosmopolitan themes and European literary arcana. When he wrote of his native country, he often turned to themes of violence, machismo, and foreboding, all of which come to bear in "The South," a vivid tale set in Patagonia.

Every Argentine knows that the South begins at the other side of Rivadavia. Dahlmann was in the habit of saying that this was no mere convention, that whoever crosses this street enters a more ancient and sterner world. From inside the carriage he sought out, among the new buildings, the iron grill window, the brass knocker, the arched door, the entrance way, the intimate patio.

At the railroad station he noted that he still had thirty minutes. He quickly recalled that in a cafe on the Calle Brazil (a few dozen feet from Yrigoyen's house) there was an enormous cat which allowed itself to be caressed as if it were a disdainful divinity. He entered the cafe. There was the cat, asleep. He ordered a cup of coffee, slowly stirred the sugar, sipped it (this pleasure had been denied him in the clinic), and thought, as he smoothed the cat's black coat, that this contact was an illusion and that the two beings, man and cat, were as good as separated by a glass, for man lives in time, in succession, while the magical animal lives in the present, in the eternity of the instant.

Along the next to the last platform the train lay waiting. Dahlmann walked through the coaches until he found one almost empty. He arranged his baggage in the network rack. When the train started off, he took down his valise and extracted, after some hesitation, the first volume of *The Thousand and One Nights*. To travel with this book, which was so much a part of the history of his ill-fortune, was a kind of affirmation that his ill-fortune had been annulled; it was a joyous and secret defiance of the frustrated forces of evil.

Along both sides of the train the city dissipated into suburbs; this sight, and then a view of the gardens and villas, delayed the beginning of his reading. The truth was that Dahlmann read very little. The magnetized mountain and the genie who swore to kill his benefactor are who would deny it?—marvelous, but not so much more than the morning itself and the mere fact of being. The joy of life distracted him from paying attention to Scheherezade and her superfluous miracles. Dahlmann closed his book and allowed himself to live.

Lunch—the bouillon served in shining metal bowls, as in the remote summers of childhood—was one more peaceful and rewarding delight.

Tomorrow I'll wake up at the ranch, he thought, and it was as if he was two men at a time: the man who traveled through the autumn day and across the geography of the fatherland, and the other one, locked up in a sanitarium and subject to methodical servitude. He saw unplastered brick houses, long and angled, timelessly watching the trains go by; he saw horsemen along the dirt roads; he saw gullies and lagoons and ranches; he saw great luminous clouds that resembled marble; and all these things were accidental, casual, like dreams of the plain. He also thought he recognized trees and crop fields; but he would not have been able to name them, for his actual knowledge of the countryside was quite inferior to his nostalgic and literary knowledge.

From time to time he slept, and his dreams were animated by the impetus of the train. The intolerable white sun of high noon had already become the yellow sun which precedes nightfall, and it would not be long before it would turn red. The railroad car was now also different; it was not the same as the one which had quit the station siding at Constitución; the plain and the hours had transfigured it. Outside, the moving shadow of the railroad car stretched toward the horizon. The elemental earth was not perturbed either by settlements or other signs of humanity. The country was vast but at the same time intimate and, in some measure, secret. The limitless country sometimes contained only a solitary bull. The solitude was perfect, perhaps hostile, and it might have occurred to Dahlmann that he was traveling into the past and not merely south. He was distracted from these considerations by the railroad inspector who, on reading his ticket, advised him that the train would not let him off at the regular station but at another: an earlier stop, one scarcely known to Dahlmann. (The man added an explanation which Dahlmann did not attempt to understand, and which he hardly heard, for the mechanism of events did not concern him.)

The train laboriously ground to a halt, practically in the middle of the plain. The station lay on the other side of the tracks; it was not much more than a siding and a shed. There was no means of conveyance to be seen, but the station chief supposed that the traveler might secure a vehicle from a general store and inn to be found some ten or twelve blocks away.

Dahlmann accepted the walk as a small adventure. The sun had already disappeared from view, but a final splendor exalted the vivid and silent plain, before the night erased its color. Less to avoid fatigue than to draw out his enjoyment of these sights, Dahlmann walked slowly, breathing in the odor of clover with sumptuous joy.

The general store at one time had been painted a deep scarlet, but the years had tempered this violent color for its own good. Something in its poor architecture recalled a steel engraving, perhaps one from an old edition of *Paul et Virginie*. A number of horses were hitched up to the paling. Once inside, Dahlmann thought he recognized the shopkeeper. Then he realized that he had been deceived by the man's resemblance to one of the male nurses in the sanitarium. When the shopkeeper heard Dahlmann's request, he said he would have the shay made up. In order to add one more event to that day and to kill time, Dahlmann decided to eat at the general store.

Some country louts, to whom Dahlmann did not at first pay any attention, were eating and drinking at one of the tables. On the floor, and hanging on to the bar, squatted an old man, immobile as an object. His years had reduced and polished him as water does a stone or the generations of men do a sentence. He was dark, dried up, diminutive, and seemed outside time, situated in eternity. Dahlmann noted with satisfaction the kerchief, the thick poncho, the long chiripá, and the colt boots, and told himself, as he recalled futile discussions with people from the Northern counties or from the province of Entre Rios, that gauchos like this no longer existed outside the South.

Dahlmann sat down next to the window. The darkness began overcoming the plain, but the odor and sound of the earth penetrated the iron bars of the window. The shop owner brought him sardines, followed by some roast meat. Dahlmann washed the meal down with several glasses of red wine. Idling, he relished the tart savor of the wine and let his gaze, now grown somewhat drowsy, wander over the shop. A kerosene lamp hung from a beam. There were three customers at the other table: two of them appeared to be farm workers; the third man, whose features hinted at Chinese blood, was drinking with his hat on. Of a sudden, Dahlmann felt something brush lightly against his face. Next to the heavy glass of turbid wine, upon one of the stripes in the table cloth, lay a spit ball of breadcrumb. That was all but someone had thrown it there.

The men at the other table seemed totally cut off from him. Perplexed, Dahlmann decided that nothing had happened, and he opened the volume of *The Thousand and One Nights*, by way of suppressing reality. After a few moments another little ball landed on his table, and now the *peones* laughed outright. Dahlmann said to himself that he was not frightened, but he reasoned that it would be a major blunder if he, a convalescent, were to allow himself to be dragged by strangers into some chaotic quarrel. He determined to leave, and had already gotten to his feet when the owner came up and exhorted him in an alarmed voice:

"Señor Dahlmann, don't pay any attention to those lads; they're half high."

Dahlmann was not surprised to learn that the other man, now, knew his name. But he felt that these conciliatory words served only to aggravate the situation. Previous to this moment, the *peones'* provocation was directed against an unknown face, against no one in particular, almost against no one at all. Now it was an attack against him, against his name, and his neighbors knew it. Dahlmann pushed the owner aside, confronted the *peones*, and demanded to know what they wanted of him.

The tough with a Chinese look staggered heavily to his feet. Almost in Juan Dahlmann's face he shouted insults, as if he had been a long way off. His game was to exaggerate his drunkness, and this extravagance constituted a ferocious mockery. Between curses and obscenities, he threw a long knife into the air, followed it with his eyes, caught and juggled it, and challenged Dahlmann to a knife fight. The owner objected in a tremulous voice, pointing out that Dahlmann was unarmed. At this point, something unforeseeable occurred.

From a corner of the room, the old ecstatic gaucho—in whom Dahlmann saw a summary and cipher of the South (his South)—threw him a naked dagger, which landed at his feet. It was as if the South had resolved that Dahlmann should accept the duel. Dahlmann bent over to pick up the dagger, and felt two things. The first, that this almost instinctive act bound him to fight. The second, that the weapon, in his torpid hand, was no defense at all, but would merely serve to justify his murder. He had once played with a poniard, like all men, but his idea of fencing and knifeplay did not go further than the notion that all strokes should be directed upwards, with the cutting edge held inwards. *They would not have allowed such things to happen to me in the sanitarium*, he thought.

"Let's get on our way," said the other man.

They went out and if Dahlmann was without hope, he was also without fear. As he crossed the threshold, he felt that to die in a knife fight, under the open sky, and going forward to the attack, would have been a liberation, a joy, and a festive occasion, on the first night in the sanitarium, when they stuck him with the needle. He felt that if he had been able to choose, then, or to dream his death, this would have been the death he would have chosen or dreamt.

Firmly clutching his knife, which he perhaps would not know how to wield, Dahlmann went out into the plain.

Translated by Anthony Kerrigan

In the Barrancas

George Gaylord Simpson

Paleontologist George Gaylord Simpson's fieldwork in South America helped unravel any number of geological mysteries related to the then-nascent theory of plate tectonics. His travels, many on behalf of the American Museum of Natural History, took him to the most unknown places, among them the canyon country of Patagonia, as Simpson (1902–1986) recounts in his 1934 memoir *Attending Marvels: A Patagonian Journal.*

OCT. 27. As I write this, just before going to bed, the Patagonian wind is living up to its reputation. Waves roar on the beach. The tent billows and snaps and then strains with the guy ropes humming, but perhaps it will stand up. The strongest wind I have ever seen was blowing on the barranca today. To climb over the crest I had to crawl on my belly and in a less cautious moment I was knocked down and almost blown over the cliff. At one time going into the wind down a slope too steep to stand on at all ordinarily, we could walk leaning forward at an apparently fatal angle, supported by the constant gale in our faces. There could hardly be a more curious sight or a stranger sensation. Just there the wind was blowing such large pebbles that we had to remove our goggles for fear of their being hit and broken.

My present field garb, ridiculous to others but practical for me, consists of boots, khaki riding breeches, flannel shirt, canvas hunting coat, air-tight goggles, and a beret or boina. In this it is possible to work in spite of the wind. Work is not simple, however, at times like today when the wind blows away even tools, and the fossils we are trying to collect.

Coley [Simpson's field assistant, C. S. Williams] put in a few good licks, but is still very weak and had to quit early. What with having to leave his bride, his severe illness, and other things he is not quite as favorably impressed with Patagonia as I am. We put in a good day of work. We found traces of the last fossil collectors—Riggs' party some six or seven years ago—and even came across a specimen which they had started to collect and then had left for some reason. They worked altogether on the richer upper beds, whereas we are about done with them and are now going to concentrate on the older and rarer things near the foot of the barranca.

European hares were introduced into Patagonia a few years ago by some very misguided soul and now have overrun the country, threatening to do in the native and more valuable fauna. This apropos of the fact that we had one for dinner tonight and that it tasted very good. Odd how the mind keeps reverting to food out here!

No one sat around after eating, all having had quite enough for one day. The wind is very trying, but we manage to keep on good terms and in good humor.

Oct. 28. The wind was even more violent today and my eyes were swollen nearly shut from the sharp grains of volcanic ash blown into them yesterday, so we stayed in camp. There was plenty to do, as several of our specimens were not completely prepared for packing and my notes and geologic sections, which consume a great deal of time, needed copying and revising.

Justino went off and bought us half a sheep, also picking up a live armadillo, pichi, on the way. It is a gravid female, intensely upset at her captivity and sulking in a pail of dirt at this moment. A shepherd came by on horseback and told us there were some bones a few kilometers away. We went there with him, but the "bones" were bits of petrified wood of no value.

OCT. 31. The last two days and today were spent working at the barranca. We have now transferred our attentions to the old beds in the lower half of the cliff. Here there is a thick bed of pure gray volcanic ash which is fairly hard and very tough when dry but which washes out easily when wet. In this way the occasional torrential downpours have honeycombed the ash bed with small caves and channels. In one of these caves, in a block fallen from the ceiling, Justino and I found the skull of a fossil crocodile. (This specimen later turned out to be very important. It is of a genus and species new to science, and it also indicates the ancestry of the caimans and jacares now living in South America and suggests that they probably wandered there from North America some sixty million years or more ago.)

We had lunch in the crocodile cave today. Justino, who prospects around like an overgrown fox terrier, but with very good results, has wormed his way into all the little caves and holes around here. He found one excellent specimen in a tiny crack in the ceiling of a cave so small and narrow that it had to be enlarged with a pick to be passable at all. He is an amazingly good prospector and seems to smell out specimens in the most unlikely places.

The armadillo has been staked out with a cord tied to one leg, and has dug herself a hole and retired permanently to it. A most unsocial creature.

NOV. 1. Justino, Manuel, and I went off, leaving Coley to hold down the camp and rest himself. The lads dropped me off at a strip of badlands on the slope of the Pampa Castillo, a few miles from the Valle Hermoso railway station and they went on to 112, on the Pampa, to make a few purchases and mail letters. Hence they came back by way of Cañadón Pedro, where they stocked up on drinking water and got a lamb. I found a few specimens but didn't accomplish as much as I wished because my eyes swelled shut after a couple of hours in the sun.

Guanaco are fairly common in that area—there was one troupe of thirteen. On the cliff there were two of the very handsome big black and white eagles, aguiluchos. They were disturbed by my climbing their perch and the male amused himself and got on my nerves by going to a great height and then dropping straight for me, turning at the last moment and buzzing by a foot above my head with the speed of a cannon ball, then banking and soaring back to repeat the maneuver. He did not strike, but whenever he swooped I could not help wondering just what his intentions toward me were.

I was also entertained by another bird which Justino calls a chuchumento—I cannot guarantee the name as Justino hates to admit that there is anything about this country that he does not know and so occasionally invents answers. This chuchumento, or what have you, builds a large nest of firmly intertwined twigs in thorn bushes several feet above the ground. The nest itself is spherical and is completely enclosed except for a small entrance tunnel about two feet long. This is set with sharp, fresh thorns so as to be almost impregnable.

Incidentally I was much surprised the other day to find the fresh, recent bones of a very small opossum. I had no idea they ranged this far south, and in fact they must be very rare and probably nocturnal, for Justino had never seen or heard of such an animal and insisted that the bones must belong to a weasel.

Nov. 5. Coley is well now and has been working full time and making some fine discoveries the last few days, and of course Justino is in good form. I have been out and have done what I could, but that was not always a great deal as my eyes are still very bad.

Today Justino and I went down to the far end of the barranca and walked back on the cliff, a good trick involving much climbing and walking on narrow ledges, jumping chasms, sliding down clay slopes, and in general a combination of Alpine and field sports. The work here is pretty well laid out now, and I think it will take till the end of the month to clean up the things within reach of our present base camp.

We had cold pichi—armadillo—meat for lunch. The meat is dark and rather pleasant, although it is very greasy. I would not care for it as a steady diet. The ostrich laying season is in full swing and we gathered some eggs. It is possible to select the fresh eggs in a nest because when new-laid they are green and have a limy crust and as they get older the color fades and the lime is worn off. There were forty-eight eggs in one nest. To return to my usual gastronomic theme, these eggs are extremely good food. They make excellent omelettes, tortillas, and are even better, and more exotic, roasted in the native manner. The top is carefully cut off and part of the white is removed and replaced with sugar. The contents, still in the shell, are then mixed thoroughly and the whole thing banked in hot ashes until cooked through. As I write it, this does not sound very enticing, but in fact it is one of the best things I ever ate.

In one place the eggs were neatly piled up several feet below the nest which, as often, was on a little knoll. Explaining this stopped Justino for only a moment, then his inventive genius came to his aid:

"You see, doctor, one egg rolled out and the bird was too lazy to put it back in the nest. So he moved all the other eggs down to it."

"And how did he carry the eggs?"

"Oh, he tucks them under his chin and holds them there with a loop in his neck!"

If Justino could only understand English I would tell him about the Side-Hill Squeegee of my native Colorado mountains.

Nov. 6. After having breakfasted on armadillo sauté, we went out to the barranca and found his oldest known ancestor, proving that armadillos were in existence, and pretty much the same as they are today, some forty-five million years ago. To all his other strange characteristics the armadillo adds that of being a "living fossil." He has hardly changed at all since the Eocene Epoch and should by all rights be an extinct and prehistoric critter, but in his quiet and dumb—how dumb!—way he keeps on anachronistically surviving. Apparently in the struggle for existence a thick skin serves just as well as brains, or better.

Speaking of food, we are almost out of meat and cannot get a sheep till tomorrow. Coley shot an abutarda near Francisco's fishing hut, but it was on the other side of a small arm of the lake. He started after it in Francisco's boat, but the boat sank when halfway across. This boat is one of the world's sad sights, made out of tin cans and a couple of old planks, with cracks as wide as a finger. Francisco goes out in it on this very tempestuous lake, but he can and does swim. When Coley finally got across the bird had recovered and flown away. We had ostrich egg omelette for supper.

This very peculiar desert even presents difficulties in navigation!

Nov. 9. The work has been going along smoothly, with the usual nasty weather and good fossils.

This morning just before dawn, when the wind had been almost quiescent for a change, the gale suddenly hit my tent with a resounding whack and then rain pelted down, the drops drumming on the taut canvas like machine gun bullets. I finally dozed off and only a second later there was a handclap outside and I heard Justino's cheery (but also sleepy) voice calling "Doctor! Linda hora pa' levantarse!" I found his belief that the hour was pretty for getting up difficult to share, but crawled out.

Then there was a clap of thunder and it began to hail, large stones carried along at tremendous velocity by the wind, now of hurricane force, so that it was positively unsafe to venture out of doors (or tent-flaps). These hail storms, which have been frequent, are quite annoying, but seldom last very long. This one let up soon and we did our usual stint at the barranca.

Lately I have been noticing some very strange birds from a distance, and today, getting a closer look, was amazed to see that they are parrots. What on earth is such a tropical-looking bird doing in this raw, cold desert? They are about the size of crows and they build nests of twigs high up on the cliffs—they are called cliff parrots, *loros barranqueros*. All day long they fly about us, very characteristic with their long tails, short necks, and large heads. This odd stream-lined body form makes them singularly like flying fish as they pass overhead. They are greenish but not brightly colored. Their cry is a very ugly coarse raucous squawk. Justino says that they can be tamed but do not talk.

As we came home the sun went out suddenly and the whole land turned a sinister gray, dark and light but without a spot of color. Streaked vicious clouds poured over us like a flood from the west. The moon rose yellow through the last band of clear sky. Rain began to patter, then to pour. Surf is roaring again on the shores of the lake. Beyond this element-tormented spot lies vast, desolate Patagonia. Beyond Patagonia lies the world of seas and plains and mountains, for complacent thousands of miles. Beyond the world wheels the dusty universe.

So, chastened, to bed.

Birds

Graciliano Ramos

As a young man, Graciliano Ramos (1892–1953) studied the work of Émile Zola and Maxim Gorki to forge a new kind of realism in Brazilian fiction, which found its highest moment in his novel *Vidas secas* (*Barren Lives*), a novel often likened to John Steinbeck's *The Grapes of Wrath*. Its protagonist is Fabiano, a tenant farmer who tends an absentee cattleman's stock in the face of a paralyzing drought in the Sertão. Desperate, Fabiano contemplates joining an outlaw band, a thinly veiled allusion to the socialist activist Limpião (1897–1940), the so-called Bandit King of Sertão.

The branches of the coral-bean tree down by the water hole were covered with birds of passage. This was a bad sign. In all probability the backhand would soon be burnt up. The birds came in flocks; they roosted in the trees along the riverbank; they rested, they drank, and then, since there was nothing there for them to eat, they flew on toward the south. Fabiano and his wife, deeply worried, had visions of misfortunes to come. The sun sucked up the water from the ponds and those cursed birds drank up what was left, trying to kill the stock.

It was Vitória who said this. Fabiano grunted, wrinkled his brow, and found the expression exaggerated. The idea of birds killing oxen and goats! He looked at his wife distrustfully; he thought she was out of her mind. He went to sit on the bench under the shed, and from there he studied the sky, filled with a brightness that boded evil, its clear expanse broken only by the lines of passing birds. A feathered creature kill stock! Vitória must be crazy.

Fabiano stuck out his lower lip and wrinkled his sweaty brow still more deeply: it was impossible for him to understand what his wife meant. He couldn't get it. A little thing like a bird! As the matter seemed obscure to him he refrained from going into it any further. He went into the house, got his haversack, made himself a cigarette, struck the flint against the stone, and took a long drag. He looked in all directions and remained facing north for several minutes, scratching his chin.

"Awful! It's like the end of the world!"

He wouldn't stay there long. In the long-drawn-out silence all that could be heard was the flapping of wings.

What was it that Vitória had said? Her phrase came back to Fabiano's mind, and suddenly its meaning was apparent. The birds of passage drank the water. The stock went thirsty and died. Yes, the birds of passage did kill the cattle. That was right! Thinking the matter over you could see it was so, but Vitória had a complicated way of putting things. Now Fabiano saw what she meant. Forgetting imminent misfortune, he smiled, enchanted at Vitória's cleverness. A person like her was worth her weight in gold. She had ideas, she did! She had brains in her head. She could find a way out of difficult situations. There, hadn't she figured out that the birds of passage were killing the stock? And they were too! At that very hour the branches of the coral-bean tree down by the water hole, though stripped of blossoms and leaves, were a mass of feathers.

Desiring to see it up close he arose, slung his haversack across his chest, and went to get his leather hat and his flintlock. He stepped down from the shed, crossed the yard, and approached the slope, thinking of the dog. Poor thing! Those horrible-looking places had appeared around her mouth, her hair had dropped out, and he had had to kill her. Had he done right? He had never thought about that before. The dog was sick. Could he risk her biting the children? Could he? It was madness to expose the boys to rabies. Poor dog! He shook his head to get her out of his mind. It was that devilish flintlock that brought the image of the little dog back to him. Yes, it was certainly the flintlock. He turned his face away as he passed the stones at the end of the yard where they had found the dog, cold and stiff, her eyes pecked out by the vultures.

Taking longer steps he went down the slope and walked across the river flat toward the water hole. There was a wild flapping of wings over the pool of dark water. The branches of the coral-bean tree couldn't even be seen. What a flock of pests! When they came in from the backhand they made an end of everything. The stock was going to waste away, and even the thorns would dry up.

He sighed. What was he to do? Flee once more, settle some place else, begin life all over again. He raised his gun and pulled the trigger without even aiming. Five or six birds fell to the ground. The rest took flight and the dry branches appeared in all their nakedness. Little by little they were covered again. There was no end to it.

Fabiano sat down dispiritedly at the edge of the water hole. Slowly he loaded the flintlock with bird shot, but did not use any wadding, so the load would spread and hit many enemies. There was a new report and new birds fell, but this gave Fabiano no pleasure. He had food there for two or three days; if he had enough munition he would have food for weeks and months.

He examined the powder horn and the leather shot holder; he thought of the trip and shuddered. He tried to deceive himself into thinking it wouldn't come about if he didn't provoke it by evil thoughts. He relit his cigarette and sought to distract himself by talking in a low voice. Old Miss Terta was a person who knew a lot about that part of the country. What could be the state of his accounts with the boss? That was something he could never figure out. That business of interest swallowed up everything, and on top of it all the boss acted as if he were doing a favor. Then there was that policeman in khaki—

Fabiano closed his fists and punched himself in the thigh for his bad luck. The devil! There he was, trying to forget one misfortune, and others came crowding upon him. He didn't want to think either of the boss or of the policeman in khaki. But to his despair they insisted on coming to his mind, and he tightened up like a rattlesnake coiling in anger. He was unlucky, the unluckiest fellow in the world. He ought to have struck the policeman in khaki that afternoon; he ought to have carved him up with his machete. But like a good-for-nothing country lout he had pulled in his horns and had showed the policeman the way. He rubbed his sweaty, wrinkled brow. Why bring his shame back to mind, though? He was just a poor devil. But was he determined to go on living like that forever? Worthless and weak, that was what he was. If he hadn't been so timid he would have joined a gang of bandits and would have gone around wreaking destruction. Eventually he would get shot in ambush, or would spend his old age serving out a sentence in jail. This was better, though, than dying by the roadside in the broiling heat, his wife and boys dying too. He ought to have cut the policeman's throat, taking his own good time about doing it. They could put him in jail then, but he would be respected—yes, respected, as a man of guts. The way he was now, nobody could respect him. He wasn't a man; he wasn't anything. He had suffered a beating and had not taken revenge.

"Fabiano, my boy, get your chin up! Get some self-respect! Kill the policeman in khaki! Policemen in khaki are a pack of scoundrels that ought to be put out of the way. Kill the policeman and the people he gets his orders from!"

He began to pant and be thirsty as a result of the energy wasted in his wild gesticulations. Sweat ran down over his red, sunburned face and darkened his ruddy beard. He came down from the bank and bent over the edge of the hole, lapping the brackish water from his cupped hands. A throng of startled birds of passage took flight. Fabiano got up with a flash of indignation in his eyes.

"Dirty, low-down—"

His anger was once again turned against the birds. Sitting back down on the bank, he fired many times into the branches of the coral-bean tree, leaving the ground covered with dead bodies. They would be salted and hung up on a line to dry. He intended to use them for food on the coming journey. He should spend the rest of his money on powder and shot and put in a day there at the water hole, then take to the road. Would he have to move? Although he knew perfectly well he would, he clung to frail hopes. Perhaps the drought wouldn't come; perhaps it would rain.

It was those cursed birds that frightened him. He tried to forget them. But how could he forget them if they were right there, flying about his head, hopping around on the mud, perching on the branches, lying scattered in death on the ground? Were it not for them, the drought would not exist. At least it would not exist just then. It would come later and last a shorter time. As things were, it was beginning now; Fabiano could feel it already. It was just as if it had arrived; he was already suffering the hunger, thirst, and endless fatigue of the trek. A few days earlier he had been calmly making whips and mending fences. Suddenly there was a dark line across the sky, then other lines, thousands of lines uniting to form clouds, and the fearful noise of wings, heralding destruction. He had already suspected something when he saw the springs diminishing, and he had looked with distrust at the whiteness of the long mornings and the sinister redness of the afternoons. Now his suspicions were confirmed.

"Miserable wretches!"

Those cursed birds were the cause of the drought. If he could kill them the drought would be choked off. He moved feverishly, loading the flintlock with fury. His thick, hairy hands, full of blotches and skinned spots, trembled as they moved the ramrod up and down.

"Pests!"

But it was impossible to put an end to that plague. He looked about the countryside and found himself completely isolated. Alone in a world of feathers, full of birds that were going to eat him up. He thought of his wife and sighed. Poor Vitória would again have to carry the tin trunk across the wasteland. It was hard for a woman with her brains to go tramping over the scorched earth, bruising her feet on the stones. The birds of passage were killing the stock. How had Vitória hit on that idea? It was hard. He, Fabiano, no matter how he might rack his brains, would never come out with an expression like that. Vitória knew how to figure accounts right; she sat down in the kitchen, consulted piles of different kinds of seeds, representing coins of varying value. And she came out right. The boss's accounts were different, drawn up in ink, against the herdsman, but Fabiano knew that they were wrong and that the boss was trying to cheat him. He did cheat him. But what could he do about it? Fabiano, a luckless half-breed, slept in jail and was beaten. Could he react? He could not. He was just a half-breed. But Vitória's accounts must be right. Poor Vitória. She would never be able to stretch her bones in a real bed, the only thing she truly wanted. Didn't other people sleep in beds? Fearing to wound her feelings, Fabiano would agree with her, though it was just a dream. They couldn't sleep like Christians. And now they were going to be eaten up by the birds of passage.

He got down from the bank, slowly picked up the dead birds, filling his haversack to overflowing with them, and gradually withdrew. He, Vitória, and the two boys would eat the birds.

If the dog were still alive, she would have a feast. Why did he feel such a stab at his heart? The poor dog! He had had to kill her, because she was sick. Then he had gone back to the whips, the fences, and the boss's mixed-up accounts. He walked up the slope and approached the jujubes. At the root of one of them the poor dog loved to wallow, covering herself with twigs and dry leaves. Fabiano sighed. He felt a tremendous weight in his chest. Had he been wrong? He looked at the burnt plain, the hill where the cavies hopped about, and he swore to the catingueira trees and the stones that the animal had rabies and threatened the children. That was why he had killed her. And he had given the matter no further thought at the time.

Here Fabiano's thoughts became mixed up. The idea of the dog mingled with that of the birds of passage, which he failed to distinguish from the drought. He, his wife, and the two boys would be eaten up. Vitória was right; she was smart and saw things a long way off. Fabiano's eyes widened; he wanted to go on admiring her, but his heart was heavy. It felt as big as a bullfrog; it was full of thoughts of the dog. The poor thing, thin and stiff, her eyes pecked out by the vultures!

Passing in front of the jujubes, Fabiano walked more quickly. How could he tell whether the dog's spirit wasn't haunting the place?

Fear was in his soul as he reached the house. It was dusk, and at that hour he always felt a vague terror. He had been discouraged and dejected of late because misfortunes had been many. He would have to consult with Vitória about the trip, get rid of the birds he had shot, explain himself, convince himself he had not done wrong in killing the dog. They would have to abandon the accursed place. Vitória would think just as he did.

Translated by Ralph Edward Dimmick

The Cactus

Manuel Bandeira

A native of the Sertão, Manuel Bandeira (1886–1953) spent most of his life working as a journalist and editor in Rio de Janeiro, where a fallen columnar cactus brought to mind his desert childhood, a theme to which his work often returned.

That cactus brought to mind the hopeless gestures of statues:
Laocoön choked by serpents,

Ugolino and his starving sons.
It evoked as well the dry northeast, the desert,
    the thorn bushes.

It was huge, even for this ridiculously fertile region.

One day a furious gust tore it loose.
The cactus fell across the street,
broke the rooftiles of the facing houses,
impeded the traffic of trams, cars, and wagons,
tore down wires, and for twenty-four hours
    robbed the city of light and power.

It was beautiful, severe, and intractable.

Atacama

Charles Darwin

Before he secured fame as the foremost proponent of the theory of organic
evolution, Charles Robert Darwin (1809–1882) traveled around the world
as a naturalist aboard the H. M. S. *Beagle*, a five-year voyage that took him
to places like the Galápagos Islands, Tierra del Fuego, Madagascar, and
Australia. In this passage from *The Voyage of the Beagle*, Darwin describes
the Atacama Desert of the Chilean coast.

JUNE 2ND. We set out for the valley of Guasco, following the
coast-road, which was considered rather less desert than the other.
Our first day's ride was to a solitary house, called Yerba Buena,

where there was pasture for our horses. The shower mentioned as having fallen a fortnight ago, only reached about halfway to Guasco; we had, therefore, in the first part of our journey a most faint tinge of green, which soon faded quite away. Even where brightest, it was scarcely sufficient to remind one of the fresh turf and budding flowers of the spring of other countries. While travelling through these deserts one feels like a prisoner shut up in a gloomy court, who longs to see something green and to smell a moist atmosphere.

JUNE 3RD. Yerba Buena to Carizal. During the first part of the day we crossed a mountainous rocky desert, and afterwards a long deep sandy plain, strewed with broken sea-shells. There was very little water, and that little saline: the whole country, from the coast to the Cordillera, is an uninhabited desert. I saw traces only of one living animal in abundance, namely, the shells of a Bulimus, which were collected together in extraordinary numbers on the driest spots. In the spring one humble little plant sends out a few leaves, and on these the snails feed. As they are seen only very early in the morning, when the ground is slightly damp with dew, the Guasos believe that they are bred from it. I have observed in other places that extremely dry and sterile districts, where the soil is calcareous, are extraordinarily favourable to land-shells. At Carizal there were a few cottages, some brackish water, and a trace of cultivation: but it was with difficulty that we purchased a little corn and straw for our horses.

4TH. Carizal to Sauce. We continued to ride over desert plains, tenanted by large herds of guanaco. We crossed also the valley of Chaneral; which, although the most fertile one between Guasco and Coquimbo, is very narrow, and produces so little pasture, that we could not purchase any for our horses. At Sauce we found a very civil old gentleman, superintending a copper-smelting furnace. As an especial favour, he allowed me to purchase at a high price an armful of dirty straw, which was all the poor horses had for supper after their long day's journey. Few smelting-furnaces are now at work in any part of Chile: it is found more profitable, on account of the extreme scarcity of firewood, and from the Chilean method of eduction being so unskilful, to ship the ore for Swansea. The next day we crossed some mountains to Freyrina, in the valley of Guasco. During each day's ride further northward, the vegetation became more and more scanty; even the great chandelier-like cactus was here replaced by a different and much smaller species. During the winter months, both in northern Chile and in Peru, a uniform bank of clouds hangs, at no great height, over the Pacific. From the mountains we had a very striking view of this white and brilliant aerial-field, which sent arms up the valleys, leaving islands and promontories in the same manner, as the sea does in the Chonos Archipelago and in Tierra del Fuego.

We stayed two days at Freyrina. In the valley of Guasco are four small towns. At the mouth there is the port, a spot entirely desert, and without any water in the immediate neighbourhood. Five leagues higher up stands Freyrina, a long straggling village, with decent whitewashed houses. Again, ten leagues further up Ballenar is situated; and above this Guasco Alto, a horticultural village, famous for its dried fruit On a clear day the view up the valley is very fine; the straight opening terminates in the far-distant snowy Cordillera; on each side an infinity of crossing lines are blended together in a beautiful haze. The foreground is singular from the number of parallel and step-formed terraces; and the included strip of green valley, with its willow-bushes, is contrasted on both hands with the naked hills. That the surrounding country was most barren will be readily believed, when it is known that a shower of rain had not fallen during the last thirteen months. The inhabitants heard with the greatest envy of the rain at Coquimbo; from the appearance of the sky they had hopes of equally good fortune, which, a fortnight afterwards, were realized. I was at Copiapó at the time; and there the people, with equal envy, talked of the abundant rain at Guasco. After two or three very dry years, perhaps with not more than one shower during the whole time, a rainy year generally follows; and this does more harm than even the drought. The rivers swell, and cover with gravel and sand the narrow strips of ground, which alone are fit for cultivation. The floods also injure the irrigating ditches. Great devastation had thus been caused three years ago.

JUNE 8TH. We rode on to Ballenar, which takes its name from Ballenagh in Ireland, the birthplace of the family of O'Higgins, who, under the Spanish government, were presidents and generals in Chile. As the rocky mountains on each hand were concealed by clouds, the terrace-like plains gave to the valley an appearance like that of Santa Cruz in Patagonia. After spending one day at Ballenar I set out, on the 10th, for the upper part of the valley of Copiapó. We rode all day over an uninteresting country. I am tired of repeating the epithets barren and sterile. These words, however, as commonly used, are comparative; I have always applied them to the plains of Patagonia, which can boast of spiny bushes and some tufts of grass; and this is absolute fertility, as compared with northern Chile. Here again, there are not many spaces of two hundred yards square, where some little bush, cactus or lichen, may not be discovered by careful examination; and in the soil seeds lie dormant ready to spring up during the first rainy winter. In Peru real deserts occur over wide tracts of country. In the evening we arrived at a valley, in which the bed of the streamlet was damp: following it up, we came to tolerably good water. During the night, the stream, from not being evaporated and absorbed so quickly, flows a league lower down than during the day. Sticks were plentiful for firewood, so that it was a good place of bivouac for us; but for the poor animals there was not a mouthful to eat.

JUNE 11TH. We rode without stopping for twelve hours, till we reached an old smelting-furnace, where there was water and firewood; but our horses again had nothing to eat, being shut up in an old courtyard. The line of road was hilly, and the distant views interesting from the varied colours of the bare mountains. It was almost a pity to see the sun shining constantly over so useless a country; such splendid weather ought to have brightened fields and pretty gardens. The next day we reached the valley of Copiapó. I was heartily glad of it; for the whole journey was a continued source of anxiety; it was most disagreeable to hear, whilst eating our own suppers, our horses gnawing the posts to which they were tied, and to have no means of relieving their hunger. To all appearance, however, the animals were quite fresh; and no one could have told that they had eaten nothing for the last fifty-five hours.

I had a letter of introduction to Mr. Bingley, who received me very kindly at the Hacienda of Potrero Seco. This estate is between twenty and thirty miles long, but very narrow, being generally only two fields wide, one on each side the river. In some parts the estate is of no width, that is to say, the land cannot be irrigated, and therefore is valueless, like the surrounding rocky desert. The small quantity of cultivated land in the whole line of valley, does not so much depend on inequalities of level, and consequent unfitness for irrigation, as on the small supply of water. The river this year was remarkably full: here, high up the valley, it reached to the horse's belly, and was about fifteen yards wide, and rapid; lower down it becomes smaller and smaller, and is generally quite lost, as happened during one period of thirty years, so that not a drop entered the sea. The inhabitants watch a storm over the Cordillera with great interest; as one good fall of snow provides them with water for the ensuing year. This is of infinitely more consequence than rain in the lower country. Rain, as often as it falls, which is about once in every two or three years, is a great advantage, because the cattle and mules can for some time afterwards find a little pasture on the mountains. But without snow on the Andes, desolation extends throughout the valley. It is on record that three times nearly all the inhabitants have been obliged to emigrate to the south. This year there was plenty of water, and every man irrigated his ground as much as he chose; but it has frequently been necessary to post soldiers at the sluices, to see that each estate took only its proper allowance during so many hours in the week. The valley is said to contain 12,000 souls, but its produce is sufficient only for three months in the year; the rest of the supply being drawn from Valparaiso and the south. Before the discovery of the famous silver-mines of Chanuncillo, Copiapó was in a rapid state of decay; but now it is in a very thriving condition; and the town, which was completely overthrown by an earthquake, has been rebuilt.

The valley of Copiapó, forming a mere ribbon of green in a desert, runs in a very southerly direction; so that it is of considerable length to its source in the Cordillera. The valleys of Guasco and Copiapó may both be considered as long narrow islands, separated from the rest of Chile by deserts of rock instead of by salt water. Northward of these, there is one other very miserable valley, called Paposo, which contains about two hundred souls; and then there extends the real desert of Atacama—a barrier far worse than the most turbulent ocean. After staying a few days at Potrero Seco, I proceeded up the valley to the house of Don Benito Cruz, to whom I had a letter of introduction. I found him most hospitable; indeed it is impossible to bear too strong testimony to the kindness, with which travellers are received in almost every part of South America. The next day I hired some mules to take me by the ravine of Jolquera into the central Cordillera. On the second night the weather seemed to foretell a storm of snow or rain, and whilst lying in our beds we felt a trifling shock of an earthquake.

The connexion between earthquakes and the weather has been often disputed: it appears to me to be a point of great interest, which is little understood. Humboldt has remarked in one part of the Personal Narrative, that it would be difficult for any person who had long resided in New Andalusia, or in Lower Peru, to deny that there exists some connexion between these phenomena: in another part, however, he seems to think the connexion fanciful. At Guayaquil, it is said that a heavy shower in the dry season is invariably followed by an earthquake. In Northern Chile, from the extreme infrequency of rain, or even of weather foreboding rain, the probability of accidental coincidences becomes very small; yet the inhabitants are here most firmly convinced of some connexion between the state of the atmosphere and of the trembling of the ground: I was much struck by this, when mentioning to some people at Copiapó that there had been a sharp shock at Coquimbo: they immediately cried out, "How fortunate! there will be plenty of pasture there this year." To their minds an earthquake foretold rain, as surely as rain foretold abundant pasture. Certainly it did so happen that on the very day of the earthquake, that shower of rain fell, which I have described as in ten days' time producing a thin sprinkling of grass. At other times, rain has followed earthquakes, at a period of the year when it is a far greater prodigy than the earthquake itself: this happened after the shock of November, 1822, and again in 1829, at Valparaiso; also after that of September, 1833, at Tacna. A person must be somewhat habituated to the climate of these countries, to perceive the extreme improbability of rain falling at such seasons, except as a consequence of some law quite unconnected with the ordinary course of the weather. In the cases of great volcanic eruptions, as that of Coseguina, where torrents of rain fell at a time of the year most unusual for it, and "almost unprecedented in Central America," it is not difficult to understand that the volumes of vapour and clouds of ashes might have disturbed the atmospheric equilibrium. Humboldt extends this view to the case of earthquakes unaccompanied by eruptions; but I can hardly conceive it possible, that the small quantity of aeriform fluids which then escape from the fissured ground, can produce such remarkable effects. There appears much probability in the view first proposed by Mr. P. Scrope, that when the barometer is low, and when rain might naturally be expected to fall, the diminished pressure of the atmosphere over a wide extent of country, might well determine the precise day on which the earth, jalready stretched to the utmost by the subterranean forces, should yield, crack, and consequently tremble. It is, however, doubtful how far this idea will explain the circumstance of torrents of rain falling in the dry season during several days, after an earthquake unaccompanied by an eruption; such cases seem to bespeak some more intimate connexion between the atmospheric and subterranean regions.

Finding little of interest in this part of the ravine, we retraced our steps to the house of Don Benito, where I stayed two days collecting fossil shells and wood. Great prostrate silicified trunks of trees, embedded in a conglomerate, were extraordinarily numerous. I measured one, which was fifteen feet in circumference: how surprising it is that every atom of the woody matter in this great cylinder should have been removed and replaced by silex so perfectly, that each vessel and pore is preserved. These trees flourished at about the period of our lower chalk; they all belonged to the fir-tribe. It was amusing to hear the inhabitants discussing the nature of the fossil shells which I collected, almost in the same terms as were used a century ago in Europe,—namely, whether or not they had been thus "born by nature." My geological examination of the country generally created a good deal of surprise amongst the Chilenos: it was long before they could be convinced that I was not hunting for mines. This was sometimes troublesome: I found the most ready way of explaining my employment, was to ask them how it was that they themselves were not curious concerning earthquakes and volcanoes?— why some springs were hot and others cold?—Why there were mountains in Chile, and not a hill in La Plata? These bare questions at once satisfied and silenced the greater number some, however (like a few in England who are a century behindhand), thought that all such inquiries were useless and impious; and that it was quite sufficient that God had thus made the mountains.

An order had recently been issued that all stray dogs should be killed, and we saw many lying dead on the road. A great number had lately gone mad. and several men had been bitten and had died in consequence. On several occasions hydrophobia has prevailed in this valley. It is remarkable thus to find so strange and dreadful a disease, appearing time after time in the same isolated spot. It has been remarked that certain villages in England are in like manner much more subject to this visitation than others. Dr. Unanùe states that hydrophobia was first known in South America in 1803: this statement is corroborated by Azara and Ulloa having never heard of it in their time. Dr. Unanùe says that it broke out in Central America, and slowly travelled southward. It reached Arequipa in 1807; and it is said that some men there, who had not been bitten, were affected, as were some Negroes, who had eaten a bullock which had died of hydrophobia. At Ica forty-two people thus miserably perished. The disease came on between twelve and ninety days after the bite; and in those cases where it did come on, death ensued invariably within five days. After 1808, a long interval ensued without any cases. On inquiry, I did not hear of hydrophobia in Van Dieman's Land, or in Australia; and Burchell says, that during the five years he was at the Cape of Good Hope, he never heard of an instance of it. Webster asserts that at the Azores hydrophobia has never occurred; and the same assertion has been made with respect to Mauritius and St. Helena. In so strange a disease, some information might possibly be gained by considering the circumstances under which it originates in distant climates; for it is improbable that a dog already bitten, should have been brought to these distant countries.

At night, a stranger arrived at the house of Don Benito, and asked permission to sleep there. He said he had been wandering about the mountains for seventeen days, having lost his way. He started from Guasco, and being accustomed to travelling in the Cordillera, did not expect any difficulty in following the track to Copiapó; but he soon became involved in a labyrinth of mountains, whence he could not escape. Some of his mules had fallen over precipices, and he had been in great distress. His chief difficulty arose from not knowing where to find water in the lower country, so that he was obliged to keep bordering the central ranges.

We returned down the valley, and on the 22nd reached the town of Copiapó. The lower part of the valley is broad, forming a fine plain like that of Quillota. The town covers a considerable space of ground, each house possessing a garden: but it is an uncomfortable place, and the dwellings are poorly furnished. Every one seems bent on the one object of making money, and then migrating as quickly as possible. All the inhabitants are more or less directly concerned with mines; and mines and ores are the sole subjects of conversation. Necessaries of all sorts are extremely dear; as the distance from the town to the port is eighteen leagues, and the land carriage very expensive. A fowl costs five or six shillings; meat is nearly as dear as in England; firewood, or rather sticks, are brought on donkeys from a distance of two and three days' journey within the Cordillera; and pasturage for animals is a shilling a day: all this for South America is wonderfully exorbitant.

JUNE 26TH. I hired a guide and eight mules to take me into the Cordillera by a different line from my last excursion. As the country was utterly desert, we took a cargo and a half of barley mixed with chopped straw. About two leagues above the town, a broad valley called the "Despoblado," or uninhabited, branches off from that one by which we had arrived. Although a valley of the grandest dimensions, and leading to a pass across the Cordillera, yet it is completely dry, excepting perhaps for a few days during some very rainy winter. The sides of the crumbling mountains were furrowed by scarcely any ravines; and the bottom of the main valley, filled with shingle, was smooth and nearly level. No considerable torrent could ever have flowed down this bed of shingle; for if it had, a great cliff-bounded channel, as in all the southern valleys would assuredly have been formed. I feel little doubt that this valley, as well as those mentioned by travellers in Peru, were left in the state we now see them by the waves of the sea, as the land slowly rose. I observed in one place, where the Despoblado was joined by a ravine (which in almost any other chain would have been called a grand valley), that its bed, though composed merely of sand and gravel, was higher than that of its tributary. A mere rivulet of water, in the course of an hour, would have cut a channel for itself; but it was evident that ages had passed away, and no such rivulet had drained this great tributary. It was curious to behold the machinery, if such a term may be used, for the drainage, all, with the last trifling exception, perfect, yet without any signs of action. Every one must have remarked how mud-banks, left by the retiring tide, imitate in miniature a country with hill and dale; and here we have the original model in rock, formed as the continent rose during the secular retirement of the ocean, instead of during the ebbing and flowing of the tides. If a shower of rain falls on the mud-bank, when left dry, it deepens the already-formed shallow lines of excavation; and so is it with the rain of successive centuries on the bank of rock and soil, which we call a continent.

We rode on after it was dark, till we reached a side ravine with a small well, called "Agua amarga." The water deserved its name, for besides being saline it was most offensively putrid and bitter; so that we could not force ourselves to drink either tea or maté. I suppose the distance from the river of Copiapó to this spot was at least twenty-five or thirty English miles; in the whole space there was not a single drop of water, the country deserving the name of desert in the strictest sense.

The Nitrate Pampa

Pablo Neruda

Pablo Neruda (1904–1973)—whose real name was Ricardo Eliezer Neftali Reyes y Basoalto—was only twenty when his debut, *Veinte poemas de amor y una canción desesperada* (*Twenty Love Poems and a Song of Despair*), was published. Three years later the Chilean government rewarded Neruda for his literary merits with consular postings in Burma, Thailand, Sri Lanka, China, India, Japan, Spain, and Mexico. In 1942 he returned home to resume his writing.

He was interrupted in late 1944 when a delegation of miners from Antofagosta, in Chile's harsh Atacama Desert asked him to represent them in parliament. For the next four years he traveled throughout the "nitrate pampa"; always passionately interested in natural history, Neruda took the opportunity to learn as much as he could about the desert, as the following passage from his autobiography *Confieso que he vivido* (*I Confess That I Have Lived*) shows.

At the end of 1943 I returned to Santiago. I settled in a house for which I took out a mortgage and stacked all my books within it, this house surrounded by tall trees, and resumed hard work.

Once again I sought my nation's beauty, the comeliness of its women, nature's great splendors, the work of my compatriots and their intelligence. The land had not changed. Fields and drowsy villages, appalling poverty in the mining regions, rich people elbowing their way into the country clubs. I had to come to a decision.

That decision brought me troubles, along with moments of glory. What poet could regret that?

Curzio Malaparte, who later interviewed me, put it well when he wrote, "I am not a Communist, but if I were a Chilean poet, I would be one, like Pablo Neruda. You have to take sides here, with the Cadillacs or with the people who have no education or shoes."

The people without education or shoes elected me senator on March 4, 1945. I will always be proud that thousands of people from Chile's most inhospitable sector, the great mining region of copper and nitrate, voted for me.

Walking over the pampa was tough going. It had not rained for half a century there, and the desert has worked its way into the miners' faces. They are men with burned features; their loneliness and remoteness shows in the darkness of their eyes. Traveling through desert and mountain, entering their humble homes, seeing the inhuman work they do, and feeling that the aspirations of isolated, broken people are in your hands is not an easy responsibility. But my poetry provided a way of talking, allowing me to walk among them and be accepted as a lifelong peer by the miners, who led such terrible lives.

I cannot recall whether it was in Paris or in Prague that I began to doubt the encyclopedic knowledge of my European friends. Most of them were writers, others students.

"We often talk about Chile," I said, "probably because I am Chilean. But do you really know anything about my faroff country? For example, how do we get around? By elephant, automobile, train, airplane, bicycle, camel, or sled?"

Most of them said assuredly, "elephant."

There are no elephants or camels in Chile. I can understand, however, how strange a country that starts at the South Pole and ends in salt marshes and long-rainless deserts must seem. As the representative of those who lived in that desolation, countless nitrate and copper miners who had never worn a collar or tie, I had to travel through those deserts for several years.

Entering those depressions, facing those expanses of sand, is like visiting the moon. This region, which looks like an unpopulated asteroid, stores my country's vast wealth, but the white fertilizer and red ore have to be torn from the scorched earth and the granite mountains. Few places on earth are so harsh; few offer so little reason to go on living. It is an incredible hardship to haul water, to nurture a plant that produces even the smallest flower, to raise a dog, a rabbit, a hog.

I came from the other end of the country. I was born in a green place with vast dark forests. My childhood was filled with rain and snow. The simple act of coming into that desert changed my life. Representing those people in parliament—representing their isolation, their endless land—was also difficult. The bare earth, plantless, waterless, is an immense puzzle. In the forests or beside rivers everything speaks to humans. The desert does not speak. I could not comprehend its tongue: its silence. . . .

Those men locked within walls of silence, in the remotest region under the most desolate sky, had a strong curiosity about politics. They wanted to know what was happening in Yugoslavia and in China. They were interested in the problems of the socialist countries, the result of the great Italian general strike, rumors of war, revolutions that were taking place in faraway lands.

At hundreds of gatherings, in places remote even from neighboring hamlets, I heard the same request: read your poems. The people often asked for them by name. I never knew if my audience understood all or even some of my poems; it was hard to tell in that absolute silence, in the sort of awe with which they listened. Does it matter? There are poems by Hölderin and Mallarmé that I, who am a learned idiot, have never been able to understand. I read them, let me say, with the same awe.

Sometimes supper took on a holiday feel and they served stewed chicken, a rare bird indeed in the pampa. I had a hard time eating the most commonly offered food: stewed guinea pig. Hardship had turned this tiny animal, born only to die in the lab, into a popular dish.

In the houses where I stayed the beds I slept in had two monastic qualities: they had white sheets so starched that they could have stood by themselves, and a hardness like the desert pavement's. These people had no mattresses, only bare boards that gave no bend.

But I still slept the sweet sleep of the blessed. I never had trouble falling into the deep sleep of my comrades. The days were always sere and glowed like coals, but night enfolded the desert with coolness, and the pampa lay under a sky beautifully embossed with stars.

SAHARA

*That narrow stretch of sand knows nothing in the world better
than it does the white waves that whip it, caress it, collapse on to
it, vanish into it. The white foam knows nothing better than
those sands that wait for it rise to it and suck it in. But what do
the waves know of the massed, hot, still sands of the desert just
twenty, no, ten feet beyond the scalloped edge?*
    Ahdaf Soueif

Sahara. The Arabic means "the brown void." Metaphorically,
my Moroccan friend Hsain Iliahane tells me, it can mean
"nothingness," something akin to the old Greek word *lethe*, the
forgetting of the world. Crisscrossed for millennia by nomadic
peoples, the Sahara—a desert less of sand than of jagged rock—
is the largest desert in the world at more than 3.3 million square
miles. It has only recently been thoroughly explored, but even with
the sophisticated methods of modern cartography it remains no
less powerful than before, the haunt of strange animals like the
doppelganger and the basilisk, strange beings like the djinn.
As recently as the last century Europeans who ventured into the
Sahara expected to find cities of gold, much as they did in the
deserts of New Spain; they found only tents and walls of mudbrick,
and little else but to despair of. Robert Laing, the first European
to reach the Malian desert oasis of Timbouktou, complained,
"The eye of the traveler roams in vain over the wide, unvaried
superficies, in search of some object to rest upon, till at length

wearied by a repetition of the bleak and tedious sameness, he is willing to pull one of the folds of his turban over his eyes, and to shroud his head in his burnousa, allowing his mind, which refuses to expand upon the desiccated objects around him, to shrink within itself, and to anticipate in imaginative hope, more genial and enlivening scenes."

Even those who live within the desert take care not to wander too far from their camps. The Taureg leader Sidati Ag Sheik observed, "In the true desert not even jackals can survive; there are only the addax and the fennec, which were made by God to remind man of his own modest capabilities," while the great poet Al Tirimmah (A.D. 660–725) wrote, "A foolish man rides in the desert's heart." Ibn Batuta, the medieval traveler and historian who wandered over much of the Mediterranean world, dutifully ventured into the interior, but noted in his memoir that the "desert is haunted by demons. . . . There is no visible road, nothing but sand blown hither and thither by the wind." For all that, the Sahara has given birth to a rich body of writing and remembrance.

The Nile

The Nile is the longest and oldest river on the face of the earth. At the very beginnings of literature it staked out its claim on the human imagination, as witness this four-thousand-year-old inscription on an Egyptian tomb on the island of Sahal, which lies in the river's first cataract.

I am mourning on my high throne for the vast misfortune, because the Nile flood in my time has not come for seven years! Light is the grain; there is lack of crops and of all kind of food. Each man has become a thief to his neighbor. They desire to hasten and cannot walk. The child cries, the youth creeps along, and the old man; their souls are bowed down, their legs are bent together and drag along the ground, and their hands rest in their bosoms. The counsel of the great ones in the court is but emptiness. Torn open are the chests of provisions, but instead of contents there is air. Everything is exhausted.

Herodotus of Halicarnassus was born about 484 B.C. and died some sixty years later. In between he traveled over much of the known ancient world, making trips to such places as southern Italy, lower Egypt, and the Caucasus. His great *History*, the first major prose work in world literature, is an account of his world at the time of the Persian Wars. In writing it he distinguished between the things he had seen with his own eyes and those that he had only heard of, but he was often too credulous of those things he heard from his peers along the way; his younger contemporary Thucydides called him "Father of Lies."

Renowned in his own time for wide-ranging curiosity and his humanity, Herodotus shows an insatiable appetite for both useful information and a good yarn. This passage from the second book of the *History*, discussing the nature and sources of the Nile River, yields plenty of both. We should not be too quick to ridicule Herodotus for his naive geography—his equating the Nile with the Danube, for instance—or unsophisticated science. After all, the source of the Nile was discovered only a little over a century ago, and the jet stream, which governs climatic patterns, was unknown until World War II, when Japanese high-altitude bombers encountered it for the first time.

When it is full, the Nile spreads over not only the Delta but also portions of Libya and Arabia for about two days' walking in either direction. I was unable to learn about the nature of this river from the priests or, for that matter, from anyone else. I wanted very much to learn why the Nile, beginning at the summer solstice, fills and floods for a hundred days, and when it approaches this length of time, it recedes again, becoming only a trickle by winter and so on until the next summer solstice. About these matters I could get nothing at all from the Egyptians, though I asked everyone I could whether this river had some special property that no other river shared. I remained anxious to learn and persisted in this inquiry, asking as well why it is that no breeze rises from the river.

Certain Greeks, wanting to be well known for resourcefulness, have ventured the three explanations about the river. Two of them I consider worthless, but will mention them anyway for their own sake. The first says that the Etesian winds [northwesterly breezes from the Mediterranean] cause the river to swell because they prevent the Nile from reaching the sea. Now, many times the Etesian winds have failed to blow, but the Nile swells anyway; besides, if this explanation were true, every other river that ran against these winds would have to behave as the Nile does, and even more so, because they are smaller and have weaker currents, and many rivers in Libya and Syria are not at all affected by the Etesian winds. The second explanation, which is even more ignorant, but also more ingenious, says that the Nile causes this itself, because it flows from Ocean, and Ocean girds the entire Earth. The third seems to be most reasonable, but is also silly: it says that the Nile swells with melting snow. Yet this river flows through Libya and the middle of Ethiopia into Egypt, and how could a river flowing from such a hot region into a cooler one carry snow? Anyone with an ounce of sense will see that the Nile does not flow because of snow. The first proof is the hot winds that blow out of the desert. The second is that the region has no rain and frost, and because rain always follows snowfall within five days, the desert would naturally be a rainy place. The third proof is that the people who live there have been burned black by the heat. Not to mention that kites and swallows live there all year, and cranes, to avoid the cold of Scythia, come there to winter. If it snowed where the Nile rises and flows, none of these things would happen.

Whoever came up with the theory of Ocean, having drawn his account from age-old legend, cannot be disproved. I do not know firsthand of any river called Ocean, but I think that Homer or one of the other ancient poets found the name somewhere and introduced it into poetry.

Still, having found other theories wanting, I ought to declare my own view in this matter, which is far from clear. The Nile floods in summer because the Sun, in winter, is driven from its normal course by storms, and it retires to upper Libya. This is it in a nutshell, for it stands to reason that the country closest to where the Sun dwells will be the hottest and most arid, with the native streams burned away.

To explain at greater length: the Sun, passing over upper Libya, produces this effect. As the air in this region is normally still, and the soil nearly always hot because no cold winds pass over it, the Sun causes the same effects in winter as in summer as he traverses the middle of the heavens. He takes for himself the water, and, having done so, takes it into the upper countries; the winds, taking it from him, scatter and dissolve it. The winds that blow from those countries, the south and southwest, are the most rainy of all. I think that the Sun does not give up all this water, but keeps some for himself. As the winter becomes milder, he returns to the middle of the heavens, and thereafter he draws water equally from every river. Up until then, those rivers flow full with rainwater, but when the rain lessens short and the Sun begins to draw on them, they flow weakly. The Nile, on which no rain falls, flows much more weakly at this time than in summer, when the other rivers share its burden; in the winter it alone feeds the Sun. I therefore consider that the Sun causes these things.

In my opinion, the Sun also causes the air to be so dry in these parts, because he scorches everything he approaches. If the order of the seasons were to change, and if that part of the sky where north and winter reside could become that of the south and summer, then the Sun, driven from the middle of the heavens by winter and the north wind, would go to the upper countries of Europe, just as he now goes to Libya, and he would have the same effect on the Danube as he does on the Nile.

As to why no winds blow from the Nile, I think it improbable that they would rise from hot places. They usually come from cold regions.

Let us leave these things as they are and have always been. No Egyptian, Libyan, or Greek with whom I have spoken pretends to know a thing about the sources of the Nile, except for a clerk at the Temple of Athena in the Egyptian city of Saïs. (It seems to me that he was not being serious when he said he knew the exact sources.) This is what he said: between the cities of Seyene, which lies in the Thebaïd, and Elephantine are two sharp-peaked mountains called Crophi and Mophi. The clerk claimed that the springs of the Nile flow between these mountains, and that these springs are bottomless; half of the water flows to Egypt and the north, the other half to Ethiopia and the south. Psammetichus, the king of Egypt, proved that the springs were bottomless by ordering that a cable many thousands of fathoms long be lowered into them. This was done, and the cable never touched bottom. Anyway, this was the clerk's opinion. If it is true, I believe he proved only that there must be a whirlpool in the springs, which flow against the mountains, that entangles sounding lines. . . .

Because the Danube flows through populous countries, many people know about it, but no one can describe the sources of the Nile because no one lives in the deserts of Libya. I have told you all that I could discover about its course. It flows into Egypt, which lies opposite the highlands of Cilicia. From there to the town of Sinope, on the Black Sea, is a straight journey of five days for a practiced traveler. Sinope lies across from the place where the Danube empties

into the sea. I think that the Nile, which passes through all of Libya,
is about the same length as the Danube.

In his *Metamorphoses*, the Roman poet Ovid, who flourished at the time of
Christ, treats the Nile as a great progenitor of life.

When the seven-mouthed Nile
falls back from the flooded fields and returns
the waters to their former course,
and fresh mud bakes underneath the sun,
farmers, turning over the soil, uncover
newborn creatures, some inchoate,
some beginning to take their natural forms,
unfinished, without proportion—in a single body
one part may be alive. while another
may still be a crumb of dirt. Confronting
each other, heat and moisture generate all life;
their union produces all things. Fire
hates water, but wet heat is the creator:
harmonious conflict is the nature of the world.

The Atlas and Beyond

Pliny the Elder

The work of the Roman explorer Pliny (A.D. 23–79) stands at the very
origins of nature writing, marked by the author's intense curiosity—he
died of asphyxiation while observing an eruption of Mount Vesuvius—

and his willingness to entertain many theories. In this passage from his *Historia Naturalis*, he relates stories of the little-known Atlas massif of northwestern Africa.

Mount Atlas has more legends attached to it than any other mountain in Africa. It is reported that it rises out of the sand desert high into the sky, rugged and jagged on the side facing the coastline of the Atlantic Ocean, which is named for the mountain, whereas on the side facing the interior of Africa it is shaded by forests and watered by gushing springs. Fruits of all kinds grow there on their own and in such abundance that no one ever wants for food.

In the Atlas region no person is ever seen in the daytime. Everything is as starkly silent there as it is in the desert, and anyone approaching the quiet summit, which reaches nearly to the moon, is dumbstruck with a certain dread. At night Atlas is covered with many fires, or so I have heard, illuminating the orgies of Goat-Pans and Satyrs, and it rings with echoes of their wild flutes, bagpipes, drums, and cymbals. Noted writers have published accounts of these things, along with the exploits of Hercules and Perseus that took place on the mountain. Mount Atlas is a tremendous distance away from Rome and must be approached across unmapped territory.

Some notes have survived made by the Punic general Hanno, who, at the height of Carthage's power, was ordered by its leaders to circumnavigate the continent of Africa. Most Greek and Roman writers follow Hanno in recounting both his legends and accounts of the many settlements he founded in Africa. No one remembers where these settlements were, and no trace of them remains.

When Scipio Aemilianus was the Roman commanding general in Africa, the historian Polybius took a fleet to explore the continent. Sailing along the coast, Polybius reported that west of Mount Atlas lie forests full of wild animals. In the River Bambolus, he said, there are many crocodiles and hippopotamuses.

The first time Roman forces fought in Mauretania was during Claudius's reign. Caligula had murdered Ptolemy, and his freeman Aedemon sought to avenge him in the desert. Most people believe that our soldiers went as far as Mount Atlas, where the natives fled from them.

Five Roman colonies now lie in the province. According to widespread reports, you might think them to be easily accessible, but that is simply not true. Well-born people, too lazy to find out the truth for themselves, are nonetheless not ashamed to tell lies if by not doing so they admit to ignorance. Credibility never more quickly collapses than when an important authority supports a lie. As for me, I am less surprised that our knights, some of whom are now entering the Senate, do not know the truth about these things than I am that they so worship Luxury, an immensely influential power that causes people to fell whole forests and the creatures within them for ivory and citrus-wood, to sift through all the rocky shores of Algeria for murex and purple-fish.

Suetonius Paulinus, who was consul in my day [A.D. 66], was the first Roman leader to cross over the Atlas Mountains, and he went further into Mauretania. His estimate of their height generally accords with what other authorities say, but he adds that the lower slopes are covered with dense forests of tall trees, the species of which he does not record; they have very tall, lustrous trunks that have no knots. The leaves, like cypress but heavily scented, are covered with a silky down from which clothing can be made, just as it can from the down of the silkworm. The summit of Mount Atlas, he says, is covered with deep snow, even in summer.

Suetonius Paulinus reached Mount Atlas in ten days, and traveled to the River Ger [Niger] across deserts of black dust strewn with sharp rocks that looked as though they had been set on fire. The region is uninhabitable because of the heat, even though he crossed it in winter. The Canarii live in the nearby forests, which are full of elephants and snakes.

Cyrenaica is thought to be good within twenty miles of the coast even for arboriculture, but further inland it is good only for growing grain. Beyond that lies a band thirty-five miles wide and about three hundred miles long that can support only silphium.

After the Nasamon tribe come the Asbytae and Macae; and beyond them, twelve days beyond the Greater Syrtes, are the Amantes. They are walled in by great dunes of sand to the west, but they take water from cistern wells only a few feet deep, for the territory is well watered by Mauretania. The Amantes make their houses from salt blocks that are quarried from the mountains.

The River Ger is like the Nile. It yields reeds, papyrus, and the same kinds of animals, and it rises at the same time of year. Some authorities locate the Atlas tribe in the middle of the desert and next to them the Goat-Pans, the Blemmyae, the Gamphasantes, the Satyrs, and the Thongfeet.

The Atlas tribe is subhuman, if what I hear is true. They have no names. When they see the sun rise or set they shout terrible curses, because they believe it will bring calamity to themselves and their fields. They do not dream at night, as humans do. The Cavedwellers live in hollows and eat only snake meat. They have no voices, properly speaking, but make high-pitched noises. The Garamantes never marry, but share their women back and forth. The Augilae worship only the gods of the underworld. The Gamphasantes go naked, do not fight, and run away from foreigners.

The Blemmyae, it is reported, have no heads, but their chests have mouths and eyes. The Satyrs are human only in their physical form. We all know what the Goat-Pans look like. The Thongfeet

have feet like thin straps and move by crawling on the sand. The
Pharusi, formerly from Persia, accompanied Hercules when he
went to the Gardens of the Hesperides. I cannot think of anything
else to write about Africa.

The Garden of Allah

Algerian saying

The desert is the Garden of Allah, from which the Lord of the
faithful removed all superfluous human and animal life, so that
there might be one place where He can walk in peace.

The Bahia of Morocco

Edith Wharton

Edith Wharton (1862–1937) is best known today for her perceptive novels
of manners, among them *The Age of Innocence* and *The House of Mirth*. She
is less well known as a traveler, but she roamed the world and explored
places uncommon for foreign women in her time to venture into. This
selection from her memoir *In Morocco* (1906) is marked by her attention to
small but telling details.

Whoever would understand Marrakech must begin by mounting
at sunset to the roof of the Bahia.

Outspread below lies the oasis-city of the south, flat and vast as the great nomad camp it really is, its low roof extending on all sides to a belt of blue palms ringed with desert. Only two or three minarets and a few noblemen's houses among gardens break the general flatness; but they are hardly noticeable, so irresistibly is the eye drawn toward two dominant objects—the white wall of the Atlas and the red tower of the Koutoubya. Foursquare, untapering, the great tower lifts its flanks of ruddy stone. Its large spaces of unornamented wall, its triple tier of clustered openings, lightening as they rise from the severe rectangular lights of the first stage to the graceful arcade below the parapet have the stern harmony of the noblest architecture. The Koutoubya would be magnificent anywhere; in this flat desert it is grand enough to face the Atlas.

The Almohad conquerors who built the Koutoubya and embellished Marrakech dreamed a dream of beauty that extended from the Guadalquivir to the Sahara; and at its two extremes they placed their watchtowers. The Giralda watched over civilized enemies in a land of ancient Roman culture; the Koutoubya stood at the edge of the world facing the hordes of the desert.

The Almoravid princes who founded Marrakech came from the black desert of Senegal, themselves leaders of wild hordes. In the history of North Africa the same cycle has perpetually repeated itself; generation after generation of chiefs have flowed in from the desert or the mountains, overthrown their predecessors, massacred, plundered, grown rich, built sudden palaces, encouraged their great servants to do the same; then fallen on them and taken their wealth and their palaces. Usually some religious fury, some ascetic wrath against the self-indulgence of the cities, has been the motive of these attacks; but invariably the same results followed, as they followed when the Germanic barbarians descended on Italy. The conquerors infected with luxury and mad with power built vaster palaces, planned grander cities; but Sultans and Viziers camped in their golden houses as if on the march, and the mud huts of the tribesmen within their walls were but one degree removed from the mud-walled tents of the bled.

This was more especially the case with Marrakech, a city of Berbers and blacks, and the last outpost against the fierce black world beyond the Atlas from which its founders came. When one looks at its site and considers its history one can only marvel at the height of civilization it attained.

The Bahia itself, now the palace of the Resident-General, though built less than a hundred years ago, is typical of the architectural megalomania of the great southern chiefs. It was built by Ba-Ahmed, the all-powerful black Vizier of the Sultan Moulay-el-Hassan (who reigned from 1873 to 1894). Ba-Ahmed was evidently an artist and an archaeologist. His ambition was to re-create a Palace of Beauty such as the Moors had built in the prime of Arab art, and he brought to Marrakech skilled artificers of Fez, the last surviving masters of the mystery of chiselled plaster and ceramic mosaics and honeycombing of gilded cedar. They came, they built the Bahia, and it remains the loveliest and most fantastic of Moroccan palaces.

Court within court, garden beyond garden, reception halls, private apartments, slaves' quarters, sunny prophets' chambers on the roofs and baths in vaulted crypts, the labyrinth of passages and rooms stretches away over several acres of ground. A long court enclosed in pale-green trellis-work, where pigeons plume themselves about a great tank and the dripping tiles glitter with refracted sunlight, leads to the fresh gloom of a cypress garden, or under jasmine tunnels bordered with running water; and these again open on arcaded apartments faced with tiles and stucco-work, where, in languid twilight, the hours drift by to the ceaseless music of the fountains.

The beauty of Moroccan palaces is made up of details of orna-
ment and refinements of sensuous delight too numerous to record;
but to get an idea of their general character it is worthwhile to cross
the tiled Court of Cypresses at the Bahia and follow a series of low-
studded passages that turn on themselves till they reach the center
of the labyrinth. Here, passing by a low padlocked door leading to a
crypt and known as the "Door of the Vizier's Treasure-House," one
comes on a painted portal that opens into a still more secret sanctuary, the apartment of the Grand Vizier's Favorite.

This lovely prison from which all sight and sound of the outer
world are excluded is built about an atrium paved with disks of tur-
quoise and black and white water trickles from a central *vasca* of al-
abaster into a hexagonal mosaic channel in the pavement. The walls,
which are at least 25 feet high, are roofed with painted beams resting
on panels of traceried stucco in which is set a clerestory of jewelled
glass. On each side of the atrium are long recessed rooms closed by
vermilion doors painted with gold arabesques and vases of spring
flowers; and into these shadowy inner rooms, spread with rugs and
divans and soft pillows, no light comes except when their doors are
opened into the atrium. In this fabulous place it was my good luck to
be lodged while I was in Marrakech.

In a climate where, after the winter snow has melted from the Atlas, every breath of air for long months is a flame of fire, these enclosed rooms in the middle of the palaces are the only places of
refuge from the heat. Even in October the temperature of the Favorite's apartment was deliciously reviving after a morning in the ba-
zaars or the dusty streets, and I never came back to its wet tiles and
perpetual twilight without the sense of plunging into a deep sea-
pool.

From far off through circuitous corridors came the scent of citron
blossom and jasmine, with sometimes a bird's song before dawn,
sometimes a flute's wail at sunset, and always the call of the muezzin

in the night; but no sunlight reached the apartment except in remote rays through the clerestory, and no air except through one or two broken panes.

Sometimes, lying on my divan, and looking out through the vermilion doors, I used to surprise a pair of swallows dropped down from their nest in the cedar-beams to preen themselves on the fountain's edge or in the channels of the pavement; for the roof was full of birds who came and went through the broken panes of the clerestory. Usually they were my only visitors; but one morning just at daylight I was waked by a soft tramp of bare feet and saw silhouetted against the cream-colored walls a procession of eight tall negroes in linen tunics, who filed noiselessly across the atrium like a moving frieze of bronze in that fantastic setting, and the hush of that twilight hour, the vision was so like the picture of a "Seraglio Tragedy," some fragment of a Delacroix or Decamps floating up into the drowsy brain, that I almost fancied I had seen ghosts of Ba-Ahmed's executioners revisiting with dagger and bowstring the scene of an unavenged crime. . . . They vanished, and when I made the mistake of asking what they had been doing in my room at that hour, I was told (as though it were the most natural thing in the world) that they were the municipal lamp-lighters of Marrakech, whose duty it is to refill every morning the two hundred acetylene lamps lighting the Palace of the Resident-General. Such unforeseen aspects, in this mysterious city, do the most ordinary domestic functions wear.

The Desert's Edge

Federico García Lorca

In most geographies southern Spain lies beyond the Sahara, but ecologically it is an extension of the desert in every respect. (Most "spaghetti westerns" were filmed in the province of Almería, about as dry a place as is to be found in Europe.) These three poems by Federico García Lorca (1899–1936) evoke the dry landscape of Andalusia.

And Later

The labyrinths
time creates
vanish.

(The only thing left
is the desert.)

The heart,
spring of wanting,
vanishes.

(The only thing left
is the desert.)

The illusion of the dawn
and of kisses
vanishes.

The only thing left
is the desert.
An undulating
desert.

Evocation

Dry land
quiet land
of immense
nights.

(Wind in the olive trees,
wind in the mountains.)

Old
land
of lantern
and misery.
Land
of deep wells.
Land
of sightless death,
of arrows.

(Wind on the high roads.
Breeze in the poplar grove.)

Village

Atop a naked hill
a cross.
Clear water
and hundred-year-old olive trees.
In the alleyways
shrouded men;
on the towers
weathervanes turning.

Eternally
turning.
O, lost village
in weeping Andalusia!

A Sandstorm

Antoine de Saint-Exupéry

Best known today for his novels *The Little Prince* and *Night Flight*, the young
Antoine de Saint-Exupéry (1900–1943) wanted nothing more than to
become a famous aviator. To that end he joined the French Air Force
immediately after graduating from college, yearning for the adventure the
military would surely provide. After a year of flying in Morocco, he was
demobilized and quickly joined the Air Mail Service, flying courier planes
throughout French North Africa, the setting for his 1929 book *Courrier
Sud* (*Southern Mail*), from which this passage is taken.

The wind is coming in from the east. Coming in from the heart of
the Sahara, the sand rising in yellow dust devils. At dawn a pale, wa-
vering sun unfastened itself from the horizon, twisted by the burning haze like a washed-out soap bubble. As it rose toward noon it
shrank ever smaller into a burning arrow, a fiery brand on the neck.

The wind is coming in from the east. Taking off from Port-
Étienne in a calm, even balmy air you go only a hundred meters upward before reaching the searing river of that wind. The needle
shoots upward.

Oil temperature: 120°.

Water temperature: 110°.

It's a matter of going upward two or three thousand meters. Obviously it can be done. You have to if you're to climb out of this sand-storm. Certainly. But five minutes of such a steep climb and the ignition and valves will burn out. It's easy to say to yourself, keep climbing. But in the stiff wind the plane doesn't perform.

The wind comes in from the east, and you're blind. The sun jumps around in the yellow cyclones. Its pale, dust-caked face comes out, burns, and goes away. Sometimes, if you look straight down, you'll get a glimpse of the earth. Sometimes. Am I ascending, descending, banking? How can I tell? I can only climb a hundred meters, it seems. We'll try to fly below the storm.

A mild north wind meets you near the ground. That's better. You dangle your arm from the cockpit, like dangling your fingers in a cool stream from the boat you're riding.

Oil temperature: 110°.

Water temperature: 95°.

Cool as a river? By comparison. The plane skims along, bounced by thermals. The lack of visibility is unnerving.

At Cape Timeris the wind is coming in from the east even at ground level. It can't be avoided. I smell burning rubber—the magneto, maybe, or one of the joints. The speed gauge drops by ten points. "Don't you start, too," I growl.

Water temperature: 115°.

I can't get the plane to climb ten meters. I see the dune ahead of me, the oil gauge. Up! Up and over, shot up by the dune. I've got the stick pulled back as far as it will go. It won't last; keeping the plane level is like trying not to spill an overflowing bowl.

Ten meters below the wheels Mauretania pours out its sand, its salts, a whirlwind of dust.

1,520 revolutions per minute.

The first air pocket whacks the plane like a fist. Just twenty kilometers ahead is a French fort, the only one in the area. The problem is getting there.

Water temperature: 120°.

Dunes, boulders, salt depressions: the sand engulfs them, whips them around. The dunes open wider, wider, and close while catastrophe awaits the wheels. The black boulders bunched up over there come up slowly, then scatter below.

1,430 revolutions per minute.

Centimeters below the wheels the final sand rivers loomed, tossing up shovelfuls of whirling gold. The plane cleared the last of the dunes. There, not far beyond them, the fortress lay. Thank God. Bernis cut the ignition.

The hurtling desert slowed. The world fell back into dusty chaos.

Rain Songs

These Judeo-Arabic rain songs come from the highlands of Morocco.

1

o the rain drop drop drop drop
o the farmers' little sons
o the landlord Bu-Sukri
o the trip down by the river
o his tumble down the well
o his mother's red tarboosh
o the one-eyed man one-eyed
down the silo in the dark

2

the wind the wind o the bellows
o my uncle o the bellows

it's the blacksmith's bellows
blacksmith gropes his way around
then calls out   children
o my children in the forest
they call   Papa
buy a shirt   or   Papa
buy a black shirt
shirt with carrot-colored sleeves
we eat it all up
whatever there is to eat

Translated by Jerome Rothenberg

God, Book, Desert

Edmond Jabés

Born in 1907 in Cairo, the poet Edmond Jabés has made the Sahara
central to his work These remarks come from his collection of interviews
with Marcel Cohen, *From the Desert to the Book.*

As far as the word *desert* is concerned, what fascinates me is to see
how far the metaphor of the void, from being used so much, has per-
meated the whole word. The word itself has become a metaphor. To
give it back its strength, one has therefore to return to the real desert
which is indeed exemplary emptiness—but an emptiness with its
own, very real dust. Think also about the word *book.* The book,
where everything seems possible through a language that one thinks
one can master and that finally turns out to be but the very place of
its bankruptcy. All the metaphors the word can inspire lie between

those two extremes. None of them really gets to the heart of it, but, between this all and this nothing, the unfathomable opening takes place, which in the end is what every writer and every reader is confronted with. Moreover you know that one of the Hebrew names of God is *Hammakom* which means *Place*. God is the place—as the book is. Bringing those two together is something that has always excited me. God, through His Name, is the book. In one of my works I noted that one writes only in the effacement of the Divine Name—of the place.

One cannot look at Egypt, at the Orient, with Western eyes without falling into an exoticism that negates the essential. People talk easily about Oriental indolence. This shows their total ignorance. The Egyptians are not indolent, far from it. One need only watch the energy, the endurance with which a construction worker carries cement on his back, in a canvas bag. No, the Egyptian is not indolent. He is simply attentive—especially the peasant—to signs that escape us. The flat landscape of the plain, punctuated by tall palm trees shooting up to the sky, opens the mind to a perception of time infinitely vaster than ours. Nowhere is there an interruption, everything goes on forever. The pharaohs barely belong to the past.

Over there, time is an artificial concept. Something artificial laid over something real. The real is made up of patiently repeated gestures. The peasant is its surest guarantor. His movements simultaneously limit and "illimit" him. True to himself, he plants what he has always planted and will continue to plant, in the heart of the seasons. He has inherited his faith from his ancestors and will transmit it to his descendants. That faith is a lighter, a larger breath, an indefinable blue in the motionless blue of the sky. God commands. Life is but incalculable goings and comings along a familiar road. Fatality liberates the peasant from the anguish of death. His words are the wisdom of millennia, drawn from the desert—they are the words of the sand, as vast as NOTHINGNESS. That's because the desert assigns its own slow rhythm—a rhythm from beyond silence, from beyond life—to the smallest gesture, the most insignificant word.

In the desert one becomes other: one becomes the one who knows the weight of the sky and the thirst of the earth; the one who has learned to take account of his own solitude. Far from excluding us, the desert envelops us. We become the immensity of sand, just as we are the book when we write. All of that is eminently present throughout Egypt, in the town dwellers as well.

Just as the countryside hits you with its bareness—it is only sand torn from the desert and fertilized by the river—so the city hits you with its many colors and its all-pervading sensuality, with its crowded streets where the smell of sweat contends with the odor of the spices, jasmine, incense; with its overcrowded, stuffy cafés beloved by flies, where customers and backgammon players share rickety tables; where water pipes awake insatiable erotic dreams in the lonely, dazed smoker.

The old quarters of Cairo with their low shanties, their badly lit filthy alleyways—the quarter of the bazaar and the mosques, kept at arm's length by the residential quarters of the island of Gherzireh or Zamalec and by that portion of the capital dotted with imposing buildings, movie theaters, large stores, banks, luxury hotels; with its prestigious squares, its spacious roads where the common man, too poor to feel at ease in such surroundings, rarely ventures, though here and there a few beggars—the one-eyed or blind, the armless or legless—bring back the reality of the surrounding poverty and squalor.

All of that is a part of my intimate landscape. Like those unforgettable spectacles, the feast days or days of mourning, that one takes part in regularly.

I'm thinking especially of the Feast of Spring, the Mouled El

Nabi, when for twelve hours, men, women, children, all gaudily dressed, crisscross the city in donkey carriages while clapping their hands, singing, dancing and brandishing sugar dolls made for the occasion, before flooding the public gardens—and its opposite: the sad, nearly daily, spectacle of the black funeral processions—no two alike—with their professional mourners, screaming, tearing their faces smudged with earth, miming pain in the face of death, miming death and the dead man or woman in their last struggle, in their ultimate embrace, like a couple locked together since the beginnings of time.

It is really one and the same popular demonstration alternatively exhibiting its joy or pain—their irresistible explosion. What is so surprising about that? In a country without twilight, where bright colors signal the end of day, doesn't starry night succeed day without visible transition?

SOUTHERN
AFRICA

The smell of the Kalahari after sudden rain is something you never forget. What blooms up, especially when the sun gets to work, and even in cool-tending June weather, is an odor so powerful and so elusive that you want to keep inhaling it in order to make up your mind which it is, foul or sweet. It seems poised midway between the two poles. It's resinous or like tar, and like the first smell of liver when it touches a hot pan. It fades as the dryness returns, and as it does you will it to persist until you can penetrate it
Norman Rush, *Mating*

At 220,000 square miles, the Kalahari Desert of South Africa and its neighbor, the coastal Namib, were mysteries until very recent times. Thanks now to the world conservation movement and continued anthropological interest in the indigenous !Kung and San peoples, these vast unknown places are becoming more familiar to us; still, the body of literature about those drylands is small. Of seemingly impossible antiquity, the deserts of southern Africa are increasingly threatened by development and the continent's rapidly growing population, and much international conservation work is aimed at preserving both desert habitats and the many endangered species living within them. For all that, the arid lands of southern Africa retain much of their old magic, which Saul Bellow so well evokes in his novel *Henderson the Rain King*: "It was hot, clear, and arid and after several days we saw no human footprints. . . . I felt I was entering the past—the real past, no history or junk like that. The prehuman past. And I believed that there was something between the stones and me. The mountains were naked, and often snakelike in their forms, without trees, and you could see the clouds being born on the slopes."

The Coming of the Sun in the Sky

Auen folktale

The so-called Bushmen fall into three main ethnic groups: the Heikum, living in Namibia; the Auen, in the southern Kalahari; and the !Kung, in the northern, central and western Kalahari. Altogether they number only about 25,000. This Auen story relates the origin of the sun.

The Sun was a man, but not one of the early Bushmen. In the beginning he gave forth brightness only around his own dwelling. In those days before the children threw him upwards from the earth, the sky was dark. The light that shone from him came from one of his armpits as he lay with his arm lifted up. When he put his arm down darkness fell everywhere; when he lifted it up again it was as if day had come. When the Sun was thrown into the sky it became round, and after that it was never a man again.

The children who performed this deed did so because their mother had requested them to do it. It was another old woman who had told the mother about it, for she herself had no children. She told the mother of the children that they should approach the Sun gently and lift his arm, so that the Sun's armpit would make everything bright. The old woman also spoke to the children, saying: "O children! You must wait for the sun to lie down to sleep, for we are cold. You shall gently approach to lift him up while he lies asleep. All together you shall lift him up and throw him into the sky." In this manner the old woman spoke to the mother of the children, and in this manner the mother also spoke to the children.

The children came, the children went away. The old woman had said: "You must go and sit down when you have found him, waiting to see if he sleeps." Therefore the children went out, they sat down while they waited. The Sun came, he lay down, he lifted up his elbow, his armpit shone on the ground. The old woman had instructed the children, saying: "O children who are going to that place! You must speak to him when you throw him up!" She had said to them: "O children! You must tell him that he must entirely become the Sun, and go forward through the sky as the Sun, which is hot, so that the Bushmen rice will dry while he is hotly passing along in the sky." Thus the white-haired woman had spoken to them. And the children listened to her. And they listened to their mother, who repeated what the old woman had said. Therefore they knew what to do.

They went out, an older child informing them what was to be done. They went out, they sat down while awaiting the old man who was the Sun. When he lay down and slept, they stealthily approached him. They stood still, they looked at him, they went forward. They stealthily reached him, they took hold of him, all of them together, they lifted him up, they raised him, feeling his hotness. Then, feeling his hotness, they threw him up, speaking to him, saying: "O Sun! You must entirely stand fast where we are throwing you. You must go along, standing fast, and remain hot." The old woman who had instructed them said that they appeared to have thrown him into the sky and that he seemed to be standing fast. In this manner she spoke. And the father of the children said: "The Sun-armpit is standing fast in the sky over there, he whom the children have thrown up. He lay intending to sleep, but the children have thrown him upwards."

The children returned. They came and one of them said: "Our companion here, he took hold of him. I also took hold of him. My younger brother took hold of him. My other younger brother also took hold of him. Our companion who is here, his younger brother also took hold of him. I said, 'Grasp him firmly.' I spoke in this manner, saying, 'Throw him up!' I said, 'Throw the old man up!' Then the children threw up the old man, that old man, the Sun, doing as the old woman instructed us." Another older child spoke, telling his grandmother: "O my grandmother! We threw him up, we told him that he must become entirely the Sun, which is hot, for we are cold. We said, 'O my grandfather Sun-armpit! Remain at the place above. Become the Sun which is hot, so that the Bushmen rice may dry for us, that the whole earth may become light, that the whole earth may become warm in the summers, that you may provide heat. Therefore you must shine completely, taking away the darkness. You must come and the darkness go away.' "

Thus the Sun comes, the darkness goes away, the Sun comes, the Sun sets, the darkness comes, the Moon comes at night. The day breaks, the Sun comes out, the darkness goes away, the Sun comes. The Moon comes out, the Moon brightens the darkness, the darkness departs. The Moon comes out, the Moon shines, taking away the darkness. It goes along, it has made bright the darkness, it sets. The Sun comes out, the Sun follows the darkness. The Sun takes away the Moon, the Moon stands, the Sun pierces it with the Sun's knife as it stands. Therefore the Moon decays on account of it. Therefore it says, "O Sun! Leave for the children the backbone!" Therefore the Sun leaves the backbone for the children. The Sun does this. The Sun says that he will leave the backbone for the children, the Sun assents to the Moon's request. The Sun leaves the backbone for the children, the Moon goes painfully away, he painfully returns home. He goes to become another Moon, which is whole. He again lives. He lives again, knowing that he seemed to die. Therefore he becomes a new Moon, feeling that he has put on a stomach, he becomes large, feeling that he is a Moon which is whole. He is alive. He goes along at night, feeling that he is the Mantis's shoe walking in the night.

The Sun is here, all the earth is bright. The people walk while the earth is light. The people perceive the bushes, they see other people; they see the meat which they are eating; they also see the springbok, they also head the springbok in summer; they also head the ostrich when they know that the Sun shines, they also steal up to the gems-bok; they also steal up to the kudu when they feel that the whole place is bright; they also visit each other when the Sun shines upon the path. They also travel in summer; they shoot in summer; they espy the springbok in summer; they go round to head the springbok; they lie down; they feel that they lie in a little house of bushes; they scratch up the earth in the little house of bushes; they lie down when the springbok come.

The Rain Tried to Kill Us

Nama Hottentot folktales

These two stories, collected in 1880, are from the Damara area of the southern Kalahari.

When the rain fell on us at night, I did thus, while the rain fell, I lay on the ground and played my gourd lute, just as the rain-sorcerer does. And my mother said to me, do you not see that the rain is let-ting up? Why did I not know that the rain-sorcerer used his power in anger to make the rain stand still? The rain would stop, when the rain-sorcerer said that it would not fall.

When my mother rebuked me, I did not heed her. I lay on the ground, playing my gourd lute, just as the rain-sorcerer does. And she became silent; seeing that I did not heed her, she lay down and slept, while I kept playing.

As I lay there playing the gourd lute, the rain shone in our eyes. When we thought that the rain would lighten, it seemed first to close and then to flood our eyes. We kept shutting our eyes, and the darkness kept our eyes closed. Before we opened them, the rain gave us green things; the rain let up, and we sensed greenness all around.

And the rain, letting up, passed over our heads.

My mother exclaimed, "N n n n n!" My father asked her, what was it? Had the blast of the storm come to her and caused her pain? And my mother told him that it seemed that the rain was ready to flay her, and she called out in pain. She said that it was our fault that we had not obeyed her over such a small thing.

I acted that way, when mother told me to stop playing the gourd lute, like the rain-sorcerer. I would not listen. And the rain tried to kill us because of it.

When he is on his way home, and he feels that he cannot make it, he throws dust up in the air so that people at home can see it.

The person who is standing guard, feeling the hot sun, scans the horizon. As she stands there, she looks out and cries, "Someone is throwing dust up there!"

And the people run out of their huts, crying, "You must run quickly and give him water! The sun is killing him! You must run quickly and give him water!" They run to the man, pouring water on him to cool him.

And he sits up straight to take the darkness from his face; for the blinding sun is as dark as night.

A Kalahari Christmas

Frederick Courteney Selous

Frederick Selous (1851–1917) was the virtual archetype of the "great white hunter." A friend of Cecil Rhodes and Theodore Roosevelt, he traveled the world as a hunter and adventurer, and he served as the model for the novelist H. Rider Haggard's swashbuckling hero Alan Quatremain. Tanzania's Selous Reserve, the second-largest wildlife sanctuary in the world, is named for him This account of a safari in the northern Kalahari is taken from his 1908 book *African Nature Notes and Reminiscences*.

Christmas time is about the hottest season of the year in South Africa, unless heavy rains happen to be falling, and at the time of which I am writing the heat was simply terrific. The country around us was an absolutely dead level in all directions, everywhere clothed with a sparse covering of low thorny bushes, whose little grey-green leaves and hard black twigs, over which little hook-shaped thorns are profusely scattered, afforded but little protection from the cruel sun. Early in the day the sand became so hot that it was quite impossible to keep the palm of one's hand upon it for more than a few seconds at a time, nor was it possible to hold one's hand on any piece of iron exposed to the sun's rays. The sand itself was so deep and soft, that our heavy bullock waggons sank in it to a depth of several inches, over the felloes of the wheels, in fact; and as our long caravan moved slowly and painfully forwards, both bullocks and waggons were almost hidden from sight in a thick cloud of fine dust which rose from the trampled ground into the still hot air. When the sun set the relief was immense, but still the heat thrown up from the scorched sand was very great, and it was only for one short hour between dawn and sunrise that the temperature became pleasantly cool.

It was about four o'clock on the afternoon of December 23 that

we finally left Tlakani, after having carefully filled our water-casks
and given all the bullocks and horses a good drink. At sundown we
outspanned, made a hasty meal of dried eland meat roasted on the
ashes, washed down with a cup of tea, and then inspanned again. All
that night we trekked on with only two short intervals of rest, and
when day broke on the morning of December 24, our oxen had done
ten hours' actual pulling through the heavy sand and covered some
fifteen miles since leaving Tlakani. All this day we travelled slowly
onwards through the frightful heat, giving the bullocks an hour's
rest after every two hours' pull. The terrific heat of the cruel pitiless
sun told upon the straining oxen very rapidly, for it must be remembered that nothing but steady hard pulling by every member of each
span, all pulling in unison, could move the heavy waggons through
the deep sand, and nothing made of flesh and blood could work very
long in such a temperature without drinking.

Towards the close of the long day it became a pitiful sight to look
at the poor oxen, as they toiled slowly and painfully along, with lowered heads and tongues hanging from their gasping mouths. The
hot air they breathed was full of fiery dust, which rose in clouds from
their feet and hung suspended in the breathless atmosphere long after the last waggon had passed. This hot dust no doubt very much
aggravated the terrible thirst from which our bullocks were now suffering, and kept them continually gasping and coughing.

At last the dreadful sun turned blood-red as it neared the western
horizon, and then soon sank from view behind the interminable
landscape of stunted thorn bushes. When outspanned during the
day, the bullocks had made no attempt to feed, but had only stood
about in clusters amongst the shadeless thorn scrub; I was in hopes,
however, that they would graze a little at sunset, albeit the grass was
scorched and scant. But they were too parched to do so; and so, hungry, weary, and terribly thirsty, the poor brutes were once more
yoked to the heavy waggons just as the short twilight of the early

tropic night was giving place to a bright moonlight, for it wanted but a couple of days to full moon. The whole of this second night we travelled slowly southwards, with short intervals of rest.

I kept awake once more throughout the night, in order to time the periods of travel and the intervals of rest. As we were four Europeans, we might have kept awake turn and turn about, and turned in for a sleep in one of the waggons when not on duty; but when travelling through the desert I am always too anxious to be able to sleep, whilst making a push from one water to another, and always make a point of timing the treks myself, and keeping the waggon-drivers and leaders up to the mark; for these latter naturally get worn out during such journeys, and often are so tired that when a halt is called, they just throw themselves down where they stand and lie there like logs till it is time to move on again.

During the night we passed the deep limestone well and shallow pan of Inkowani, both of which were perfectly dry, and presently Christmas Day 1879 dawned upon us, and the cruel sun was soon once more shining over the desolate wilderness around us. By this time it had become evident that our bullocks could not possibly pull the heavy waggons much farther. One or other of them was constantly lying down, and had to be mercilessly beaten or its tail twisted or bitten before it could be induced to get up again and struggle on a little farther. Although the waggons of our Bamangwato friends were much less heavily laden than ours, their bullocks were much inferior, and on the whole in quite as sorry a plight.

About ten o'clock it became impossible to get the waggons along at all, and we had to give up the idea of reaching the pools of Mahakabi, from which we were only about six miles distant, with them, as we had hoped to have done. We therefore outspanned, and prepared to drive all our cattle and horses to the water, let them have a good drink and feed there, and return to fetch the waggons in the afternoon. Collison was not very well, so he and Sell remained with the waggons, whilst Miller and I—both of us mounted—and all our coloured boys, with the exception of the waggon-drivers, accompanied Tinkarn and his people to Mahakabi, taking all our cattle, horses, and dogs with us. Tinkarn, I think, only left a couple of boys to look after the five waggons belonging to his people. I let him start first with all his people and their troop of cattle, Miller and I following with our own herd, driven by our own boys, about a quarter of an hour or twenty minutes later. I rode my own favourite shooting horse "Bob," and led Collison's best nag "Big Bles," his after-rider, a Mangwato boy, named Dick, being mounted on his second horse. I had had a cup of coffee when we outspanned just before daylight, but had eaten nothing since the previous evening, and had not even tied a piece of "biltong" on my saddle, when leaving the waggons with the oxen, as I had hoped to get back again before sundown, and was besides too full of anxiety to think much about food just then.

Although the bullocks were unable to drag our heavy waggons any farther through the deep sand, they stepped out briskly enough along the road when unencumbered, and evidently knew that they were being taken to water. We were just approaching the first of the two pools of Mahakabi, and could see the cattle of our Mangwato friends standing round about it, when I saw Tinkarn coming riding back to meet me. "Metsi utin?" ("Is there water?"), I asked. "Metsi haio" ("There is no water"), he answered; almost immediately adding, "But we shall find water. I have two Bushmen here who will show us water." From the appearance of the grass, it was evident that a heavy shower of rain must have fallen over this part of the country about a month before our arrival, and Tinkarn told me that there must then have been a good supply of water in the Mahakabi vleys, which, however, had been very rapidly sucked up by the intense heat which had lately prevailed. When the Mangwatos' troop of cattle first reached the nearest and biggest vley, there was still a little water in it, but the thirsty beasts just rushed into the shallow pool, and of course soon trampled it into mud. Two Bushmen, however, had been found at the water, who, of course, knew Tinkarn and feared him, as one of Khama's most influential headmen, and these savages reported that heavy rain had fallen farther to the east during the last moon, and thought that a certain vley they knew of would probably still have some water in it. If there should prove to be no water there, said they, they would guide us to the place where the road from Shoshung to Pandamatenka crossed the Luali river.

It was now past midday, and the heat intense. Our horses, as well as the oxen, had been nearly forty-eight hours without drinking, but as they had done no work during that time, they were not suffering like the latter animals. However, I did not like to go away with the cattle, and perhaps have to take them right through to Luali, without letting Collison know what had happened, so I sent Miller back to the waggons, telling him to give the horse he was riding a few pannikins of water as soon as he got there, as our two largest casks had, I knew, been scarcely touched. Should the vley spoken of by the Bushmen prove to contain a good supply of water, I told Miller I would rest the oxen there until after midday on the 26th, and drive them back to the waggons, after they had had a good drink, on the afternoon of that day, in time to start for Klabala the same evening. Should I not turn up by that time, however, I told him not to expect me for at least another twenty-four hours, as he would then know I had had to go on to Luali.

Having bade good-bye to Miller, I started Dick (who was mounted) and all our boys with our cattle on the track of those belonging to Tinkarn and his people, who had already set off eastwards under the guidance of the Bushmen. After a very hot and weary tramp, we at last reached the vley where our guides had hoped to be able to show us water. As in the pools of Mahakabi, so here there were still a few gallons of liquid left, but not enough, unfortunately, to be of any use, as the thirsty oxen just rushed into it and trampled it into mud immediately.

There was now nothing for it but to push on for Luali as speedily as possible during the cool of the night. Soon the scorching sun once more went down, but as the moon was near the full, we had no difficulty in keeping a good line through the open thorn scrub, and got on at a good quick walk, as our thirsty cattle stepped out briskly, and weary though they must have been, showed no signs now of flagging. About midnight we called a halt, and off-saddling the horses—about six of Khama's headmen were mounted—lit fires, round about which the oxen were collected in two herds, the one composed of those belonging to the Mangwatos, from which I kept ours a little separate. We rested for about an hour, during which time I sat talking with Tinkarn. My boys had all lain down near the fires and gone fast asleep, as soon as they had seen the cattle begin to lie down, and I would fain have followed their example, but was afraid to do so lest any of the thirsty beasts should wander away. Luckily, the bright moonlight enabled me to keep an eye on all the cattle as they lay scattered about in the thin bush, from where I sat. Presently Tinkarn suggested that we should saddle up again and get on towards the river. He had been giving me a lot of interesting information about the desert Bushmen, their modes of hunting, etc., and asked me to ride with him, instead of remaining behind with my own troop of cattle.

This I agreed to do; so, after waking up Dick and all my boys and telling them to come on with the cattle at once, I rode forwards, always leading Collison's horse "Big Bles," on the tracks of the Mangwatos' cattle, which had trampled broad paths in the soft sandy ground, that were very plainly discernible in the moonlight. I soon joined Tinkarn, who was right in front with the two Bushmen, and his pleasant companionship and cheery talk helped very materially to relieve the tedium of the long, weary ride. At last, just as day was dawning on the morning of December 26, we reached the little Lu-ali river just where the waggon road crossed it. Here there was plenty of good water, so Tinkarn, the Bushmen, and I had a refreshing drink, before the thirsty cattle had fouled it, for though there were several good-sized pools amongst the rocks of the river's bed, there was no running stream. The Mangwatos' cattle were close behind us, and my own troop I thought would not be far behind them. However, when an hour had passed and they had not arrived, I began to feel uneasy; but Tinkarn reassured me, saying that Dick and the herd-boys must have loitered round the fires after we had left, but were bound to be here before very long, as they had drunk nothing since leaving the waggons, and their very lives now therefore depended on their getting to the water quickly. I said I would wait till midday, and then, if they had not turned up by that time, ride back on the cattle tracks to look for them. In the meantime the only thing to do was to rest, as we had no food of any sort with us, and were therefore unable to satisfy our hunger. I was very tired and sleepy, as well as hungry, having had no rest whatever for three consecutive nights, nor any food for more than thirty-six hours, so when I lay down in a sort of little cave amongst the rocks, where the sun would not reach me the whole day, I soon went off into a deep dreamless sleep, from which I was awakened late in the afternoon by Tinkarn, who informed me that Dick had just turned up, riding Collison's spare horse, but without the cattle.

I soon learned what had happened. "After you woke me and the herd-boys at the place where we rested in the night," said Dick, "I saddled up my horse, and then said to my companions, 'Let us go; the master has gone on with Tinkarn, and all the Mangwato cattle have started.' But some of the herd-boys said, 'No, Dick, let us rest a little longer, for we are very tired. Then we will drive the cattle on fast, as we can see the tracks of the big herd that has gone on ahead very plainly in the moonlight.' I was tired too," said Dick, "and did not think a little delay would matter, so I tied my horse to a tree and sat down again by one of the fires. Our cattle were still all lying down then. It was very foolish of me to sit down again, for, as you know, I had led my master's oxen for two nights previously through the deep sand, and was therefore very tired and sleepy. After sitting down again I don't remember anything, sleep must have overcome me, as well as my companions. When at last I woke again, the fires had all gone out, and I could see that the dawn was just breaking. The oxen were gone. 'Wake, wake,' I cried to my companions. 'The oxen have got up and gone away.' Then we took up their tracks, which led us away to the north and had not followed on the spoor of the Mang-watos' cattle. I remained with the rest of the boys, following on the tracks of the cattle until the sun stood there"—pointing to a part of the heavens which the sun must have reached at about 10 A.M.— "and then I thought I must let the white man, my master's friend, know what had happened. Ki peto" ("that is all"). "And how about the herd-boys, will they not all die of thirst?" I asked Dick; for, as they had been walking in the sun for the greater part of the preced-ing day, I knew from experience that, if they had not yet reached water, they were probably all dead by now; as, although a man may live for three or four days without water during the winter season, no man that is born of a woman can live much more than two days, if walking hard all the time, when exposed to the intense heat of the sun during the hottest time of year in the deserts of Western Africa. "If God wishes it," said Dick, "the sun has now killed them all; but I do not think they are dead. When we all halted in the middle of the night, you remember there was no wind; but when I awoke before dawn this morning there was a light wind blowing from the north; and our oxen, on getting up from where they had been lying, instead of following on the tracks of the other cattle, went off in a bee-line dead against the wind. I think, therefore, that they must have smelt water and were making straight for it. The boys that I left following them up on foot thought so too. They were terribly thirsty when I left them, but thought their only chance for life was to stick to the cattle tracks they were following, as they did not think they would have the strength to retrace their steps to where we rested last night and then follow up the tracks of the Mangwato cattle to the Luali river, as I have done on horseback."

This was Dick's story, and how much or how little to believe of it, I did not know. He had always been a good, trustworthy boy, and a great favourite with his master. I never imagined that he and all my boys would have gone to sleep again after I had roused them, but I felt more angry with myself than with them, for not having actually seen my cattle started before riding forward. As, according to Dick's account, he must have ridden at least twelve miles on the tracks of our cattle without their having come to the water which he thought they had smelt whilst the herd-boys slept, I could not believe it possible that they had really scented water. Tinkarn, however, whose experience was far greater than mine in such matters, stoutly maintained that cattle, when thirsty, could scent water at extraordinary distances, and arguing from the abstract to the concrete, thought that had the lost oxen not done so, they would assuredly have followed up the tracks of his own herd and arrived by themselves at the Luali river.

Tinkarn and his people were now, after the day's rest, about to start back with their cattle to the place where their waggons had been left standing in the desert, but I did not care to go with them, and take the chance of my oxen having found water, and having then been driven back to the waggons. Supposing the oxen and the herd-boys had died of thirst—or been killed by the sun, as the Kafirs express it—what was to happen to our waggons then? Collison, Miller, Sell, and the four waggon-drivers would, I knew, be all right, as well as the horse that Miller had ridden, as they would go on to Klabala with Tinkarn, but our waggons would in that case have to remain standing in the desert with no one to look after them for several days at least. This would be known to the two Bushmen who had guided us to the Luali, and be communicated by them to other Bushmen, who, I feared, might rob the stranded waggons before I could get back to them with fresh cattle from Shoshong.

I soon made up my mind what to do. Shoshong itself was about sixty miles from where I then was at the crossing of the Luali river, and there was a good waggon track leading to it, so I resolved to ride there that night, borrow four spans of bullocks either from the white traders living on the station or from Khama, and after getting something to eat, start back with them at once on the desert road by which we had been travelling from the Botletlie river. Should my oxen have found water, and after having drunk, been driven back to the waggons on the night of the 27th, I should meet them on the road, and no harm would have been done; whilst, on the other hand, should the worst have happened, and our four spans of bullocks and the poor herd-boys prove to have succumbed to thirst, heat, and fatigue, I should be able to reach our waggons before they had been long deserted, and take them into Shoshong with the spans that had been lent to me.

Sixty miles, much of it in heavy, sandy ground, is a good long ride, so I resolved to take my friend's horse "Big Bles," a very powerful animal, in excellent condition. My own horse "Bob" I entrusted to Tinkarn, and sent Dick back to the waggons with him also.

The full moon was just rising as I bade good-bye to Tinkarn and my Mangwato friends, and rode off on my lonely journey. All our shooting horses had been well looked after during the past season, and well fed daily on half-boiled maize, and "Big Bles" was not only a very powerful animal, but accustomed to hard work, and in splendid hard condition. Keeping up an average pace of about seven miles an hour—a very good one in heavy, sandy ground—and only off-saddling twice during the whole journey, I reached Shoshong about an hour before daylight on the morning of December 27. I rode straight to the store of a trader named Jim Truscott, and roused him, as well as another old friend named Fred Drake. My story was soon told. No food had passed my lips since the evening of December 24—some sixty hours—and with the exception of the sleep I had had at the Luali river during the 26th, I had had no rest either during all that time. I was thin and hard naturally from the life I had been leading, but I suppose I looked unusually worn and haggard, as Truscott insisted on my lying down on his bed at once, whilst he had some food prepared for me, and Fred Drake undertook to get the oxen together that I required, and kindly offered to go back with me to where I had left the waggons beyond Klabala.

At the time of which I am writing, South Africa was a very different country to the South Africa of to-day. Gold had not then been discovered on the Witwaters Rand, and there were therefore comparatively but few Englishmen living even in the Transvaal; whilst north of the Limpopo there were no European settlements whatever, and the few white traders and hunters who earned a precarious livelihood amongst the native tribes might have been counted on the fingers of one's two hands. Amongst these few scattered whites a bond of brotherhood existed such as cannot endure under more civilised conditions. Any white man in distress was sure of the warmest sympathy and most generous assistance on the part of all the few others of the same colour scattered here and there over a vast country. But now the times are changed. What was once the "far interior" has been opened up to the civilisation of Western Europe, and the old-time traders and hunters, with their indifferent morals, unbusiness-like habits, but hearts of gold, have passed away from South Africa for ever.

By ten o'clock Fred Drake had got together four spans of good oxen, all lent by the few white men on the station, and had also got a cart and eight oxen to carry some water-casks and provisions. I had gone fast asleep on Truscott's bed as soon as I had had something to eat, and they let me sleep on till midday. Then I had another meal, and at about 1 P.M. started back for my waggons with Fred Drake. We travelled very quickly with the light cart and fresh oxen, even during the heat of the afternoon, and keeping at it all through the night and the next day, were nearing the wells of Klabala on the afternoon of December 29 when we heard a waggon whip crack close ahead of us, and presently saw the fine cloud of dust rising above the low trees which we knew portended the arrival of a waggon. I thought it must be Tinkarn's waggons. We pulled up, and Drake and I jumped off the cart and walked on ahead. As soon as we saw the front oxen I knew them for the leaders of my own fine Damara span, and very soon we were shaking hands with Collison, Miller, and Sell.

The explanation was simple. Our oxen, when they wandered away from the resting-place on the night of December 25, had found their way to water at last before midday on the 26th. Whether they really smelt it, or were made aware by a certain freshness in the air that water lay in the direction from which the wind was blowing, or whether they only hit off the water by chance, I cannot say, but they reached a vley or pool in which there was a good supply of recent rain-water. The herd-boys who followed them had, it appeared, had a very hard time of it, and on coming to a small vley in which there was only mud but no water, a short time before reaching the larger pool, two of them had declared that they could go no farther, and had thrown themselves down and rolled in the mud, and would doubt-less have died there, had not their comrades, who shortly afterwards reached the larger pool with the cattle, carried them back some water in a calabash and revived them. The cattle were driven back to the waggons on the night of the 26th, and arrived there before Tin-karn's cattle returned from the Luali river. Collison at once gave the order to inspan, and pushing on through the heat of the day, reached

Klabala on the night of the 27th, Tinkarn and his people turning up a few hours later. At Klabala the cattle were given a rest till the afternoon of the 27th, and soon after again making a start for Shoshong, met me coming back with my unnecessary relief spans—as it turned out. Well, all's well that ends well; though I hope I may never experience such an uncomfortable Christmas again as the one I spent in the desert in the year 1879.

The Rain Sacrifice

Wahungwe folktale

This story comes from the Wahungwe people of southern Zimbabwe, in the northernmost region of the arid Kalahari.

A long, long time ago no rain fell for a whole year. Thereupon the Wanganga ordered that a Mukaranga be sacrificed. The Wanganga said: "It must be a marriageable musarre [princess] who has never lain with a man. The musarre must be virgin." The Mambo called his first wife and said: "Seek among the musarre for one who is marriageable and innocent of man, one whom we can sacrifice." The king's first wife summoned all the wasarre [princesses] and asked: "Which of you has not yet slept with a man?" The king's daughters laughed and said: 'Is it our business to live as other maidens live?" The king's first wife said: "Lie down." The wasarre lay down, each on a mat. The king's first wife found among the marriageable wasarre not one who had not had intercourse with a man.

The king's first wife went to the king and said: "Mambo, among the marriageable wasarre there is not one who has not had intercourse with a man." The Wahungwe Legend king summoned the Wanganga and said: "Among the wasarre is not one who has not had intercourse with a man. Tell me, what shall be done?" The Wanganga said: "Mambo, the Mukaranga must be sacrificed. If there is no marriageable musarre who is still innocent of man, then we must seek the oldest of the wasarre who have not yet reached marriageable age. This musarre must be imprisoned at the place of sacrifice and must remain imprisoned till she has reached a marriageable age. And then she can be sacrificed as a Mukaranga." The king called his first wife and said: "Seek among the unmarriageable wasarre for a musarre who is innocent of man." The king's first wife summoned the small girls of the Simbawoye (royal court). She found a child who was still innocent of man. Her breasts were not yet grown.

The young musarre was brought to the place of sacrifice. The place of sacrifice was a high wall. . . . In the centre stood a large antheap. On the antheap grew a tree. The maiden was brought into the place of sacrifice. The entrance was closed with heavy stones. Every day the grown wasarre brought the Mukaranga food and drink. They handed it down over the wall. The Wakaranga kept watch to see that no man approached the place of sacrifice.

The maiden grew. Two years passed before the maiden was grown and had breasts. In the course of these two years no rain fell. All the cattle died. Many people died. The rivers dried up. The grain did not take root. One day the maiden was marriageable.

The Wanganga went to the king. The Wanganga said: "The Mukaranga is marriageable. The Mbila can begin." The king summoned all his people. The people gathered at the place of sacrifice. The Wanganga opened the entrance to the place of sacrifice. The Wanganga dug out a chamber beneath the roots of the tree on the antheap. The Wanganga shouted the Mizimu. The Wanganga strangled the Mukaranga. The people danced around the place of sacrifice. The Wanganga buried the maiden in the antheap beneath the roots of the great tree. The priests shouted the Mizimu. The people danced around the place of sacrifice.

As soon as the Mukaranga was buried beneath its roots, the tree began to grow. The tree grew and grew. It grew the whole night through. The tree grew for three days. For three days the people danced. As the morning drew near again the crown of the tree reached the sky. In the sky there appeared the morning star [Venus] for the first time (after having set as the evening star some time before). The crown of the tree spread out along the sky. One could no longer see the stars and the moon. A great wind came. The leaves of the tree turned into clouds. It began to rain. It rained for thirty days.

Since then the Wazezuru sacrifice a maiden whenever there is a long drought.

Translated by Leo Frobenius

Uranium

Delia Owens

Delia and Mark Owens spent seven years in a remote desert outpost in Botswana developing and maintaining a wildlife sanctuary. In alternating chapters, they recount their experiences—including this confrontation with the forces of development—in their 1984 book *Cry of the Kalahari*.

The small, round water hole on Springbok Pan had been dry for months. Its cracked grey bottom was patterned with perfect footprints of those animals, large and small, who had come in search of water. There were old prints, made when the water was fresh: A brown hyena had knelt to drink, a lion had slid in the mud, a porcupine had swished its bristly tail. Then there were the deep spoor left by those who had plunged through the mud to the last stagnant puddles in the center and the desperate hoof marks of a gemsbok who had pawed deep into the sludge for the last few drops of seepage. Finally, there were the tracks of animals who had come, smelled around, and left, with only the memory of how it feels to drink.

The water hole was surrounded by large acacia bushes and small ziziphus trees, and kneeling beside it, we were well hidden. We had driven to Springbok Pan hoping to collect lion and brown hyena fecal samples. Analysis of the scats was important because it supplemented our direct observations of what the predators were eating during the drought.

Suddenly a loud whop, whop, whop drifted toward us. Startled, we looked up to see a helicopter circling the trees. We backed deeper into the bushes, hoping we wouldn't be seen. We were confused, threatened, curious, annoyed. What was a helicopter doing here?

The chopper blew up a storm of dust as it landed. The rotor wound down, and three young men dressed in baggy jeans stepped onto the riverbed. Blue plastic bags full of soil samples were tied to metal trays mounted on the skids of the aircraft. We introduced ourselves, and they explained that they were field geologists on contract with an international mining company.

"What are you prospecting for?" Mark asked. The chief geologist answered, his nervous glance dropping to Mark's shoulder and then to the ground. "Uh—well, we're really not supposed to say—but, uh—diamonds," he stammered.

A heavy pressure filled my chest, and my palms began to sweat. The vision of a massive diamond mine, with its great open pit, mounds of tailings, conveyers, trucks, and shantytowns looming over the gutted ancient river valley, flashed into my head. Perhaps there would be a parking lot where the brown hyena den had once been.

"Do you have a permit to prospect here?" I asked.

The geologist answered too quickly, "We're not operating in Deception Valley; we use it only for navigation. We're prospecting in the southern part of the reserve."

After a few stilted comments on how beautiful they thought the Kalahari was, the men walked to their helicopter and took off. Afterward we found sample holes and blue plastic bags littered at intervals all along Deception Valley.

A few weeks later a red-and-white Beaver—a single-engine bush plane of a type used in Alaska for years—circled our airstrip several times and landed. As it taxied to camp, I could feel that same tight feeling in my chest.

The pilot and his navigator introduced themselves as Hal and Caroline, mineral surveyors from Union Carbide. Caroline had sandy hair, a broad smile, and freckles. Hal, who was from Michigan, was tall, dark, and exceptionally polite. He explained that they were using a magnetometer to search for uranium in the Kalahari. We asked them into camp for tea, to discuss their operation. No one had notified us that they were coming or told us what they would be doing in the reserve.

The hornbills, flycatchers, and tit-babblers gathered in the trees above our heads, raising their usual cheerful ruckus. Our visitors were amazed at how tame the birds were and told us with great excitement that they had seen a lion from the plane that morning. How wonderful it was, they said, to be in a real, pristine wilderness among such wildlife. Pouring the tea, I quashed the urge to glare at them. How long did they think the Kalahari wilderness would last if they discovered minerals in Deception Valley?

They proudly explained that for the next several weeks they and others would be flying along the pans and dry river channels in the game reserve. The ancient riverbeds looked particularly promising for uranium deposits If it were found in significant quantities, a drilling team would follow, to investigate the possibility of establishing an open-pit mine in Deception Valley—perhaps right where we were sitting.

We were horrified. After nearly six years of living alone in the Kalahari, suddenly we were being inundated by people in aircraft, who sat drinking their tea and cheerfully telling us how they hoped to contribute to the destruction of all that we had worked to protect.

"That's quite an airstrip you've made for yourself," Hal remarked. "We were wondering if we could use your camp area as a fuel station—the choppers and planes could easily land here to refuel."

"No," I answered abruptly. "I'm sorry, but we're working with sensitive animals here. That would cause too much disturbance."

"Oh, I see. Well, that's too bad. It would have been a big help, but we understand your position."

I thought to myself, The last thing we want to do is help you strip-mine the Kalahari, you stupid SOB. Out loud, I asked, "Would you care for more tea?" and smiled far too sweetly.

After a few more minutes of small talk they said goodbye and took off again in their Beaver.

One of the most important considerations for the conservation of Kalahari wildlife was the critical need to preserve pans and ancient river channels like Deception Valley. During years of adequate rainfall, the old river bottoms were covered with nutritious grasses, primary food for plains antelope during calving. The woodlands surrounding the valleys were essential browse for giraffe, kudu, steenbok, and eland, and for grazing antelope, who must switch to browsing in dry season and drought. These ungulates attracted predators, most of whose ranges were centered along the dry river systems.

Fossil river channels meandering through the dunes represent only a tiny fraction of the entire range area, but they are of the most crucial habitats in the desert. An open mine, with its associated development, in Deception Valley or any of the other fossil channels, would be a disaster for Kalahari wildlife.

And now, seemingly overnight, Deception Valley held great interest for the mining industry. Surface uranium deposits had been discovered in dry riverbeds in Australia; the same could be true of the Kalahari.

We could hear the planes and helicopters flying over the desert every day for several weeks. Our reports to the Botswana government, urgently requesting that the game reserve be spared mineral exploration, received no response. All we could do was wait. The skies finally quieted down, but we had no idea what the results of the mineral survey had been.

Then one morning a deep rumble sounded from beyond East Dune, and we saw a column of dust that stretched for miles above the savanna. Standing on the riverbed near camp, we watched a convoy of trucks, ten-ton trailers, and a twenty-five-ton drilling rig roll single file into the valley. Union Carbide had come to the Kalahari to drill test holes for uranium, to determine if a mine would be profitable. We met the convoy at Mid Pan and talked to the drillers about their plans.

Doug, the geologist in charge, a young man with a plump face and a hang-dog expression, scuffed at the ground with the toe of his boot as he spoke. He promised not to allow his truck drivers to speed along the riverbed, not to chase animals or to frighten any brown hyenas that came to their camps at night, and not to drive at night, when the lions and hyenas were on the move along the valley.

"I know how important your research is—the Wildlife Department has told me—and I'll try not to interfere with your work."

We were greatly relieved with his apparent concern and shook hands warmly before he climbed into his truck. But we soon learned that his offer to cooperate had only been an attempt to placate us.

For years we had tiptoed around the old river at five to ten miles per hour. Now, ignoring our pleas and protests, heavy vehicles roared up and down the valley at fifty miles per hour, day and night, along the same paths Pepper and Cocoa used. They chewed deep ruts in the fragile surface of the riverbeds, scars that will last at least 100 years. Over and over again we cajoled, begged, and finally threatened, until we were given assurances that the trucks would slow down and not drive at night. The promises were never kept. The few springbok and gemsbok that had come back to the valley to re-establish their territories galloped away from the riverbed.

Discarded drums, beer cans, and other litter were left at each campsite the drillers set up along the valley. Long strands of blue plastic ribbons marked sites worthy of further investigation at some later date. Fluttering from the limbs and branches of acacia trees, they were a driller's trademark, a laying of claim to the valley.

We drove to the rig every afternoon, wherever it was operating, and asked anxiously about the results. Drawing lines in the sand with his boots, Doug assured us that they had not found uranium in significant quantities. He would not show us the official graphs.

Eleven days after they had come into the valley, the long convoy of heavy trucks pulled up next to camp. They had completed their tests, and they told us that they had not found significant amounts of uranium. We watched them disappear over East Dune, on their way to another fossil river for more drilling. We wondered if we could believe them.

Our research was beginning to show what it would take to conserve the Kalahari. But were we too late? Would it all be lost to man's greed for more minerals and for cattle? We were a lobby of two against powerful forces of exploitation. We had learned a lot about this ecosystem, but that was not enough. Other people had to care. The Botswana government had to view the Kalahari as a precious natural heritage rather than just a tract of exploitable resources.

We would do whatever we could. For starters, we tore down as many of the blue plastic survey ribbons as we could find.

The East Wind

Henno Martin

Henno Martin spent most of his service as an officer in the Wehrmacht in the relative security of the Namib Desert, then occupied by Germany. The duty was far from easy, and Martin and his fellow soldiers lived in constant fear of an Allied attack. This passage comes from his memoir *The Sheltering Desert.*

I awoke abruptly. The wind was booming, the stars were flickering in the sky like wind-blown torches, sand was running into my ears, and my mouth and nose were dry. Every new gust of wind poured fresh sand over us. Hermann woke up too. "An east wind," he muttered and snuggled deeper into his sleeping-bag. Half awake I could hear the gusts of wind becoming more regular and finally developing into a rhythmic soughing.

When the sun rose we were half buried. Our hair, eyes and ears were full of sand and at breakfast the springbok meat crunched between our teeth. The wind had become noticeably warmer and on the chalk plateau it was so strong that we could lean against it. A red veil of sand rose from a small dune into the blue sky. To the south a sandstorm was raging and the dunes were covered with a reddish mist.

In the ravines and gulleys the wind howled and roared, and the storm boomed over ridges, summits and crests. It was a wild cacophony of stone instruments.

When we entered the canyon the grey sand was whirled into our faces and we could hardly distinguish the other side. A few hundred yards farther on we unexpectedly came across a sheltered spot, but that made the tremendous concern all around seem even louder. Waves of sand lashed up the sides like the sea beating against the shore, and the rock face was scoured and polished sixteen feet high in many places. Tiny particles of mica seemed to be raining from a blue sky.

When we clambered back again to our quarters we had to carry a full load of water and we were thankful when we were at last sheltered from the wind. Panting, we put our loads down and Hermann made coffee. We celebrated our return with an extra teaspoonful of jam and a small piece of chocolate each, including Otto. The wind continued to roar and howl across the rocky ridges and the air was so full of sand that we could hardly see the Rotstock across the canyon. It must have frozen hard in the uplands and the east wind would certainly blow for at least three days.

This winter east wind of the Namib belongs to those great movements of air which maintain a changing equilibrium between the air masses over land and sea. When, as a result of one or two frosty nights, the air over the uplands grows colder than the air over the Atlantic then this colder air begins to brim over the edge of the uplands, rushing like a waterfall over the mountains, gaining speed and growing warmer as it sweeps unhindered over the broad smooth plains of the Namib, until it finally races out over the sea. The wind that began as a cold blast in the uplands finally ends over the Atlantic as a hot, sand-laden storm which squashes the great breakers until the sea laps the sandy edge of the desert as a lazy blue swell.

Owing to the great volume of air involved it usually takes three days for a new equilibrium to be established between land and sea. In summer the same process takes place but in the opposite direction. The suction of the warm air rising above the land draws in cooler air from over the sea which rushes inland as a west wind. For these reasons the prevailing winds in the Namib are east in winter and west in summer.

Due to the warmth of the sun during the day the east wind fell a little towards evening, but in the cool night air the strength of the wind increased and we could hear it roaring again. The following morning it was still whistling and howling amongst the rocks and caves of the long cliff ridge, and clouds of whirling sand covered the floor of the canyon like mist.

At breakfast we discussed our game chances, for we hadn't seen much from the Rotstock. "We mustn't let those loose sights waste any more ammunition," I said. "We can't possibly afford to use four bullets on one springbok. At that rate we'd soon have no ammunition left at all."

Hermann agreed. "It means we must solder it in one position, but then we shan't be able to adjust for range, that's all. In any case we never had much luck at long ranges."

We therefore heated up our soldering iron and soldered the sights for a range of fifty-five yards. Hermann painted a target which we set up against the rock face and we then carefully measured off a distance of fifty-five yards. For our target practice we sacrificed four cartridges, but at least it gave us some idea of how the pistol behaved with the fixed sights.

The storm had charged our battery to the full and we were able to listen to the wireless as much as we liked. We found that a Beethoven concert fitted in perfectly with the howling of the desert wind; they seemed to be made for each other. Then a German announcer came through with a summary of the week's events, and we learned that "reprisal raids" had begun against Britain two days previously. We were depressed. Was it the preliminary to an invasion? And how long would it be before there were reprisals for the reprisal raids?

The wind blew strongly all that night and it was not until the following afternoon that it dropped a little. We went down into the canyon to fetch water and at the water-hole we had an unpleasant surprise; the level of the water had sunk by about three inches; obviously less water was filtering through the gravel of the river bed than was being lost by evaporation. If that were already happening now, what would it be like when it got really hot?

Our garden had been protected from the worst of the storm by a bush, but it was half buried under sand, and the leaves of the mangel-wurzel were drooping because the ground water had sunk. If this went on we should have to water the beds every day. Whilst we were drawing water Otto was sniffing at something in the soft ground near the carp pond; it turned out to be a half-covered hyaena spoor. Apprehensively we counted our carp and discovered that two were missing. We did our best to protect the pool from such depredations with branches and stones, but we weren't very optimistic about the result.

THE ARABIAN AND
INDIAN DESERTS

For me how tiny the world,
This ant's egg—and the sky!
  Mirza Asadullah Khan Ghalib

Geographers generally divide the deserts of the Arabian peninsula
from those of South Asia, more for cultural than topographical
reasons. Taken together, the Arabian Desert (1 million square
miles), the Thar or Great Indian Desert of Rajahstan (230,000
square miles), and Iranian Desert (150,000 square miles) form a
vast arid belt in which humans have long been active. The Arabian,
the birthplace of many of the world's great religions, is the sandiest
desert in world and contains perhaps the fewest natural watercourses; the Iranian Desert shades off into the wild country of
the Hindu Kush and the folded mountains of Afghanistan,
joining the Mediterranean world to those of Central Asia and
subcontinental India; and the Great Thar Desert gave rise to the
powerful Rajputrah warrior clans, whose movement into the
drylands more than a millennium ago sent the Rom, or gypsies,
into their westward flight. On the southern edge of that desert,
lying along the old caravan route to Central Asia, stood Mahatma
Gandhi's ashram at Kocherab, from which he started his famous
"salt satyagraha" of 1930.

Ruins

Percy Bysshe Shelley

Expelled from Oxford University in 1811 for his pamphlet *On the Necessity of Atheism*, Percy Bysshe Shelley (1792–1822) abandoned England for France and later Italy in the company of his wife, the writer Mary Wollstonecraft. Long interested in archaeology, Shelley found in a report on Arabia Petrea the makings for his Ecclesiastes-like denunciation of vain human wishes, "Ozymandias."

I met a traveller from an antique land
Who said: Two vast and trunkless legs of stone
Stand in the desert . . . Near them, on the sand,
Half sunk, a shattered visage lies, whose frown,
And wrinkled lip, and sneer of cold command,
Tell that its sculptor well those passions read
Which yet survive, stamped on these lifeless things,
The hand that mocked them, and the heart that fed:
And on the pedestal these words appear:
"My name is Ozymandias, king of kings:
Look on my works, ye Mighty, and despair!"
Nothing beside remains. Round the decay
Of that colossal wreck, boundless and bare
The lone and level sands stretch far away.

A Prayer & Invocation to the Prince of Rain

Eleazar ha-Kallir

The rabbi and mystic Eleazar ha-Kallir (flourished 7th century A.D.) offers this remarkable petition for that rarest of all things, a desert downpour.

Af-Bri
    sign
        name of
            rain's angels

clouding
    vaporing
        emptying
            raining
sprouts
    of water
        crown
            this valley
won't stop
    compact
        goes on
            unyielding
shielding them
    faithful
        beggars for
            rain

& you my hero forever Yahweh my god you wake the dead many
                                                    times you
save us

be watchful
        send down
                rain from
                        rain rivers
melt
        the face of
                earth
                        with clear opals
water
        your power
                your mark
                        written down
like drops
        reviving
                those who blow
                        breath
you restore
        who invoke
                powers of
                        rain
. . . .
(invocation thru the fathers priests & tribes)

: our Elohim & Elohim of our fathers
remember the father
                you drew behind you
                                like water
you blessed like a tree

      planted by streams
            of water
you shielded
    saved h_m from fire
      & water
you would guard
    when he seeded beside
        every water
because of him don't stop your water
remember words of his birth
      let him drink
        the small water
you told his father to kill him
     his blood spilt
       like water
as he was ready to spill
     his heart
      like water
to dig & to find
    wells
     of water
because of him pour down your water
remember
    who carried his stick across
        Jordan's water
one-hearted
    rolled stones from the mouth of the well
         of water
when he wrestled the prince
     mixed from fire
        & water
till you promised

you would stay with him
in fire & water
because of him don't stop your water
remember the one they drew out
from a reed boat
in the water
they commanded
& didn't he water his flock
with water
the people you chose
when they thirsted
for water
he beat on the rock
it opened & gave out
water
because of him pour down your water
remember the temple priest
who bathed 5 times
in water
who walked
who washed his hands in holiness
of water
reading
sprinking purifying
water
kept distant
from a people violent
as water
because of him don't stop your water
remember the 12 tribes
you made to cross
the water

for whom you sweetened
                    bitterness
                              of water
whose generations
                    spilt their blood for you
                                        like water
o turn our minds
                    encircled by
                              that water
because of them pour down your water
for you are Yahveh are our elohim you make the wind blow & the
                                                    rain fall
down

Translated by Jerome Rothenberg and Harris Lenowitz

The Wilderness of Judea

Gertrude Bell

A remarkable autodidact, Gertrude Bell (1868–1926) trained herself
through travel and reading to become one of the leading Arabists of her
time. She spent many years in Persia and Ottoman Syria, the latter an
area comprising the modern states of Syria, Lebanon, Jordan, and
Israel. In 1919 she was named Oriental Secretary to the British Civil
Administrator of Iraq, where she lived until her death. This account
comes from her book *The Desert and the Sown* (1907).

It was a stormy morning, the 5th of February. The west wind swept
up from the Mediterranean, hurried across the plain where the Ca-

naanites waged war with the stubborn hill dwellers of Judea, and leapt the barrier of mountains to which the kings of Assyria and of Egypt had lain vain siege. It shouted the news of rain to Jerusalem and raced onwards down the barren eastern slopes, cleared the deep bed of Jordan with a bound, and vanished across the hills of Moab into the desert. And all the hounds of the storm followed behind, a yelping pack, coursing eastward and rejoicing as they went.

No one with life in his body could stay in on such a day, but for me there was little question of choice. In the grey winter dawn the mules had gone forward carrying all my worldly goods—two tents, a canteen, and a month's provision of such slender luxuries as the austerest traveller can ill spare, two small mule trunks, filled mostly with photographic materials, a few books and a goodly sheaf of maps. The mules and the three muleteers I had brought with me from Beyrout, and liked well enough to take on into the further journey. The men were all from Lebanon. . . .

I had a great desire to ride down the desolate road to Jericho, as I had done before when my face was turned toward the desert, but Mikhail was of opinion that it would be inconsistent with my dignity, and I knew that even his chattering companionship could not rob that road of solitude. At nine we were in the saddle, riding soberly round the walls of Jerusalem, down into the valley of Gethsemane, past the garden of the Agony and up to the Mount of Olives. Here I paused to recapture the impression, which no familiarity can blunt, of the walled city on the hill, grey in a grey and stony landscape under the heavy sky, but illumined by the hope and unquenchable longing of generations of pilgrims. Human aspiration, the blind reaching out of the fettered spirit towards a goal where all desire shall be satisfied and the soul find peace, these things surround the city like a halo, half glorious, half pitiful, shining with tears and blurred by many a disillusion. The west wind turned my horse and set him gallop ng over the brow of the hill and down the road that winds through the Wilderness of Judea.

At the foot of the first descent there is a spring, 'Ain esh Shems, the Arabs call it, the Fountain of the Sun, but the Christian pilgrims have named it the Apostles' Well. In the winter you will seldom pass there without seeing some Russian peasants resting on their laborious way up from Jordan. . . .

Beyond the fountain the road was empty, and though I knew it well I was struck again by the incredible desolation of it. No life, no flowers, the bare stalks of last year's thistles, the bare hills and the stony road. And yet the Wilderness of Judea has been nurse to the fiery spirit of man. Out of it strode grim prophets, menacing with doom a world of which they had neither part nor understanding; the valleys are full of the caves that held them, nay, some are peopled to this day by a race of starved and gaunt ascetics, clinging to a tradition of piety that common sense has found it hard to discredit.

Before noon we reached the khan half way to Jericho, the place where legend has it that the Good Samaritan met the man fallen by the roadside, and I went in to lunch beyond the reach of the boisterous wind. Three Germans of the commercial traveller class were writing on picture-postcards in the room of the inn, and bargaining with the khanj for imitation Bedouin knives. I sat and listened to their vulgar futile talk—it was the last I was to hear of European tongues for several weeks, but I found no cause to regret the civilization I was leaving.

The road dips east of the khan, and crosses a dry water-course which has been the scene of many tragedies. Under the banks the Bedouin used to lie in wait to rob and murder the pilgrims as they passed. Fifteen years ago the Jericho road was as lawless a track as is the country now that lies beyond Jordan: security has travelled a few miles eastward during the past decade. At length we came to the top of the last hill and saw the Jordan valley and the Dead Sea, back by the misty steeps of Moab, the frontier of the desert. Jericho lay at our feet, an unromantic village of ramshackle hotels and huts wherein live the only Arabs the tourist ever comes to know. . . . I left my horse with the muleteers whom we had caught up on the slope— "Praise God you prosper!" "Praise be to God! If your excellency is well we are content."—and ran down the hill into the village. But Jericho was not enough for that first splendid day of the road. I desired eagerly to leave the tourists behind, and the hotels and the picture-postcards. Two hours more and we should reach Jordan bank, and at the head of the wooden bridge that leads from Occident to Orient we might camp in a sheltered place under mud hillocks and among thickets of reed and tamarisk. A halt to buy corn for the horses and the mules and we were off again across the narrow belt of cultivated land that lies around Jericho, and out on to the Ghor, the Jordan valley.

The Jericho road is bare enough, but the valley of Jordan has an aspect of inhumanity that is almost evil. If the prophets of the Old Testament had fulminated their anathemas against it as they did against Babylon or Tyre, no better proof of their prescience would exist; but they were silent, and the imagination must travel back to flaming visions of Gomorrah and of Sodom, dim legends of iniquity that haunted our own childhood as they haunted the childhood of the Semitic races.

A heavy stifling atmosphere weighed upon this lowest level of the earth's surface; the wind was racing across the hill tops above us in the regions where men breathed the natural air, but the valley was stagnant and lifeless like a deep sea bottom. We brushed through low thickets of prickly sidr trees, the Spina Christi of which the branches are said to have been twisted into the Crown of Thorns. They are of two kinds, these sidr bushes, the Arabs call them zakum and dom. From the zakum they extract a medicinal oil, the dom bears a small fruit like a crab apple that ripens to a reddish brown not uninviting in appearance. It is a very Dead Sea fruit, pleasant to look upon and leaving on the lips a taste of sandy bitterness.

The sidrs dwindled and vanished, and before us lay a sheet of hard mud on which no green thing grows. It is of a yellow colour, blotched with a venomous grey-white salt: almost unconsciously the eye appreciates its enmity to life. As we rode here a swirl of heavy rain swooped down upon us from the upper world. The muleteers looked grave, and even Mikhail's face began to lengthen, for in front of us were the Slime Pits of Genesis, and no horse or mule can pass over them except they be dry. The rain lasted a very few minutes, but it was enough. The hard mud of the plain had assumed the consistency of butter, the horses' feet were shod in it up to the fetlocks, and my dog Kurt whined as he dragged his paws out of the yellow glue. So we came to the Slime Pits, the strangest feature of all that uncanny land.

A quarter of a mile to the west of Jordan . . . the smooth plain resolves itself suddenly into a series of steep mud banks intersected by narrow gullies. The banks are not high, thirty or forty feet at the most, but the crests of them are so sharp and the sides so precipitous that the traveller must find his way across and round them with the utmost care. The shower had made these slopes as slippery as glass; even on foot it was almost impossible to keep upright. My horse fell as I was leading him: fortunately it was on a little ridge between mound and mound, and by the most astonishing gymnastics he managed to recover himself. I breathed a short thanksgiving when I saw my caravan emerge from the Slime Pits: we might, if the rain had lasted, have been imprisoned there for several hours, since if a horseman falls to the bottom of one of the sticky hollows he must wait there till it dries.

Light

Pierre Loti

The French novelist—and sometime soldier, painter, and acrobat—Julien Viaud (1850–1923) traveled by camel caravan from Suez to Gaza in 1894 on a lark. The 1895 book that he wrote of his trip, *Le Désert*, takes many liberties with the facts, but it marks a then-new trend in European literature: an aesthetic appreciation for the lonely drylands.

Every morning you wake up in a different setting of the vast desert. You leave your tent and are surrounded by the splendor of the virginal morning. You stretch your arms and half-naked body in the cold pure air. Out on the sand, you wrap your turban and drape yourself in your white woolen veils. You get drunk on light and space. At the time of waking, you know the heady intoxication of just being able to breathe, just being alive . . .

And then off you go, perched atop the ever-moving camel that steadily plods along until nighttime. You go along, go along, go along, and you see in front of you a hairy head decorated with shells and its long neck, cutting the air like the prow of a ship at sea. Wasteland follows wasteland. You stretch your ears into the silence and you hear nothing, not a birdsong, nor the buzz of a fly, because there is nothing alive anywhere . . .

After a chilly dawn, the sun suddenly climbs and warms. The four hours of our morning travel as we go east into the sun are the most dazzling time of the day. Then we have our noon stop at a randomly chosen spot, in a flimsy tent that was set up quickly. The slower caravan of our Bedouin and baggage camels catches up, goes by with shouts as if at a wild party, and disappears into the unknown ahead. Then, after the four hours of our afternoon trek, we finally arrive at our new place for the night, and we have the simple physical joy of finding our tents again, where our gentle dromedaries kneel to set us down.

This morning we start off into hot valleys between claustrophobic mountains. The sun is dreary, dreary; it is like a big dying ember that could fall from the sky. Your tired eyes follow the shadows of the camels as they move along the reflecting sand. And as always happens when you approach distant mountains, the mountains seem black in contrast with the sheen of the sand nearby.

Toward afternoon we are very high up in the remote wastes of the Sinai peninsula. New spaces unfold on all sides; this tangible sign of their immensity increases our understanding of what wilderness is, but it also intimicates us more.

And it is an almost terrifying magnificence . . . In a distance that is much clearer than usual earthly distances, mountain chains join and overlap. They are in regular arrangements that man has not interfered with since the creation of the world. And they have harsh brittle edges, never softened by the least vegetation. The closest row of mountains is a reddish brown; then, as they stand closer to the horizon, the mountains go through elegant violet, turning a deeper and deeper blue, until they are pure indigo in the farthest chain. And everything is empty, silent, and dead. Here you have the splendor of fixed perspectives, without the ephemeral attraction of forests, greeneries, and grasslands; it is also the splendor of almost eternal stuff, freed of life's instabilities. The geological splendor from before the Creation . . .

From another height at evening, we discover a plain with no visible limits, composed of sand and stone, speckled with spindly reddish bushes. The plain is flooded with light, burning with the sun's rays, and our camp, already set up out there with its infinitely tiny white tents, becomes a pygmy village dwarfed by this magnificent wilderness.

Oh! The sunset this time! Never had we seen so much gold spread out around our lonely camp for us alone. And as our camels are doing their usual evening foraging, they loom strangely large against the empty horizon and have gold on their heads, on their legs, and on their long necks. They are completely edged with gold. The plain is all gold. And the bushes are gold . . . Then comes the night, the clear silent night . . .

And now you feel an almost religious fear if you wander away and lose sight of the camp. But in order to be absolutely alone in the black emptiness, you separate yourself from your little handful of living things lost in this dead land. The stars shine in the cosmic void but are closer and more accessible than before. In this desert the stars are permanent and ageless; looking at them here, one feels closer to understanding their inconceivable infinity; one almost has the illusion of truly being united with universal permanence and time . . .

For they were departed from Rephidim, and were come to the desert of Sinai, and had pitched in the wilderness.
(Exodus xix:2)

Five days now without finding water. But we still have enough from the Nile.

Traveled all morning in yesterday's plain, where the broom has been replaced with sparser clumps of plants, whitish green, half-buried in sand, balls of thorns that could pierce feet like iron spikes.

We are beginning to come upon big black stones standing upright on the sand, set up like men or menhirs. At first rather sparse, they become more and more numerous—and also taller and taller. Then little by little, as we go on gently swaying, they take on the dimensions of dungeons, towers, and fortresses; finally they group, forming corridors, like the streets of some destroyed cyclopean city—and they enclose us with dark walls.

The noon stop is in one of these forbidding valleys . . .

While we are sleeping on our carpets, raucous loud voices suddenly resound from the reflecting stones. Our guards, our drivers, and our camels are letting us know they are going by. It's the slower caravan that follows us every morning and gets ahead of us during our noon rest, so that it can beat us to the evening stop. Both animals and men usually greet us with shrieks as they go by, and today their voices are more piercing, due to surprisingly loud echoes from these dry rocks that resonate like dead wood.

We proceed until the hour of evening prayer through narrow winding valleys. But their walls are constantly changing shape and color. They become pink granite, veined with broad bands of blue or green rock.

This region is less desolate than before, because here we have trees, the first we have seen in five days. Oh, wretched little trees, a kind of thorny mimosa like those you find in the Sahara, in Senegal, and Obock; during this early spring they have just turned light green, with barely visible pale leaves. And strewn about occasionally among chunks of granite, there are delicate little white flowers.

At a fork in these valleys, we came upon two adorable Bedouin youngsters, brother and sister, who watched us approaching with fright in their dark velvet eyes. They tell us there are campsites up in the mountain. Indeed we hear distant guard dogs barking to announce our presence. Soon afterwards we see herds of goats shepherded by Bedouin dressed and veiled in black.

Our old driver-sheik then comes and requests my permission to leave us until tomorrow, so that he can visit this tribe, where he has sons.

We come close to the "Myrrh Mountain" and suddenly the whole desert has a delightful scent, because skinny little plants release delicious, strange odors as they are crushed by the hooves of our camels.

The ground of these interminable mountain passes is slowly climbing toward the central plateau in almost unnoticeable degrees. We will continue to go up for two more days, slowly heading for the Sinai Convent at a height of two thousand meters.

We are still in rough terrain. Very recently mountains must have crumbled, breaking up on the sand with apocalyptic noise, for gigantic ruins with fresh fractures give evidence of past catastrophes. And we continue our ascent on crumbled blue and pink granite, between stands of the same rock that are cracked at the bottom, seemingly on the verge of tumbling down.

For the night we camp in a high valley beside stark and frightening embankments of red granite, where the air is turning cold as ice.

And it came to pass on the third day in the morning, that there were thunders and lightnings, and a thick cloud upon the mount, and the voice of the trumpet exceeding loud; so that all the people that was in the camp trembled.
(Exodus XIX:16)

In the middle of the night, we are awakened by the racket of thunder made outsize and terrible here in this resonant echoing valley. A violent wind shakes our fragile canvas houses and threatens to blow us away. And our camels moan in the sudden and torrential downpour . . .

Wind more than rain is the enemy of the nomads. You have to get up and drive the stakes deeper, while the tents swell up, rip loose, and tear—and then you wait, trying to face up to losing your shelter in the frigid deluge: this is the impotent stress of the infinitely small faced with massive sovereign forces . . .

As the forbidding valley explodes outside with almost continual light, there is a terror of apocalypse. The valley seems shaken to its core, giving off muffled and crackling noise. You could say it is shuddering, opening up, caving in . . .

And then the bolts are slower and farther away. It all becomes something deep and cavernous, as if one could hear worlds turn in far-off voids . . .

And at last all is peaceful and calm . . .

Little by little we regain our silence, safety, and sleep.

In the cool, quiet morning at sunrise, when I open my tent, the outside air carries a whiff of perfume, so that it seems as if someone has broken a vial of aromatics in front of my door. And all this forlorn valley of granite is also perfumed, as if it were an oriental temple. Its few little pale plants, held back by drought, have awakened because of the night's deluge and waft their odors like countless incense burners. You could say that the air is ripe with benjamin, citronella, geranium, and myrrh . .

Right off I look at the deserted valley, so strange and superb under the morning sun that is striking the red peaks into flame, against a backdrop of black, tattered clouds, fleeing fast to the north. The storm is still up there, while down here the air is slack and still.

Then I look at the ground, the source of all these perfumes; it is covered with white spots, like hailstorms after a storm . . .

And when the dew that lay was gone up, behold, upon the face of the wilderness there lay a small round thing, as small as the hoar frost on the ground.

(Exodus XIX:14)

What was shredded and left by wind and rain around our tents last night appears to be manna . . . I pick up some of these "small round things," these very hard white seeds, smelling something like cheese—they are the dried fruit of the thorny little plants that carpet these mountains here and there.

By collecting this manna, I have stirred up the perfumes of the soil, and for some time my hands give off an exquisite scent.

Translated by Jay Paul Minn

From Jum'a al-Fararja to Jazi Al 'Aradi

Jum'a al-Fararja

This seemingly innocuous bedouin poem, recorded about 1951, signals notice that a caravan shipment of wax-encased hashish would soon be passing through the Sinai from Turkey to Cairo along the flanks of Goz Khelat, a tall mountain. The Pleiades rise in November and usher in the rainy season, pinpointing the passage even more directly.

Lightning flashed over Goz Khlelat;
I saw it and thought it the Pleiades' sign.

She poured forth her rain sprouting grasses so high,
Filling wells at the spring after these had run dry.

O Rider racing along hidden ways,
Far from all souls, be they friend be they foe,

Tell Jazi a camel passed bearing his sign;
If he thinks that she's thin, assure him she's fine.

And to Jazi and gang my greetings convey;
This news, good or bad, is what I have to say.

Translated by Clinton Bailey

Lawrence Comes to Arabia

T. E. Lawrence

At the outbreak of World War I, T. E. Lawrence (1888–1935) was given
a commission in the British Army and posted to Cairo. Lawrence was a
gifted linguist—he had translated Homer, the major Provençal and
Occitan poets, and several Roman writers—and a trained archaeologist
who had made a thorough study of Crusader castles in the Middle East,
but the high command saw fit to put him to work coloring artillery and
survey maps. When the Arabs under King Faisal rose up against their
Turkish masters, however, Lawrence successfully petitioned to be sent to
Arabia as a liaison officer. He eventually assumed command of the king's
troops, and in many ways Lawrence can be considered the author of the
modern Middle East.

In this passage from his memoir *Seven Pillars of Wisdom*, he describes
his first grueling trip into the Arabian interior.

While [an Arab elder] spoke we scoured along the dazzling plain,
now nearly bare of trees, and turning slowly softer under foot. At first
it had been grey shingle, packed like gravel. Then the sand increased and the stones grew rarer, till we could distinguish the colours of the separate flakes, porphyry, green schist, basalt. At last it

was nearly pure white sand, under which lay a harder stratum. Such going was like a pile carpet for our camels' running. The particles of sand were clean and polished, and caught the blaze of sun like little diamonds in a reflection so fierce, that after a while I could not endure it. I frowned hard, and pulled the head-cloth forward in a peak over my eyes, and beneath them, too, like a beaver, trying to shut out the heat which rose in glassy waves off the ground, and beat up against my face. Eighty miles ahead of us, the huge peak of Rudhwa behind Yenbo was looming and fading in the dazzle of vapour which hid its foot. Quite near in the plain rose the little shapeless hills of Hesna, which seemed to block the way. To our right was the steep ridge of Beni Ayub, toothed and shaped like a saw-blade, the first edge of the sheaf of mountains between the Tehema and the high scarp of the tableland about Medina. These Tareif Beni Ayub fell away on their north into a blue series of smaller hills, soft in character, behind which lofty range after range in a jagged stairway, red now the sun grew low, climbed up the towering central mass of Jebel Subh with its fantastic granite spires.

A little later we turned to the right, off the pilgrim road [to Mecca], and took a short cut across gradually rising ground of flat basalt ridges, buried in sand until only their topmost piles showed above the surface. It held moisture well enough to be well grown over with hard wiry grass and shrubs up and down the slopes, on which a few sheep and goats were pasturing. There Tafas [a bedouin guide] showed me a stone, which was the limit of the district of the Masruh [tribe], and told me with grim pleasure that he was now at home, in his tribal property, and might come off his guard.

Men have looked upon the desert as barren land, the free holding of whoever chose; but in fact each hill and valley in it had a man who was its acknowledged owner and would quickly assert the right of his family or clan to it, against aggression. Even the wells and trees had their masters, who allowed men to make firewood of the one and drink the other freely as much as was required for their need, but who would instantly check anyone trying to turn the property to account and to exploit it or its products among others for private benefit. The desert was held in a crazed communism by which Nature and the elements were for the free use of every known friendly person for his purposes and no more. Logical outcomes were the reduction of this licence to privilege by the men of the desert, and their hardness to strangers unprovided with introduction or guarantee, since the common security lay in the common responsibility of kinsmen. Tafas, in his own country, could bear the burden of my safe-keeping lightly.

The valleys were becoming sharply marked, with clean beds of sand and shingle, and an occasional large boulder brought down by a flood. There were many broom brushes, restfully grey and green to the eye, and good for fuel, though useless as pasture. We ascended steadily until we rejoined the main track of the pilgrim road. Along this we held our way until sunset, when we came into sight of the hamlet of Bir el Sheikh. In the first dark as the supper fires were lighted we rode down its wide open street and halted. Tafas went into one of the twenty miserable huts, and in a few whispered words and long silences bought flour, of which with water he kneaded a dough cake two inches thick and eight inches across. This he buried in the ashes of a brushwood fire, provided for him by a Subh woman whom he seemed to know. When the cake was warmed he drew it out of the fire, and clapped it to shake off the dust; then we shared it together, while Abdulla went away to buy himself tobacco.

They told me the place had two stone-lined wells at the bottom of the southward slope, but I felt disinclined to go and look at them, for the long ride that day had tired my unaccustomed muscles, and the heat of the plain had been painful. My skin was blistered by it, and my eyes ached with the glare of light striking up at a sharp angle from the silver sand, and from the shining pebbles. The last two years I had spent in Cairo, at a desk all day or thinking hard in a little overcrowded office full of distracting noises, with a hundred rushing things to say, but no bodily need except to come and go each day between office and hotel. In consequence the novelty of this change was severe, since time had not been given me gradually to accustom myself to the pestilential beating of the Arabian sun, and the long monotony of camel pacing. There was to be another stage to-night, and a long day tomorrow before Faisal's camp would be reached.

So I was grateful for the cooking and the marketing, which spent one hour, and for the second hour of rest after it which we took by common consent; and sorry when it ended, and we re-mounted, and rode in pitch darkness up valleys and down valleys, passing in and out of bands of air, which were hot in the confined hollows, but fresh and stirring in the open places. The ground under foot must have been sandy, because the silence of our passage hurt my straining ears, and smooth, for I was always falling asleep in the saddle, to wake a few seconds later suddenly and sickeningly, as I clutched by instinct at the saddle post to recover my balance which had been thrown out by some irregular stride of the animal. It was too dark, and the forms of the country were too neutral, to hold my heavy-lashed, peering eyes. At length we stopped for good, long after midnight; and I was rolled up in my cloak and asleep in a most comfortable little sand-grave before Tafas had done knee-haltering my camel.

Three hours later we were on the move again, helped now by the last shining of the moon. We marched down Wadi Mared, the night of it dead, hot, silent, and on each side sharp-pointed hills standing up black and white in the exhausted air. There were many trees. Dawn finally came to us as we passed out of the narrows into a broad place, over whose flat floor an uneasy wind span circles, capriciously in the dust. The day strengthened always, and now showed Bir ibn Hassani just to our right. The trim settlement of absurd little houses, brown and white, holding together for security's sake, looked doll-like and more lonely than the desert, in the immense shadow of the dark precipice of Subh, behind. While we watched it, hoping to see life at its doors, the sun was rushing up, and the fretted cliffs, those thousands of feet above our heads, became outlined in hard refracted shafts of white light against a sky still sallow with the transient dawn.

We rode on across the great valley. . . . The sand and detritus of last night and of Bir el Sheikh had vanished. We were marching up a valley, from two hundred to five hundred yards in width, of shingle and light soil, quite firm, with occasional knolls of shattered green stone cropping out in its midst. There were many thorn trees, some of them woody acacias, thirty feet and more in height, beautifully green, with enough of tamarisk and soft scrub to give the whole a charming, well kept, park-like air, now in the long soft shadows of the early morning. The swept ground was so flat and clean, the pebbles so variegated, their colours so joyously blended that they gave a sense of design to the landscape; and this feeling was strengthened by the straight lines and sharpness of the hills. They rose on each hand regularly, precipices a thousand feet in height, of granite-brown and dark porphyry-coloured rock, with pink stains; and by a strange fortune these glowing hills rested on hundred-foot bases of the cross-grained stone, whose unusual colour suggested a thin growth of moss.

We rode along this beautiful place for about seven miles, to a low watershed, crossed by a wall of granite slivers, now little more than a shapeless heap, but once no doubt a barrier. . . . Across the wall we were in an affluent of Wadi Safra, a more wasted and stony valley among less brilliant hills. It ran into another, far down which to the west lay a cluster of dark palm-trees, which the Arabs said was Jedida, one of the slave villages in Wadi Safra. We turned to the right, across another saddle, and then downhill for a few miles to a corner of tall cliffs. We rounded this and found ourselves suddenly in Wadi Safra, the valley of our seeking, and in the midst of Wasta, its largest village. Wasta seemed to be many nests of houses, clinging to the hill-sides each side of the torrent bed on banks of alluvial soil, or standing on detritus islands between the various deep-swept channels whose sum made the rich parent valley.

Riding between two or three of these built-up islands, we made for the far bank of the valley. On our way was the main bed of the winter floods, a sweep of white shingle and boulders, quite flat. Down its middle, from palm-grove on the one side to palm-grove on the other, lay a reach of clear water, perhaps two hundred yards long and twelve feet wide, sand-bottomed, and bordered on each brink by a ten-foot lawn of thick grass and flowers. On it we halted a moment to let our camels put their heads down to drink their fill, and the relief of the grass to our eyes after the day-long hard glitter of the pebbles was so sudden that involuntarily I glanced up to see if a cloud had not covered the face of the sun.

We rode up the stream to the garden from which it ran sparkling in a stone-lined channel; and then we turned along the mud wall of the garden in the shadow of its palms, to another of the detached hamlets. Tafas led the way up its little street (the houses were so low that from our saddles we looked down upon their clay roofs), and near one of the larger houses stopped and beat upon the door of an uncovered court. A slave opened to us, and we dismounted in privacy. Tafas haltered the camels, loosed their girths, and strewed before them green fodder from a fragrant pile beside the gate. Then he led me into the guest-room of the house, a dark clean little mud-brick place, roofed with half palm-logs under hammered earth. We sat down on the palm-leaf mat which ran along the dais. The day in this stifling valley had grown very hot; and gradually we lay back side by side. Then the hum of the bees in the gardens without, and of the flies hovering over our veiled faces within, lulled us into sleep.

Arabia Deserta

Charles M. Doughty

"I have studied [*Travels in Arabia Deserta*] for ten years," wrote T. E.
Lawrence in 1908, when an abridged version appeared, "and have grown
to consider it a book not like other books, but something particular, a bible
of its kind. To turn round now and reckon its merits and demerits seems
absurd. I do not think that any traveller in Arabia before or after Mr.
Doughty has qualified himself to praise the book—much less to blame it."
The demerits in question centered on the seemingly strange literary style
Charles M. Doughty (1843–1926) employed to convey something of the
syntax, idiom, and archaisms of classical Arabic, a language that he had
come to know better than any earlier explorer. He was also the first known
nasriny, or Christian, to enter Mecca across the "wild waste earth" of the
Arabian desert. Here he describes "the setting forth from Damascus."

The new dawn appearing we removed not yet. The day risen the
tents were dismantled the camels led in ready to their companies,
and halted beside their loads. We waited to hear the cannon shot
which should open that year's pilgrimage. It was near ten o'clock
when we heard the signal gun fired, and then, without any disorder
litters were suddenly heaved and braced upon the bearing beasts,
their charges laid upon the kneeling camels, and the thousands of
riders, all born in the caravan countries, mounted in silence. As all is
up, the drivers are left standing upon their feet, or sit to rest out the
latest moments on their heels: they with other camp and tent servants must ride those three hundred leagues upon their bare soles,
although they faint; and are to measure the ground again upward
with their weary feet from the holy places. At the second gun, fired a
few moments after, the Pasha's litter advances and after him goes the
head of the caravan column: other fifteen or twenty minutes we, who
have places in the rear, must halt, that is until the long train is un-

folded before us; then we must strike our camels and the great pilgrimage is moving. There go commonly three or four camels abreast and seldom five: the length of the slow-footed multitude of men and cattle is near two miles, and the width some hundred yards in the open plains. The hajjaj were this year by their account (which may be above the truth) 6,000 persons; of these more than half are serving men on foot; and 10,000 of all kinds of cattle, the most camels, then mules, hackneys, asses and a few dromedaries of Arabians returning in security of the great convoy to their own districts. We march in an empty waste, a plain of gravel, where nothing appeared and never a road before us. Hermon, now to the backward, with his mighty shoulders of snows closes the northern horizon; to the nomads of the East a noble landmark of Syria, they name it *Towîl éth-Thalj*, "the height of snow" (of which they have a small experience in the rainless sun-stricken land of Arabia). It was a Sunday, when this pilgrimage began, and holiday weather, the summer azure light was not all faded from the Syrian heaven; the 13th of November, 1876; and after twelve miles away (a little, which seemed long in the beginning), we came to the second desert station, where the tents which we had left behind us at Muzeyrib, stood already pitched in white ranks before us in the open wilderness. Thus every day the light tent-servants' train outwent our heavy march, in which, as every company has obtained their place from the first remove, this they observe continually until their journey's end. Arriving we ride apart, every company to their proper lodgings: this encampment is named *Ramta*.

It is their caravan prudence, that in the beginning of a long way the first shall be a short journey: the beasts feel their burdens, the passengers have fallen in that to their riding in the field. Of a few sticks (gathered hastily by the way), of the desert bushes, cooking fires are soon kindled before all the tents; and since here are no stones at hand to set under the pots as Beduins use, the pilgrim hearth is a scraped-out hole, so that their vessels may stand, with the brands put under, upon the two brinks, and with very little fuel they make ready their poor messes. The small military tents of the Haj escort of troopers and armed dromedary riders, *Ageyl* (the most *Nejd* men), are pitched round about the great caravan encampment, at sixty and sixty paces: in each tent fellowship the watches are kept till the day dawning. A paper lantern after sunset is hung before every one to burn all night where a sentinel stands with his musket, and they suffer none to pass their lines unchallenged. Great is all townsmen's dread of the Beduw, as if they were the demons of this wild waste earth, ever ready to assail the Haj passengers; and there is no Beduwy durst chop logic in the dark with these often ferocious shooters, that might answer him with lead and who are heard, from time to time, firing backward into the desert all night; and at every instant crying down the line *kerakô kerakô* (sentinel) the next and the next men thereto answering with *haderûn* (ready). I saw not that any officer went the rounds. So busy is the first watch, whilst the camp is waking. These crickets begin to lose their voices about midnight, when for aught I could see the most of their lights were out; and it is likely the unpaid men spare their allowance: those poor soldiers sell their candles privily in the Haj market.

In the first evening hour there is some merrymake of drum-beating and soft fluting, and Arcadian sweetness of the Persians singing in the tents about us; in others they chant together some piece of their devotion. In all the pilgrims' lodgings are paper lanterns with candle burning; but the camp is weary and all is soon at rest. The hajjies lie down in their clothes the few night hours till the morrow gun-fire; then to rise suddenly for the march, and not knowing how early they may hear it, but this is as the rest, after the Pasha's good pleasure and the weather.

At half past five o'clock was the warning shot for the second journey. The night sky was dark and showery when we removed, and cressets of iron cages set upon poles were borne to light the way, upon serving men's shoulders, in all the companies. The dawn discovered the same barren upland before us, of shallow gravel and clay ground upon limestone.

The *Derb el-Haj* is no made road, but here a multitude of cattle-paths beaten hollow by the camels' tread, in the marching thus once in the year, of so many generations of the motley pilgrimage over this waste. Such many equal paths lying together one of the ancient Arabian poets has compared to the bars of the rayed Arabic mantle. Commonly a shot is heard near mid-day, the signal to halt; we have then a short resting-while, but the beasts are not unloaded and remain standing. Men alight and the more devout bow down their faces to say the canonical prayer towards Mecca. Our halt is twenty minutes; some days it is less or even omitted, as the Pasha has deemed expedient, and in easy marches may be lengthened to forty minutes. "The Pasha (say the caravaners) is our *Sooltan.*" Having marched twenty miles at our left hand appeared *Mafrak*, the second Haj road tower, after the great kella at Muzeyrib, but it is ruinous and as are some other towers abandoned. The kellas are fortified water stations weakly garrisoned; they may have been built two or three centuries and are of good masonry. The well is in the midst of a kella; the water, raised by a simple machine of drum and buckets, whose shaft is turned by a mule's labour, flows forth to fill a cistern or *birket* without the walls. Gear and mules must be fetched down with the Haj from Damascus upon all the desert road, to Medain Salih. The cisterns are jealously guarded; as in them is the life of the great caravan. No Aarab (nomads) are suffered to draw of that water; the garrisons would shoot out upon them from the tower, in which closed with an iron-plated door, they are sheltered themselves all the year from the insolence of the nomads. The kellas stand alone, as it were ships, in the immensity of the desert; they are not built at distances of camps, but according to the opportunity of water; it is more often two or even three marches between them. The most difficult passage of the pilgrim road before Medina, is that four or five marches in high ground next above Medain Salih where are neither wells nor springs, but two ruined kellas with their great birkets to be filled only by torrent water, so that many years, in a nearly rainless country they lie dry. *A nejjab* or post, who is a Beduin dromedary-rider, is therefore sent up every year from Medain Salih, bringing word to Damascus, in *ramathan* before the pilgrimage, whether there be water run in the birket at *Dar el-Hamra*, and reporting like-wise of the state of the next waters. This year he was a messenger of good tidings (showers and freshets in the mountains had filled the birket), and returned with the Pasha's commandment in his mouth (since in the garrisons there are few or none lettered), to set a guard over the water. But in years when the birket is empty, some 1,500 girbies are taken up in Damascus by the Haj administration to fur-nish a public supplement of five days water for all the caravan: these water-skins are loaded betwixt the distant waterings, at the govern-ment cost, by Beduin carriers.

The caravaners pass the ruined and abandoned kellas with curses between their teeth, which they cast, I know not how justly, at the Haj officers and say "all the birkets leak and there is no water for the hajjaj; every year there is money paid out of the treasury that should be for the maintenance of the buildings; these embezzling pashas swallow the public silver; we may hardly draw now of any cistern be-fore Maan, but after the long marches must send far to seek it, and that we may find is not good to drink." Turkish peculation is noto-rious in all the Haj service, which somewhat to abate certain Greek Christians, Syrians, are always bursars in Damascus of the great Mohammedan pilgrimage:—this is the law of the road, that all look through their fingers. The decay of the road is also, because much less of the public treasure is now spent for the Haj service. The impoverished Ottoman government has withdrawn the not long established camp at Maan, and greatly diminished the kella allowances; but the yearly cost of the Haj road is said to be yet £50,000, levied from the province of Syria, where the Christians cry out, it is tyranny that they too must pay from their slender purses, for this seeking hallows of the Moslemîn. A yearly loss to the empire is the *surra* or "bundles of money" to buy a peaceful passage of the abhorred Beduins: the half part of Western Arabia is fed thereby, and yet it were of more cost, for the military escort to pass "by the sword." The destitute Beduins will abate nothing of their yearly pension: that which was paid to their fathers, they believe should be always due to them out of the treasures of the "Sooltan" and if any less be proffered them they would say "The unfaithful pashas have devoured it!" the pilgrimage should not pass, and none might persuade them, although the *Dowla* (Sultan's Empire) were perishing. It were news to them that the Sultan of Islam is but a Turk and of strange blood: they take him to be as the personage of a prophet, king of the world by the divine will, unto whom all owe obedience. Malcontent, as has been often seen, they would assault the Haj march or set upon some corner of the camp by night, hoping to drive off a booty of camels: in warfare they beset the strait places, where the firing down of a hundred beggarly matchlocks upon the thick multitude must cost many lives; so an Egyptian army of Ibrahîm Pasha was defeated in the south country of Harb Beduins.

The Historic Fart

Iraqi folktale

Not all of the thousand and one tales Scheherezade spun out to save her life carried profound moral visions or complex, mythically laden plots. This simple story pokes fun at the scruples of city dwellers as against the freedoms of the nomads—for, as the noted Arabist Wilfred Thesiger remarked, "Among the Bedu only the broken are stranded among the cultivations on the desert's shore."

They recount that in the City Kaukaban of Al-Yaman there was a man of the Fazli tribe who had left Badawi life, and become a townsman for many years and was a merchant of the most opulent merchants. His wife had deceased when both were young; and his friends were insistent with him to marry again, ever quoting to him the words of the poet,

Go, gossip! re-wed thee, for Prime draweth near:
A wife is an almanac—good for the year.

So, being weary of contention, Abu Hasan entered into negotiations with the old women who procure matches, and married a maid like Canopus when he hangeth over the seas of Al-Hind. He made high festival therefor, bidding to the wedding-banquet kith and kin, Olema and Fakirs; friends and foes and all his acquaintances of that countryside. The whole house was thrown open to feasting: there were rices of five several colours, and sherbets of as many more; and kids stuffed with walnuts and almonds and pistachios and a camel-colt roasted whole. So they ate and drank and made mirth and merriment; and the bride was displayed in her seven dresses and one more, to the women, who could not take their eyes off her. At last, the bridegroom was summoned to the chamber where she sat enthroned; and he rose slowly and with dignity from his divan; but in so doing, for that he was over full of meat and drink, lo and behold! he let fly a fart, great and terrible. Thereupon each guest turned to his neighbour and talked aloud and made as though he had heard nothing, fearing for his life. But a consuming fire was lit in Abu Hasan's heart; so he pretended a call of nature; and, in lieu of seeking the bride-chamber, he went down to the house-court and saddled his mare and rode off, weeping bitterly, through the shadow of the night. In time he reached Lahej, where he found a ship ready to sail for India; so he shipped on board and made Calicut of Malabar. Here he met with many Arabs, especially Hazramis, who recommended him to the King; and this King (who was a Kafir) trusted him and advanced him to the captainship of his bodyguard. He remained ten years in all solace and delight of life; at the end of which time he was seized with homesickness; and the longing to behold his native land was that of a lover pining for his beloved; and he came near to die of yearning desire. But his appointed day had not dawned; so, after taking the first bath of health, he left the King without leave, and in due course landed at Makalla of Hazramaut. Here he donned the rags of a religious; and, keeping his name and case secret, fared for Kaukaban afoot; enduring a thousand hardships of hunger, thirst and fatigue; and braving a thousand dangers from the lion, the snake and the Ghul. But when he drew near his old home, he looked down upon it from the hills with brimming eyes, and said in himself, "Haply they might know thee; so I will wander about the outskirts, and hearken to the folk. Allah grant that my case be not remembered by them!" He listened carefully for seven nights and seven days, till it so chanced that, as he was sitting at the door of a hut, he heard the voice of a young girl saying, "O my mother, tell me the day when I was born; for such an one of my companions is about to take an omen for me." And the mother answered, "Thou

wast born, O my daughter on the very night when Abu Hasan
farted." Now the listener no sooner heard these words than he rose
up from the bench, and fled away, saying to himself, "Verily thy fart
hath become a date, which shall last for ever and ever; even as the
poet said,

As long as palms shall shift the flower;
As long as palms shall sift the flour."

And he ceased not travelling and voyaging and returned to India;
and there abode in self-exile till he died; and the mercy of Allah be
upon him!

Translated by Sir Richard Francis Burton

The Persian Desert

Marco Polo

The Venetian traveler Marco Polo (1254?–1324?) spent the years from
1275 to 1295 in the service of Kublai Khan of China, acting as his
representative in western China, India, Persia, and what is now Vietnam.
He returned to Italy to petition the pope to send missionaries to the khan,
who had professed an interest in Nestorian Christianity, and then wrote
a memoir of his travels, which earned him the sobriquet *Il Milione*—The
Millions—for the number of lies his contemporaries supposed him to have
told. Polo may have been overly credulous, but his account is nonetheless of
great importance to historians and geographers. Note the mention of the
mythological hero Aladdin (whom Polo calls "Alo-eddin") in these remarks
on the topography of Persia.

Upon leaving Kierman and traveling three days, you reach the
borders of a desert extending to the distance of seven days' journey,

at the end of which you arrive at Kobiam. During the first three days of these seven little water is to be met with, and that little is impregnated with salt, green as grass, and so nauseous that none can use it as drink. Should even a drop be swallowed frequent calls of nature will be occasioned; and the effect is the same from eating a grain of the salt made from this water. In consequence of this, persons who travel over the desert are obliged to carry a provision of water along with them. The cattle, however, are compelled by thirst to drink such as they find, and a flux immediately ensues. In the course of these three days not one habitation is to be seen. The whole is arid and desolate. Cattle are not found there, because there is no subsistence for them. On the fourth day you come to a river of fresh water, but which has its channel for the most part under ground. In some parts, however, there are abrupt openings, caused by the force of the current, through which the stream becomes visible for a short space, and water is to be had in abundance. Here the wearied traveler stops to refresh himself and his cattle after the fatigues of the preceding journey. The circumstances of the latter three days resemble those of the former, and conduct him at length to the town of Kobiam. . . .

Leaving Kobiam you proceed over a desert of eight days' journey exposed to great drought; neither fruits nor any kind of trees are met with, and what water is found has a bitter taste. Travelers are therefore obliged to carry with them so much as may be necessary for their sustenance. Their cattle are constrained by thirst to drink such as the desert affords, which their owners endeavor to render palatable to them by mixing it with flour. At the end of eight days you reach the province of Timochain, situated towards the north, on the borders of Persia, in which are many towns and strong places. There is here an extensive plain remarkable for the production of a species of tree called the tree of the sun, and by Christians *arbor secco*, the dry or fruitless tree. Its nature and qualities are these: It is lofty, with a large stem, having its leaves green on the upper surface, but white or glaucous on the under. It produces husks or capsules like those in which the chestnut is enclosed, but these contain no fruit. The wood is solid and strong, and of a yellow colour resembling the box. There is no other species of tree near it for the space of a hundred miles, excepting in one quarter, where trees are found within the distance of about ten miles. It is reported by the inhabitants of this district that a battle was fought there between Alexander, King of Macedonia, and Darius. The towns are well supplied with every necessary and convenience of life, the climate being temperate and not subject to extremes either of heat or cold. The people are of the Mahometan religion. They are in general a handsome race, especially the women, who, in any opinion, are the most beautiful in the world.

Having spoken of this country, mention shall now be made of the old man of the mountain. The district in which his residence lay obtained the name of Mulehet, signifying in the language of the Saracens, the place of heretics, and his people that of Mulehetites, or holders of heretical tenets; as we apply the term of Patharini to certain heretics amongst Christians. The following account of this chief, Marco Polo testifies to having heard from sundry persons. He was named Alo-eddin, and his religion was that of Mahomet. In a beautiful valley enclosed between two lofty mountains, he had formed a luxurious garden, stored with every delicious fruit and every fragrant shrub that could be procured. Palaces of various sizes and forms were erected in different parts of the grounds, ornamented with works in gold, with paintings, and with furniture of rich silks. By means of small conduits contrived in these buildings, streams of wine, milk, honey, and some of pure water, were seen to flow in every direction. The inhabitants of these palaces were elegant and beautiful damsels, accomplished in the arts of singing, playing upon all sorts of musical instruments, dancing, and especially those of dalliance and amorous allurement. Clothed in rich dresses they were seen continually sporting and amusing themselves in the garden and pavilions, their female guardians being confined within doors and never suffered to appear. The object which the chief had in view in forming a garden of this fascinating kind, was this: that Mahomet having promised to those who should obey his will the enjoyments of Paradise, where every species of sensual gratification should be found, in the society of beautiful nymphs, he was desirous of its being understood by his followers that he also was a prophet and the compeer of Mahomet, and had the power of admitting to Paradise such as he should choose to favor. In order that none without his license might find their way into this delicious valley, he caused a strong and inexpugnable castle to be erected at the opening of it, through which the entry was by a secret passage. At his court, likewise, this chief entertained a number of youths, from the age of twelve to twenty years, selected from the inhabitants of the surrounding mountains, who showed a disposition for martial exercises, and appeared to possess the quality of daring courage. To them he was in the daily practice of discoursing on the subject of the Paradise announced by the prophet, and of his own power of granting admission; and at certain times he caused opium to be administered to ten or a dozen of the youths; and when half dead with sleep he had them conveyed to the several apartments of the palaces in the garden. Upon awakening from the state of lethargy, their senses were struck with all the delightful objects that have been described, and each perceived himself surrounded by lovely damsels, singing, playing, and attracting his regards by the most fascinating caresses, serving him also with delicate viands and exquisite wines; until intoxicated with excess of enjoyment amid actual rivulets of milk and wine, he believed himself assuredly in Paradise, and felt an unwillingness to relinquish its delights. When four or five days had thus been passed, they were thrown once more into a state of somnolence, and carried out of the garden. Upon their being introduced to his presence, and questioned by him as to where they had been, their answer was, "In Paradise, through the favor of your highness": and then before the whole court, who listened to them with eager curiosity and astonishment, they gave a circumstantial account of the scenes to which they had been witnesses. The chief thereupon addressing them, said: "We have the assurances of our prophet that he who defends his lord shall inherit Paradise, and if you show yourselves devoted to the obedience of my orders, that happy lot awaits you." Animated to enthusiasm by words of this nature, all deemed themselves happy to receive the commands of their master, and went forward to die in his service. The consequence of this system was, that when any of the neighboring princes, or others, gave umbrage to this chief, they were put to death by these his disciplined assassins; ncne of whom felt terror at the risk of losing their own lives, which they held in little estimation, provided they could execute their master's will. On this account his tyranny became the subject of dread in all the surrounding countries. He had also constituted two deputies or representatives of himself, of whom one had his residence in the vicinity of Damascus, and the other in Kurdistan; and these pursued the plan he had established for training their young dependents. Thus there was no person, however powerful, who, having become exposed to the enmity of the old man of the mountain, could escape assassination. His territory being situated within the dominions of Ulau (Hulagu), the brother of the grand khan (Mangu), that prince had information of his atrocious practices, as above related, as well as of his employing people to rob travelers in their passage through his country, and in the year 1262 sent one of his armies to besiege this chief in his castle. It proved, however, so capable of defense, that for three years no impression could be made upon it; until at length he was forced to surrender from the want of provisions, and being made prisoner was put to death. His castle was dismantled, and his garden of Paradise destroyed. And from that time there has been no old man of the mountain.

Leaving this castle, the road leads over a spacious plain, and then through a country diversified with hill and dale, where there is herbage and pasture, as well as fruits in great abundance, by which the army of Ulau was enabled to remain so long upon the ground. This country extends to the distance of full six days' journey. It contains many cities and fortified places, and the inhabitants are of the Mahometan religion. A desert then commences, extending forty or fifty miles, where there is no water; and it is necessary that the traveler should make provision of this article at his outset. As the cattle find no drink until this desert is passed, the greatest expedition is necessary, that they may reach a watering place. At the end of the sixth day's journey, he arrives at a town named Sapurgan, which is plentifully supplied with every kind of provision, and is particularly celebrated for producing the best melons in the world. These are preserved in the following manner. They are cut spirally, in thin slices, as the pumpkin with us, and after they have been dried in the sun, are sent, in large quantities, for sale, to the neighboring countries; where they are eagerly sought for, being sweet as honey. Game is also in plenty there, both of beasts and birds.

Leaving this place, we shall now speak of another named Balach; a large and magnificent city. It was formerly still more considerable, but has sustained much injury from the Tartars, who in their frequent attacks have partly demolished its buildings. It contained many palaces constructed of marble, and spacious squares, still visible, although in a ruinous state. It was in this city, according to the report of the inhabitants, that Alexander took to wife the daughter of King Darius. The Mahometan religion prevails here also. The dominion of the lord of the Eastern Tartars extends to this place; and to it the limits of the Persian empire extend, in a north-eastern direction. Upon leaving Balach and holding the same course for two days, you traverse a country that is destitute of every sign of habitation, the people having all fled to strong places in the mountains, in order to secure themselves against the predatory attack of lawless marauders, by whom these districts are overrun. Here are extensive waters, and game of various kinds. Lions are also found in these parts, very large and numerous. Provisions, however, are scarce in the hilly tract passed during these two days, and the traveler must carry with him food sufficient both for himself and his cattle.

At the end of these two days' journey you reach a castle named Thaikan, where a great market for corn is held, it being situated in a fine and fruitful country. The hills that lie to the south of it are large and lofty. They all consist of white salt, extremely hard, with which the people, to the distance of thirty days' journey round, come to provide themselves, for it is esteemed the purest that is found in the world; but it is at the same time so hard that it cannot be detached otherwise than with iron instruments. The quantity is so great that all the countries of the earth might be supplied from thence. Other hills produce almonds and pistachio nuts, in which articles the natives carry on a considerable trade. Leaving Thaikan and traveling three days, still in a north-east direction, you pass through a well inhabited country, very beautiful, and abounding in fruit, corn, and vines. The people are Mahometans, and are bloodthirsty and treacherous. They are given also to debauchery, and to excess in drink, to which the excellence of their sweet wine encourages them. On their heads they wear nothing but a cord, about ten spans in length, with which they bind them round. They are keen sportsmen, and take many wild animals, wearing no other clothing than the skins of the beasts they kill, of which materials their shoes also are made. They are all taught to prepare the skins.

INNER ASIA

Thou didst create the deserts, mountains, and forests,
but I produced the orchards, gardens, and groves.
    Turkmeni folk song

The deserts of what was once called Soviet Central Asia (750,000
square miles), the Taklamakan of China (200,000 square miles),
and the Gobi of Mongolia (600,000 square miles) make up a huge
inland belt of drylands separated by vast mountain chains like the
Pamirs, Tien Shan, and Hindu Kush. Europeans came to them
early on to trade along the Silk Route—ancient Greek goods have
even turned up in northwestern Siberia—but in late medieval
times they slipped into a kind of geographical void. Only in the
nineteenth and twentieth centuries did Europeans return there to
map the regions systematically, and even today parts of the inland
deserts are all but terra incognita to outsiders, who may have yet to
appreciate their majesty. The Scottish traveler Alexander Burnes
wrote, for example, of the Karakum (Black Sand Desert) of
Turkestan that "all other deserts are insignificant in comparison to
this endless ocean of sands. I cannot imagine a sight more terrible."
For his part, a *kumli*, one of the "sand people" of that desert, offers
this rejoinder: "Every time I think about the sunset in the desert,
my heart bleeds for those poor people who have never seen that
beauty."

The Road to Ashkabad

Ella R. Christie

Ella Christie (1871–1939) was one of the few women of her time to be admitted with full privileges to the ranks of the Royal Geographical Society. A wide-ranging traveler, she was also one of the first Englishwomen to venture into Central Asia, and this during a period of civil war and famine. In this passage from her 1925 book *Through Khiva to Golden Samarkand* she describes the arduous rail trip across the Transcaspian Desert.

After unrolling one's bundles and settling oneself as comfortably as circumstances permitted in the somewhat restricted space of a Central Asian railway carriage, on the ringing of the last of the three warning bells, the train glided out of Krasnovodsk at eight P.M. At stopping-places by the way these bells were a constant source of anxiety, it was so easy to miss one. Ashkabad was reached next day at midday; not a very rapid transit considering the distance, which is 200 miles; but I found on long journeys this slower mode of progression to be much less tiring than are our express trains, and besides I do not suppose the line as laid would stand their vibration.

The stations along the route are well built of stone, the platforms paved with brick, set edge up in herringbone pattern, and crowds are always assembled at them, as the Russians encourage railway travel among the natives, while they in turn think nothing of waiting for hours, or even days if need be, and happily camp on the platform during the enforced delay. Their name for the railway train is "Sheitan Arba," or the devil's coach!

For a considerable distance after leaving Krasnovodsk the journey presents few features of interest, as about two-thirds of the country of Turkestan is desert through which oases are scattered. It is bounded on the south by a continuous chain of mountains which contribute the water supply of the five rivers by which the country is intersected. Of these rivers the Amu Daria or Oxus and the Syr Daria or Jaxartes, both falling into the Aral Sea, are the most important, while the other three, the Mourghab, the Tedjen and the Zerafshan, are lost in marshes or form small lakes. The desert between the Caspian Sea and Amu Daria is known as the Kara-Kum, but one must not imagine it as all a flat plain, for in parts it rather resembles a troubled sea of sand whose dunes reach as high as sixty feet, their crescent-shaped surface rippled as by a tidal wave. These dunes are of so shifting a nature as to endanger the lives of any who seek to find a track across these desolate wastes. An interesting allusion to these sand-holes is to be found in an account of his journey by an ambassador to the Court of Tamerlane, in which he states that on the banks there were great plains of sand, and the sand was moved from one spot to the other by wind, and was thrown up in curious semicircular mounds, and the wind blew the sand from one mound to another, for it was very light, and on the ground where the wind had blown away the sand the marks of the mounds were left.

In another description a Roman historian Quintus Curtius (translated in 1553) notes: "To observe the starres as they do, that sayle the seas, and by the course of them direct their journey, wherefore in the daye time the country is wild and impassable, when they can finde no track or way to go in, nor marke or sign whereby to passe."

These descriptions apply absolutely to the present-day condition of that treeless waste, as well as to the time in which they were written. At intervals, instead of sand-dunes there are flatter stretches, whitened by saline deposits, with but scanty signs of vegetation, and yet amid this apparent desolation one knows that wherever irrigation is introduced a Garden of Eden is sure to follow. In parts the railway has to be protected from sand-blocks by thick fences of thorn and scrub planted at each side, which somewhat check the inroads made by sandstorms, especially at that part known as "the caravans' graveyard," a name that tells its own tale.

The Russians in laying out their new towns have made the invariable rule of building them entirely apart from the native ones; it might be two or it might be ten miles off according to circumstances. This has enabled them to build unhampered by space, and regardless of the extent of ground required for their laying out. Wide avenues of trees in double and even treble rows, with rivulets trickling between the rows, are much to be commended, the general plan being not unlike that of our Indian cantonments, while the railway station at Ashkabad was, like most of those already passed, a well-built stone one, with quite a pretentious façade on the town side.

Ashkabad boasts of avenues of poplars and acacias, with one-storey bungalows buried in greenery, and rather feeble attempts at gardens. Nasturtiums, stocks and most of our garden flowers would grow if encouraged, but the average Russian officer's wife either has other things of more real importance to occupy her, or lacks a pride in making her home look attractive. In the town are various public buildings, such as schools and technical colleges, and in the principal square there is a Russian church, with its fine gilded domes; in front of it in this square are some old brass guns, with the royal monogram of our King George IV—a strange place to meet them, and evidently they must at some period have been taken from the Afghans, to whom we had given artillery. There was also at the time of my visit a large temple in process of creation by the sect of the Bahais, which has many adherents among the Persians. There is a considerable trade with Persia, as the frontier is only a few miles distant, and Mesehed, 180 miles to the south, draws many Mahometan pilgrims to its shrine.

The chief attraction of the native quarter is its market, for there may be seen the many varieties of inhabitants of the country; prominent among them are of course the Tekke Turcomans, a fine-looking race in their dark-red-striped *khalats*, as their long robes are called, very similar in shape to a dressing-gown, a gaily coloured sash-band tied round their waists, on the head a huge fur cap of either black or white astrakhan, and high soft leather boots. The market is a very extensive one, held on a large open place, where the more luxurious merchants erect sheds or tents for themselves. One side of the square is devoted to quadrupeds, of which the camels form the noisiest and most noisome section. They are of the Bactrian breed, larger and heavier than those of Arabia, and in winter are covered with immensely thick brown wool, which as the warmer weather approaches is shed in handfuls, leaving large unsightly-looking bare patches. Their cast coats are not, in another sense, thrown away, for the wool is carefully collected and skilfully woven into the long robes of their owners, or else it is used for stuffing quilts, which are the native substitutes for blankets, deliciously warm and light. This reminds one of the thrifty days in Scotland long ago, when sheep's wool was carefully collected off hedges and bushes and spun into material for household use.

In another part of the market is to be seen cotton in its raw state, as well as cotton seed, both whole and crushed, testifying to a growing industry, of which the climax is reached in Ferghana, the most easterly province of Russian Central Asia. A rather uncommon use is made of the cotton seed, besides the ordinary one of oil-cake. The seed is crushed and then moulded into the form of a jug with a short spout, in which is contained the oil which has been already expressed from the small brown seeds.

Earthenware dishes for household use are displayed by another dealer—the inside of the flat dishes are coloured blue or green, with a fine glaze—while a collection of unglazed water-jars, whose artistic forms are strongly reminiscent of the Greek occupation, stand on the ground. A pile of rather squat ones, with a knob at the bottom, are intended for use on irrigation wheels, and this projection enables them to be securely tied on.

In a corner in a shed is found a copper mender, where fluted copper and brass jugs, or perhaps more strictly ewers, known as *kungana* by the natives, in every stage of dilapidation have been entrusted to his repairing powers. With the simplest of tools and means at his command, he appears to be able to make every dent vanish; a hammer and crooked stick seem to do the trick, while leakages are stopped with equal success. The copper vessels, sometimes plated with zinc and ornamented with tracery, are not unlike Kashmir work, the true Central Asian specimens depending solely on form and fluting for decoration. By way of additional adornment, jugs or ewers are sometimes chased by modern workers to imitate Indian work, which quite spoils the original design. So attractive are the purely fluted ewers that one hopes it may be long before the enamelled iron introduced by the Russians takes possession of the homes of such an artistic race.

In another corner of the mender's shed I was suddenly confronted with a sight that for a moment filled me with horror. Tales of decapitation in public places flashed into my mind as I seemed to see a place of execution. Rows of astrakhan heads on poles turned out after all to be nothing more alarming than a hat stall. It shows what imagination can do, when I pictured a head inside each one of them.

The fruit stalls of the market offer immense choice in raisins; on one stall alone I counted seven varieties. Their uses are many: they are sold mixed with parched peas, which the natives crunch in handfuls; they are also cooked in the national dish of pillau, and further are employed in making raisin wine, a somewhat sweet syrup. A fruit new to me was the *puchara*, rather like an undersized Tunis date, with a reddish yellow papery skin, the inside being of a floury consistency and a pleasant acid flavour. The melon stall has many customers: one cannot think of any market in Turkestan without associating it with large rose-pink slices whose black seeds give an accentuating note of colour. By means of some secret of preserving them they can be had in a fresh state all the year round. The process is said to consist of burying them in the sand, and doubtless the extreme dryness of the atmosphere assists to bring about the result.

Seeing several stalls furnished with sacks of what at first I took to be fragments of dark coloured cement bricks, I asked what species of building material they represented, and was told they were the refuse of black bread discarded by the soldiers months previously, and sold in this state to make *kvas*, a favourite Russian drink somewhat resembling very light beer, but such previous treatment did not make one specially anxious to sample it when occasion offered.

Strolling among the crowd is a prominent object, the itinerant smoke vender, offering a smoke of his chilim or native pipe for the fraction of a farthing, but how many draws are allowed I never ascertained. The pipe itself is a gourd of artificial shape, mounted in brass. On the top is fixed a terra-cotta receptacle to hold the ashes and tobacco, or else it may be *makhora*, a preparation of hemp seed, somewhat narcotic in its effect. At the side is inserted a bamboo stem, and it is the business of the vender to see that it is in proper working order, and if the smoke be not to his satisfaction a customer may return the pipe and ask him to make it draw. This indiscriminate use of the same mouthpiece seems to offer no objections, and these can hardly be raised when the price of a smoke is less than a quarter of a farthing.

After all this was no worse than what was the practice in my youth of the general "merchant" of a certain country village. Being of an obliging nature, when it came to selling tooth-brushes, he used to beg his customers: "Tak' hame twa three o' them an' see which ye like, all gie me back the rest!" Or again, I remember seeing in America a pawnshop in whose window was a small tray laid out with plates of false teeth with this tempting invitation on a large label: "Try us!"

Amid all the throng there are few foot-passengers. Like the southern Irish, no self-respecting native would dream of being seen otherwise than on the back of a quadruped, even if only a donkey, and two and even three may be seen riding an animal at the same time. How the third manages to cling on to some diminutive pony's back was at all times a problem to me. One of the most remarkable features in a native crowd is the almost total absence of women. A figure swathed in a long cloak and peeping through a horsehair face-covering may be noticed at rare intervals, but for the most part the women are never seen unless in the tents of nomadic tribes. Ashkabad has the advantage of a river near by, the Mourghab, which the interpreter informed me was one of the four that flowed out of the Garden of Eden!

A Nightmare on the Turkmeni Dunes

Andrei Platonov

Andrei Platonov was born in 1899 in southern Russia, the son of a railroad worker. He fought in the Red Cavalry during the Civil War, but was never a Communist. Suspect therefore, Platonov had difficulty finding publication for his work, especially after a rising power, Joseph Stalin, publicly criticized a story in Platonov's first collection. In 1946, perhaps recognizing the veiled criticism of the regime carried through such symbols as the eagle—a corruption of the Tsarist standard—in this selection, Joseph Stalin ordered that Platonov be forbidden to publish his work. He quickly faded from public view and disappeared, perhaps into the gulags.

During the era of Khruschev's anti-Stalinist reforms, two volumes of

Platonov's stories appeared. One of those stories, "Dzhan"—meaning, in Turkmeni folklore, a wandering soul in search of happiness—offers a bleak vision of the forced relocation of tribespeople during the great purges of the 1930s. Its protagonist, an indigene named Nazar Chagateyev, has been assigned by his superiors at the Moscow Institute of Economics to bring socialism to his now-embattled people. His path, however, lies elsewhere.

A dark desert wind blew in the night and the sand started wandering under this wind and gradually closed over forever the faint traces where the sheep had run. Early in the morning Chagatayev walked away from the sleeping, drowsy people when he realized that the herd of sheep was now gone for good and that to go after them made no sense, so that his enfeebled people found itself in the middle of the desert, without food or help, without the strength to go on to Sari-Kamish and at the same time unable to turn back to the flood-lands of the Amu-Darya.

A queer morning wind was blowing into Chagatayev's face, sand swirled around his feet and groaned like a Russian blizzard outside the shutters of a peasant hut. Sometimes you could hear the plaintive sound of a musical cow's horn, sometimes a harmonica was playing, or a faraway trumpet, or most often of all a two-stringed instrument called a dutar All this was really the sand singing, tortured by the wind, one grain of sand being reduced to powder by rubbing against another. Chagatayev lay down on the ground, to think about the future of his job: he hadn't been sent here for this, to die himself and to give his people nothing better than death. . . . He felt his face with his hand, it was covered with hair; lice had settled on his head; his unwashed, thin body was mourning from neglect. Chagatayev thought of himself now as a sorry, uninteresting person. Who even remembered him now, except for Ksenya? And probably even she had started to forget him; youth was too excited about its own happy problems. Chagatayev fell asleep in the unquiet sand, apart and fairly far from all the unsleeping people. Everything was standing stock-still inside him, deep down and for a long time, holding its breath inside his body, in order not to die completely. He woke up in darkness, half covered with sand; the wind was still blowing and it was already a new night. He had slept the whole day through. Chagatayev walked back to the camping place, but his people were not there. All of them had wakened long before and gone on farther and faster, away from death. Only Nazar-Shakir was lying there; he had died, his mouth was wide open and now the wind and the sand were saying something inside it. When Chagatayev found the dead man he felt him for a long time to be sure that he was really dead, and then he covered the man with sand so he would be invisible to anybody.

Chagatayev walked all night. Sometimes when he leaned over he could see the tracks of his people in front of him, and sometimes when the tracks had been wiped out by the wind, he went on by hunch. In the morning Chagatayev noticed a place where there should be water, and he found an old well which had been filled in with sand. He dug with his hands into its damp bottom and began to chew the sand, but he had to lose more in spitting than he managed to swallow; then he started to gulp the wet sand itself, and the torment of his thirst left him. For the next four days Chagatayev tried to go forward across the desert but his weakness never let him go far and he would return to the wet sand so that, weak as he was from hunger, he should not die of thirst. On the fifth day he stayed where he was, determined to recover his strength in drowsing and unconsciousness and then to catch up to his people. He ate the two quinine powders he had left, and some crumbs from the lining of his pockets, and this made him feel better. He realized that his people must be close by, for they too had no strength to go far, but he didn't know the direction in which they had gone. Chagatayev pictured to himself the secret satisfaction with which Nur-Mohammed would mark down his death in his notebook. He smiled over one of his old ideas: why people counted so much on grief and destruction when

happiness is just as inevitable and often easier to find than despair. . . . Chagatayev protected himself from the sun with wet sand
and tried to sink into unconsciousness, to rest and save his strength,
but he couldn't, and he kept right on thinking all the time, living a
little, and watching the sky where a warm wind blew from the south-
east through a weak haze, and where everything was so empty that
there was no believing in the existence of a hard, real world, anywhere.

Still lying down, Chagatayev crawled to the nearest sandhill
where he had noticed a tumbleweed bush half covered with sand.
He crawled up to it, broke off several of its dried-out twigs, and
chewed them, and then he pulled the rest of the bush out of the sand
and set it off rolling with the wind. The bush bumped its way along
and disappeared behind the dunes, headed off somewhere into distant places. Meanwhile Chagatayev, crawling around the vicinity,
found some dried-out blades of grass growing in little sandy crevices, and he ate these, too, just as he found them. Sliding down the
sandhill, he fell asleep at its base, and different memories flooded
over him in his sleep, useless, forgotten impressions, the faces of uninteresting people he had seen at one time or another—all the life
he had lived through turned back upon him. Chagatayev followed
it helplessly and quietly, unable to forget for good the small unim-
portant things which had later been covered over by important happenings—and now he realized that everything had stayed intact, in-
destructible and safe. Here his friend Vera was leaning over him,
hardly seen by him then, leaning over him and not going away, tor-
turing the awareness of this man drowsing in the desert and not
going away; and behind her, against a bank of clay were moving the
shadows of silver branches which had grown at some time in the
sunshine, perhaps at Chardzhoui, perhaps somewhere else; a Khiva
donkey was looking at Chagatayev with familiar eyes and crying out
plaintively, without interruption, as if reminding him that he should

untie it and set it free; many more eternal little things like rotting trees, a village post office, unpopulated hills under the noonday sun, the sounds of a wasting wind, and tender embraces with Vera—all of this flooded into Chagatayev at the same time and stayed inside him motionless and stubborn, even though in the past, in actuality, these happenings and people had been gentle ones, doing no harm to the conscience or the feelings of a man. But now these images, these thoughts, gnawed at Chagatayev's brain, and he wanted to scream but didn't have enough strength to do so. He started to listen hard— for infrequent, dripping, resonant sounds in the distance, from beyond the black, dead horizon, out of the dark, free night where the last shining of the sun was being swallowed whole, like a river falling down into the desert sands. Sometimes he heard the sounds of nature far away, not knowing the reason for them or their full meaning.

Chagatayev stood up on his feet, to get rid of sleep and this whole world sticking to the inside of his head like a prickly bush. Sleep flowed out of him, but all the strange thickness of memory and thought stayed alive in him even when he was awake. He saw something on a sand dune next to him, either an animal or a tent, but he couldn't understand what it was, and he fell backwards out of weakness. And whatever it was on the neighboring sand dune, an animal or a tent or a machine, moved now into Chagatayev's consciousness and boldly began to torment him, though he did not understand it or even have a name for it. This new phenomenon, tied in with all that had preceded it, overpowered Chagatayev, and he fell into unconsciousness again, to save his soul.

He woke early on the following day. The wind had disappeared without a trace, a shy silence stood all around him, so empty and so weak that a storm might suddenly have burst out inside it. The shadow of night moved up into the sky and lay there across the world, higher than the light of day. Chagatayev was well by now, his mind had cleared, and he thought about his problems as he had before; his weakness had not left him but it no longer tortured him. He foresaw that he would probably die here, and his people, too, would be lost as corpses in the desert. Chagatayev did not regret this for himself, his bigger nation would still be alive, and it would still bring general happiness to the unhappy, but it was hard that the Dzhan people, which stood in need of life and happiness more than all the other peoples of the Soviet Union, should be dead.

"It won't be," Chagatayev whispered.

He began to lift himself, pressing with all his body on his trembling hands placed flat against the sand, but immediately he fell back again: behind him, right behind the back of his neck, something was moving; Chagatayev could hear the quick, retreating steps of something alive.

Chagatayev closed his eyes and felt in his pocket for the handle of his revolver; now he was only afraid that he might not be able to cope with the heavy weapon because his hand had only a child's strength left in it. He lay there for a long time, not moving, pretending to be dead. He knew about a lot of animals and birds which eat dead people on the steppes. Probably wild animals were moving in a long, unseen procession behind his people, eating those who fell. Sheep, his people, wild animals—this triple train was moving in order across the desert. But the sheep, having lost their accustomed grazing ground, began sometimes to follow the wandering tumbleweed being blown by the wind, so the wind became the true guiding force, of everything from grass to men. Probably they should be following the wind, in order to catch up with the sheep, but Nur-Mohammed didn't know anything, and Sufyan had become bored with living, and had stopped thinking. Chagatayev wanted to jump up at once, shoot at the animal, kill it, and eat it, but he was afraid he might miss, out of weakness, and frighten the animal away for good. He decided to let the animal come right up to his body, and kill it at point-blank range.

Light, careful steps could be heard all this time behind Chagatayev's head, now coming closer, now going away. Nazar waited, holding his breath, for this slinking thing to hurl itself upon him, not yet
sure that he was dead. He worried only that the animal might sink its
fangs into his throat at its first pounce, or that, wounded, it might
run far away. He could now hear the little steps right next to his head.
Chagatayev pulled the revolver a little more out of his pocket, feeling
inside him a real strength compounded out of all the little scraps of
life left in him. But the steps moved past his body, and went beyond.
Nazar half-opened his eyes: just beyond his feet two enormous
birds were walking, moving away toward a sand dune opposite him.
Chagatayev had never seen such birds; they looked like the eagle-
carrion vultures of the steppes and at the same time like wild, dark
swans. Their beaks were like vultures' beaks, but their thick, powerful necks were longer than those of eagles, and their solid legs carried high the delicate, airy bodies of true swans. The strong wings of
one bird were a pure gray in color, while the other had blue, red, and
gray feathers. This one was probably the female. Both birds seemed
to have on trousers of snowy-white down. Even from one side, Chagatayev noticed little black spots on the female; these were fleas digging through the down into the stomach of the bird. Both birds
looked like enormous nestlings which were not yet used to being
alive, and were moving with extreme care.

The day had grown hot and dreary, little sandstorms were whirling across the surface of the sand, evening still stood high in the sky,
above the light and the warmth. The two birds walked onto the sand
dune opposite Chagatayev and looked at him with their thoughtful,
farseeing eyes. Chagatayev watched the birds from under his half-
closed eyelids, and he could see even the gray, thin color of their eyes
as they looked at him full of thought and of attention. The female
was cleaning the talons of its feet with its beak, and spitting out of its
mouth some kind of old leavings, perhaps a remnant of the clawed-

up Nazar-Shakir. The male rose into the air, but the female stayed where it was. The enormous bird flew low to one side, then soared upward with several flappings of its wings, and almost at once began to fall straight toward him. Chagatayev felt the wind in his face before the bird hit him. He could see its white, clean breast in front of his face, and its gray, clear eyes, not wicked but thoughtful, because the bird had now noticed that the man was alive, and watching it. Chagatayev lifted his revolver, held it with both hands, and fired straight at the head of the bird dropping down upon him. In the white down of the bird's breast, blown out by the speed of its downward flight, a dark spot appeared, and then the wind blew all the down and wisps of feathers around the spot of the direct hit, and for a moment the body of the eagle held itself motionless in the air above him.

The bird closed its gray eyes, and then they opened by themselves, but they no longer saw anything—the bird was dead. It lay across Chagatayev's body in the same position in which it had been falling, its breast against the man's breast, its head on his head, burying its beak in Chagatayev's thick hair, spreading wide its black, helpless wings on both sides of him, with its feathers and down strewed all over Chagatayev. Chagatayev himself fainted from the force of the blow, but he was not wounded; the bird had simply stunned him since the dangerous speed of its fall had been braked by the bullet. Chagatayev started up with sharp pain: the second bird, the female, had driven its beak into his right leg and having pulled out some of his flesh was flying off into the air. Chagatayev, holding the revolver with both hands again, fired twice but missed; the gigantic bird disappeared behind the sand dunes, and then he saw it flying away at a great height.

The dead eagle was no longer on top of Chagatayev, but lying on the sand at his feet. The female must have pushed it there in an effort to make sure that it was dead, and to say good-bye to it. Chagatayev crawled over to the dead bird and began to eat at its throat, tearing the feathers away from it. The female eagle was still to be seen, but it had already climbed high up in the sky where the shadow of night, the dusk of dawn and sunset, stands even at full noon, and it seemed to Chagatayev that the bird would never come back, that there it had found the happy land in the air of all the birds that fly.

When he had eaten a little, Chagatayev tied one leg of the dead bird to his belt and he put the other end of the belt deep inside his trousers, so he would know it if some beast of prey tried to steal the eagle away from him. Then he treated the wound torn in his leg, wrapped it in cloth, and lay down quickly, in order to recover a little of his strength.

Translated by Joseph Barnes

The Tebbad

Arminius Vámbéry

The Hungarian orientalist Arminius Vámbéry (1832–1913) overcame a crippling childhood illness to become one of his country's great explorers; he was also a linguist who was interested in the historical links among Hungarian and Finnish, Turkish, Mongolian, and the other Ural-Altaic languages. In 1863 he traveled from Tehran to Samarkand on a mapping expedition for the Hungarian Academy of Pesth, disguising himself as a dervish on the way home from Mecca. This passage from his 1865 book *Travels in Central Asia* recounts some of the excitement he faced.

A few stars began to gleam in the heavens when we reached the sandy desert. We maintained the stillness of death during our march, in order that we might escape the notice of the Turkomans probably then in our vicinity. They might perhaps not see us on account of the darkness of the night, the moon not rising till later. We wished also that no sound might betray our position to them. On the soft ground the tread of the camels produced no echo. We feared, however, that some freak of braying might occur to our asses, for their voices would echo far and wide in the still night. Toward midnight we reached a place where we were all obliged to dismount, as both asses and camels were sinking down to their knees in the fine sand. This, indeed, formed there an uninterrupted chain of little hills. In the cool night-march I could just manage to tramp on through this endless sand, but toward morning I felt my hand beginning to swell from continually resting upon my staff. I consequently placed my baggage on the ass, and took its place upon the camel, which, although breathing hard, was still more in his element in the sand than I with my lame leg.

Our morning station bore the charming appellation of Adamkyrylgan (which means "the place where men perish"), and one needed only to cast a look at the horizon to convince himself how appropriate is that name. Let the reader picture to himself a sea of sand, extending as far as eye can reach, on one side formed into high hills, like waves lashed into that position by the furious storm; on the other side, again, like the smooth waters of a still lake, merely rippled by the west wind. Not a bird visible in the air, not a worm or beetle upon the earth; traces of nothing but departed life, in the bleaching bones of man or beast that has perished, collected by every passer-by in a heap, to serve to guide the march of future travelers! Why add that we moved on unnoticed by the Turkomans? The man does not exist on earth that could make a station here on horseback; but whether the elements would not oppose our progress was a point the consideration of which shook even the *sang froid* of the Oriental, and the sombre looks of my fellow-travelers during the whole way best betrayed their anxiety.

According to what the kervanbashi told us, we should have had al-together on this way, from Tünüklü to Bokhara, only six days' jour-ney, half through sand, the rest over firm and even ground, where here and there grass is met with and shepherds resort. Conse-quently, after the examination of our skins, we calculated that we should only have to apprehend a deficiency of water during one day and a half; but the very first day I remarked that the Oxus water did not bear out our calculations; that that most precious liquid, al-though we made a most sparing use of it, diminished every moment, either from the heat of the sun, its own evaporation, or some such cause. This discovery made me watch my stores with double care-fulness; in this I was imitated by the others, and, in spite of our anx-iety, it was even comical to see how the slumberers slept, firmly embracing their water vessels.

Notwithstanding the scorching heat, we were obliged to make, during the day also, marches of from five to six hours' duration, for the sooner we emerged from the region of sand, the less occasion we had to dread the dangerous wind tebbad; for on the firm plain it can but bring with it the torture of fever, whereas in the region of sand it can in a moment bury every thing. The strength of the poor camels was taxed too far; they entered the desert wearied by their nocturnal journey; it was not, therefore, surprising that some fell ill through the torments of the sand and the heat, and that two died even at this day's station. It bears the name of Shorkutuk. This word signifies salt fountain, and one, in fact, is said to exist here, adequate for the refreshment of beasts, but it was entirely choked up by the stormy wind, and a day's labor would have been necessary to render it again serviceable.

But, let alone the tebbad, the oppressive heat by day had already left us without strength, and two of our poorer companions, forced to tramp on foot by the side of their feeble beasts, having exhausted all their water, fell so sick that we were forced to bind them at full length upon the camels, as they were perfectly incapable of riding or sitting. We covered them, and as long as they were able to articulate they kept exclaiming "Water! water!" the only words that escaped their lips. Alas! even their best friends denied them the life-dispensing draught; and when we, on the fourth day, reached Medemin Bulag, one of them was freed by death from the dreadful torments of thirst. It was one of the three brothers who had lost their father at Mecca. I was present when the unfortunate man drew his last breath. His tongue was quite black, the roof of his mouth of a grayish white; in other respects his features were not much disfigured, except that his lips were shriveled, the teeth exposed, and the mouth open. I doubt much whether, in these extreme sufferings, water would have been of much service; but who was there to give it to him?

It was a horrible sight to see the father hide his store of water from the son, and brother from brother; each drop is life; and when men feel the torture of thirst, there is not, as in the other dangers of life, any spirit of self-sacrifice, or any feeling of generosity.

. We passed three days in the sandy parts of the desert. We had now to gain the firm plain, and come in sight of the Khalata Mountain, that stretches away toward the north. Unhappily, disappointment again awaited us. Our beasts were incapable of farther exertion, and we passed a fourth day in the sand. I had still left about six glasses of water in my leathern bottle. These I drank drop by drop, suffering, of course, terribly from thirst. Greatly alarmed to find that my tongue began to turn a little black in the centre, I immediately drank off at a draught my remaining store, thinking so to save my life; but oh! the burning sensation, followed by headache, became more violent toward the morning of the fifth day; and when we could just distinguish, about midday, the Khalata Mountains from the clouds that surrounded them, I felt my strength gradually abandon me. The nearer we approached the mountains the thinner the sand became, and all eyes were searching eagerly to discover a drove of cattle or shepherd's hut, when the kervanbashi and his people drew our attention to a cloud of dust that was approaching and told us to lose no time in dismounting from the camels. These poor brutes knew that it was the tebbad that was hurrying on; uttering a loud cry, they fell on their knees, stretched their long necks along the ground, and strove to bury their heads in the sand. We intrenched ourselves behind them, lying there as behind a wall; and scarcely had we, in our turn, knelt under their cover, than the wind rushed over us with a dull, clattering sound, leaving us, in its passage, covered with a crust of sand two fingers thick. The first particles that touched me seemed to burn like a rain of flakes of fire. Had we encountered it when we were six miles deeper in the desert, we should all have perished. I had not time to make observations upon the disposition to fever and vomiting caused by the wind itself, but the air became heavier and more oppressive than before.

Where the sand comes entirely to an end, three different ways are visible: the first (22 miles long) passes by Karakol; the second (18 miles) through the plain to the immediate vicinity of Bokhara; the third (20 miles) traverses the mountains where water is to be met with, but it is inaccessible to camels on account of its occasional steepness. We took, as it had been previously determined, the middle route, the shortest, particularly as we were animated by the hope of finding water among those who tended their flocks there. Toward evening we reached fountains that had not yet been visited this year by the shepherds; the water, undrinkable by man, still refreshed the beasts. We were ourselves all very ill, like men half dead, without any animation but that which proceeded from the now well-grounded hope that we should all be saved!

I was no longer able to dismount without assistance; they laid me upon the ground; a fearful fire seemed to burn my entrails; my headache reduced me almost to a state of stupefaction. My pen is too feeble to furnish even a slight sketch of the martyrdom that thirst occasions; I think that no death can be more painful. Although I have found myself able to nerve myself to face all other perils, here I felt quite broken. I thought, indeed, that I had reached the end of my life. Toward midnight we started. I fell asleep, and on awaking in the morning found myself in a mud hut, surrounded by people with long beards; in these I immediately recognized children of Iran. They said to me, "Shuma ki hadji nistid" (You, certainly, are no hadji). I had no strength to reply. They at first gave me something warm to drink, and a little afterward some sour milk, mixed with water and salt, called "airan": that gave me strength and set me up again.

High Desert

Theodore Roosevelt and Kermit Roosevelt

An ardent hunter and conservationist—then as now, the two are not mutually exclusive—Theodore Roosevelt traveled widely in search of exotic game animals over the course of his long life. In this passage from *East of the Sun and West of the Moon* (1901), written with his brother and traveling companion Kermit, he describes a venture into the Taklamakan Desert of western China in quest of mountain bighorn sheep undertaken shortly before Roosevelt became the twenty-sixth president of the United States.

For a couple of days we travelled through the plains. We passed from oasis to oasis. Burned and forbidding, the desert lay between. There was an endless succession of scrub bushes and sun-scorched rock, with dust-devils dancing between. Time and again we passed small oases on which the desert was marching. On their outskirts were houses half buried in sand, and dead trees whose gray, gnarled upper limbs alone stuck out of sand-dunes. Closer in, where the sand had not yet conquered, were half-submerged fields and partially covered trees whose tops were still green with leaves.

On the third day we turned due south. Soon we were among the foot-hills. The plains of Turkestan were behind us.

Turkestan, though it has been comparatively civilized for a long time, has changed but little in the last thousand years. The leaders still practise mediaeval directness in dealing with those they dislike. Last year the General at Kashgar became too efficient and raised too large an army. The Governor of Turkestan descended on Kashgar unannounced, and the General's head presently appeared over one of the gates of the city.

Perhaps the most unpleasant sight we saw in this country was the prisoners. The state considers that it has done its duty when it has thrown them into prison. It does not provide them with food. They are led each day to the gates of the city, chained there, and left to beg their food from charitable passers-by. Moaning and gibbering in their chains, their wild eyes peering from beneath their tangled black hair, their gaunt limbs showing through the filthy rags in which they were clothed, they were a gruesome sight.

The hills were more than welcome after the long weeks we had spent in the plains. Bare and red, they suggested the buttes of Colorado. We marched up the bed of a rocky stream, the trail weaving from side to side over numerous fords. About noon we saw two men approaching on horseback, who turned out to be Nadir Beg and the mail-runner from India.

Nadir Beg was the native that Gillan had got us as a guide for the ovis poli country. He was an important citizen of the town of Tash-kurgan, a fine-looking man with a light complexion, a black beard and a hawk-like nose. He was a Sarikol, one of a people who live in the valleys and mountains of that name. These Sarikoli, because of their Aryan features and light complexions, are said to be descendants of the soldiers of Alexander the Great, whose "distant footsteps" still echo down the corridors of time in northwestern India. In the East, where nothing is entirely forgotten, and little remembered with accuracy, the tradition of the great Macedonian remains as the myth of a demigod.

That evening we camped by a little Kirghiz settlement on a small plain in the valley. The principal building was a mud-walled square around a great cottonwood-tree. In it was bivouacked a caravan from Tashkurgan on its way to Kashgar. The men were good-looking lean fellows and very friendly. Around the camp-fire we worked out our plans for the poli-hunting. Nadir Beg said that though goolja (rams) were scarce, he had seen a fine head shot by a Kirghiz near Subashi the previous winter. We accordingly decided to try that point first.

For the next two days we pushed on up the river. At times the trail was very bad. It wound along the steep sides of the mountain. The valley narrowed into a gorge through which the stream rushed so rapidly that fording was very difficult. A small boy, perhaps fourteen years old, led the head pony of our caravan. At one of the fords he fell in, but was pulled out by Nadir Beg and some of the others. After the water had been tilted out of him he seemed all right. His clothes, however, could not be worn wet in the bitter cold, so he was fitted out from various surplus stores. As he was by all odds the smallest of the party, the fit was far from good. The final touch to his attire was given by an enormous pair of knee-high boots which made him look, as he paddled along, like the Puss-in-boots of the fairy-tale.

After crossing the ford where the boy fell in, I noticed the head pony man stoop down and put a stone on a small pile that was there. That was Tauism, or nature-worship. The people of this country are nominally Mohammedans, but, like most people who live in the lonely places of the world, their religion is largely overlaid with primitive nature-worship. Wherever there was a bad ford we saw these piles of rocks. At times we saw trees with bits of rag or paper fluttering from their branches.

At one place we were delayed many hours because a part of a bridge had been destroyed. Before we could get the caravan over, we had to rebuild much of the road. Even then it took the efforts of three or four men, pushing and pulling, to get each pack-pony across. Just beyond, on the other side of the river, there were holes sunk in the rocks. I asked Nadir Beg what they were. He told me they were the remains of a bridge built in Yakoob Beg's time. Yakoob Beg was a very competent Mohammedan who headed a successful revolt some sixty or seventy years ago. He ruled in Turkestan for a number of years. It was only after his death that China regained her control. I noticed that improvements and public works were very often credited to him by the natives. It would seem that he must have been a very able man, but perhaps it is only a case of the far hills being the greenest.

As we wound our way along, we met an occasional caravan moving toward the plains. The men were generally so bundled up that they looked like animated bolsters. A number of times we noticed poliskins, either on their saddles or covering their bales. This encouraged us very much. When we questioned them they told us that these were the skins of arkal (female sheep) from both the Chinese and the Russian Pamirs.

Sometimes we came on great woolly Bactrian camels, which lifted their heads from their grazing and eyed us incuriously. They were in splendid shape, fat and strong. It was a constant source of wonder to us that these great animals were able to keep in such good condition feeding on the withered bushes and scant dry grass of the country.

Here we saw a type of shelter we had not seen before, a mud-and-stone yourt. The bottom was built of rough rocks, the top was of dry clay. Generally they clustered in the lee of some large rock, like chickens around a hen.

One bitter cold morning Loosa brought in a small gray mouse that he had caught in his hands. It was a new species so Kermit conscientiously skinned it, though skinning is far from pleasant when the steel cleaves to your hands from cold.

One afternoon as we were riding along we noticed a hawk pursuing a large blue rock pigeon. The latter took refuge in a hole in a crumbling mud-bank by the side of the trail. Nadir Beg and Fezildin galloped up, and a chase for the pigeon started. They scrambled down and tried to catch it by reaching into the hole where it had gone. It was really very heavy odds, for whenever they scared the pigeon out of the hole the hawk would swoop at it. At last, I am glad to say, it got off scot-free, eluding all pursuers, bird and man alike, and disappeared behind a cliff.

It had now begun to be bitterly cold. The snow lay thick on the mountains. Snow flurries and sleetstorms swept across the valley nearly every afternoon. The wind blew with gusty fury. At night the tin cup of water that Kermit and I had left between us in the tent froze solid. As the trees and large bushes had all disappeared, our fires consisted nearly entirely of yak dung, with occasionally a few scrubbush roots called bursa by the natives. Yak dung burns with a pungent odor that is rather pleasant. It serves only for cooking, and does not warm you when the weather is really cold. It is one thing to camp in our own North woods where fuel is plentiful, and where, when the hunter comes in chilled and tired, he builds a roaring fire of birch and pine; but it is a very different matter in the Pamirs, when he arrives in camp to no fire at all. We went to bed immediately after getting to camp, for it was the only place where we could be reasonably comfortable. Even there all we could do was to lie still and think, for it was too cold to hold a book even if a candle could be kept alight in the wind. Getting up in the gray light of early morning was also far from pleasant. Everything was frozen. Very often the snow was deep outside of the tent. Every piece of clothing was damp and cold. As time wore on, we took off less and less when we went to bed, until the phrase "undressed for the night" might better have been changed to "dressed for the night."

Prester John

Sir John Mandeville

Although his published work was instantly famous, no one knows who John Mandeville was. He is believed to have been born in 1322 and to have died fifty years later, and to have spent many years of his life working in the service of the Great Khan of China. His *Travels*, published in 1361, became the first bestselling travel book in history, a favorite of Columbus, Sir Francis Drake, and other later explorers.

In this passage, Mandeville writes of the legendary king Prester John, supposedly a Christian ruler who lived in the desert far from any contact with other Christian nations. Much European travel was fueled by the search for Prester John; even the seventeenth- and eighteenth-century quests to find a Northwest Passage were undertaken to find the kingdom. In Latin, "prester" means the electrical discharge of a lightning storm, and it may be that the European travelers who first brought the tale back from their travels on the Silk Route had simply interpreted the legend of an ancient desert storm god to suit their own doctrine. And storm it does along those desert paths; as John of Plano Carpini, a thirteenth-century Franciscan missionary to Mongolia, writes, "In the middle of summer when other places are normally enjoying very great heat, there is fierce thunder and lightning which cause the death of many men, and at the same time there are very heavy falls of snow. There are also hurricanes of bitterly cold wind so violent that at times men can ride on horseback only with great effort."

This Emperor Prester John is Christian, and a great part of his country also. But yet, they have not all the articles of our faith as we have. They believe well in the Father, in the Son and in the Holy Ghost. And they be full devout and right true to one another. . . .

And he hath under him seventy-two provinces, and in every province is a king. And these kings have kings under them, and all be tributaries to Prester John. And he hath in his lordships many great marvels.

For in his country is the sea that men clepe the Gravelly Sea, that is all gravel and sand without any drop of water, and it ebbeth and floweth in great waves as other seas do, and it is never still ne in peace, in no manner season. And no man may pass that sea by navy, ne by no manner of craft, and therefore may no man know what land is beyond that sea. And albeit that it have no water, yet men find therein and on the banks full good fish of other manner of kind and shape, than men find in any other sea, and they be of right good taste and delicious to man's meat.

And a three journeys long from that sea be great mountains, out of the which goeth out a great flood that cometh out of Paradise. And it is full of precious stones, without any drop of water, and it runneth through the desert on that one side, so that it maketh the sea gravelly; and it beareth into that sea, and there it endeth. And that flome runneth, also, three days in the week and bringeth with him great stones and the rocks also therewith, and that great plenty. And anon, as they be entered into the Gravelly Sea, they be seen no more, but lost for evermore. And in those three days that that river runneth, no man dare enter into it; but in the other days men dare enter well enough.

Also beyond that flome, more upward to the deserts, is a great plain all gravelly, between the mountains. And in that plain, every day at the sun-rising, begin to grow small trees, and they grow till mid-day, bearing fruit; but no men dare take of that fruit, for it is a thing of faerie. And after mid-day, they decrease and enter again into the earth, so that at the going down of the sun they appear no more. And they do so, every day. And that is a great marvel.

In that desert be many wild men, that be hideous to look on; for they be horned, and they speak nought, but they grunt, as pigs. And there is also great plenty of wild hounds. And there be many popinjays, that they clepe psittakes in their language. And they speak of their proper nature, and salute men that go through the deserts, and speak to them as apertly as though it were a man. And they that speak well have a large tongue, and have five toes upon a foot. And there be also of another manner, that have but three toes upon a foot, and they speak not, or but little, for they can not but cry.

Distances of the Gobi

Mongolian wedding song

Even the peerlessly nomadic Ordos Mongols, long famed for Genghis Khan's having recruited his household guard only from Ordos regiments, recognize how dauntingly vast their Gobi homeland is. This traditional song was sung at the wedding of the translators, which took place in the Ordos section of the Gobi Desert.

Riding my horse Zandanhorum
We'll go to Zandanzhu
"How is everybody?"
Running across the sand

This horse is good
Whitefaced horse
Festooned with silk
My daughter lives so far away
With her husband's family
Running across the ice
This horse with silver spots
At the wedding my girl wore
Jewels and silver in her hair
Then she wore out her shoes
Crossing distant hills.

Translated by Paul and Sarengowa Maxwell

The Lake Among
the Singing Dunes

Mildred Cable

Mildred Cable lived in the northern Chinese province of Shuangxi
for more than twenty years in the early years of the twentieth century.
With her friends Eva and Francesca French, she then spent three years
traveling through Mongolia while working as a Christian missionary.
Their collective book *The Gobi Desert* (1942) is a remarkable account of a
land that, then as now, has seen few nonnative explorers—and even fewer
women from beyond the sand dunes.

The constant hurricanes which sweep the sandy plains have piled
up a long line of dunes stretching from Tunhwang away to the Des-

ert of Lob. The range is so long, and the hills are so lofty, and so massed one behind the other, that it seemed incredible such a mighty rampart could be composed wholly of shifting sand. From season to season the contour of the dunes changes, for under the breath of even the lightest breeze the shifting surface runs like sand in an hour-glass, and every wind lifts the clear-cut ridge like spray, though the solid body of the sand-mountain resists the fiercest winter storms.

Behind the great rampart death reigns, and there is not so much sign of life as the track of a passing antelope. Not even a beetle or a lizard would find sustenance in that sterility, yet it was in search of a lake that we first explored the desolate region.

"The skill of man made the Caves of the Thousand Buddhas, but the Hand of God fashioned the Lake of the Crescent Moon," is a popular saying at Tunhwang, and when I asked where to find this Lake of the Crescent Moon, the answer was:

"It lies behind the first range of those sand-hills."

"Is it so very beautiful?" I enquired.

"More beautiful than words can tell," was the answer.

"How far off is the lake?" I asked, remembering the fatigue of toiling through loose sand.

"It is barely four miles from the town, and once there you will find fresh sweet water, a small temple with clean guest-rooms, and a quiet place in which to rest."

This was an encouraging answer, and a few days later we left the city gate with faces turned toward the dunes. Within an hour we were standing at the base of the outermost hill, and where the range was at its lowest we started to climb the steep side, ploughing upwards through sands which buried our feet to the ankle at each step. Near the top, where the slope was almost perpendicular, exhaustion overcame us and every few steps we sank to the ground. All around us we saw tier on tier of lofty sand-hills, giving the lie to our quest, yet when, with a final desperate effort, we hoisted ourselves over the last ridge and looked down on what lay beyond, we saw the lake below, and its beauty was entrancing.

Small, crescent-shaped and sapphire blue, it lay in the narrow space dividing us from the next range like a jewel in folds of warm-tinted sand. On its farther shore stood a small temple surrounded with silvery trees, and on the surface of the lake a flotilla of little black-headed divers were swimming. The downward stretch of the soft slope was an irresistible inducement to slide, and we all came down with a rush, bringing the sand with us like a cataract. Then, for the first time, we experienced the strange sensation of vibrant sands, for as we slid, a loud noise came from the very depths of the hill on which we were, and simultaneously a strong vibration shook the dune as though the strings of some gigantic musical instrument were twanged beneath us. We had, unknowingly, chosen for our slide one of the resonant surfaces of the hill, for, curiously enough, only a few of the dunes are musical and most of them are as silent as they are dead.

The long descent landed us on the edge of the lake and a short distance from the temple door, where the priest received us and led us to a pleasant room in the guests' courtyard.

"You heard the *lui-ing* (thunder-roll) of the hills as you came down," he said. "The sound reached us here, for you chose the right spot to set the sands thundering. Had you been a little farther to east or west, the noise would have been much fainter, and had you come down that farther hill, nothing would have been heard."

"I never knew sands with a 'thunder voice' before," I said.

"You will hear it often while you stay here," was his answer.

This was true, and whenever the wind blew in a certain quarter a roaring came from the dunes. Once, at midnight, we were awakened by a sound like a roll of drums. On that occasion there were brigands in the neighbourhood, and I jumped up in alarm, fearing an attack, but the priest heard me and called out:

"Don't be anxious, Lady. It is only the drum-roll of our sand-hills. Rest your heart."

The old man was quite satisfied to attribute the mysterious noise to the action of the gods whose shrine he tended so carefully, but we were curious to know more about it and began to study the subject. Marco Polo passed this way nearly seven hundred years ago, and he reported desert sand-hills which emitted a sound like distant thunder. These very dunes must have been the "rumbling sands" to which he referred. We also read of "singing sands" in the Arabian desert where Dr. Bertram Thomas and his companions heard a loud noise, which he describes as being like the sound of a ship's siren, coming from some steep sand-hills of which the wind was lifting the crest with a curl like a centurion's helmet. The Arab desert dwellers were familiar with the sound and called that dune "the bellowing sand-hill" because its voice reminded them of the loud bellow of a bull camel. In the Sinai Peninsula, also, travellers have spoken of a locality called "the Hill of the Bell" where a clanging noise is sometimes heard.

The musical sands which are found in these various localities all present special features of dryness and smoothness, for in deserts the transport of sand is effected solely by the wind, and the grains are so constantly rolled to and fro along the ground that each particle becomes smooth, rounded and polished. No such easy explanation, however, is forthcoming of the undoubted fact that one slope "sings" when another, close by, remains silent, and that one course will give a much louder sound than the other. The sands of the Tun-hwang dunes are composed of the tiniest fragments of multi-coloured quartz, blue, green, red, purple, grey and white, and this blend of colours gives an iridescent sheen to the sand-hills which responds to every change of light and shade. The sand-girt lake is referred to in many Chinese books as one of the beauty spots of Central Asia, and an envoy sent to Khotan from the Imperial Court in A.D. 938 spoke of its charm and of the towering dunes, which he estimated as five hundred feet in height. A modern explorer quotes this calculation as evidence of the careful, reliable observations made by these early travellers.

All the temple buildings were on the south side of the lake and terraced down to a flight of steps which led to the water's edge. The shrines were neither very large nor very noteworthy, but they filled the narrow level space between the water and the second range of sand-hills. A grove of trees shaded the courtyard, and the lake water lapped the narrow shore at the foot of some steps which led to a *loggia*. All was bathed in peace, silence and utter restfulness. The hostel was seldom without a pilgrim guest. There were no rules for visitors, but the enclosure was instinct with quiet, and the atmosphere of pervading peace exercised its own control. There were no loud voices and no hasty movements among those who came and went, for the lake was regarded as a place of peculiar sanctity, and was commonly referred to as the "back door of Paradise." Sick people sometimes came from the city to seek healing of the body at the sacred spring, and renewal of the mind in the quiet of meditation.

One of the most frequent pilgrim visitors was a fantastic figure who spent most of his time travelling among Tibetan lamaseries and constantly spoke of an impending journey to Lhasa on which, according to him, the fortunes of the world depended. Two mirrors were fixed above his forehead, and in them he liked to think that he could discern the past and gaze into the future. A passport to Lhasa was draped round his broad-brimmed hat, and his pretensions to occult knowledge were considerable. Very devout in all religious observances, he declared himself to have been appointed "Messenger of Peace to all nations." He said that at a given signal he must rally the peoples of the world to unity and concord, but until that hour there would be strife and tumult. In the course of our many long talks he professed to be deeply impressed by what he heard, and he certainly read the gospels carefully, and carried them when he went on pilgrimage. "I must tell all this to the lamas," he would often say, but he remained convinced that the issues of world peace were committed to his keeping, and that the hour for action would only be revealed to him through the reflections in his magic mirrors.

The guardian priest was a self-respecting, hard-working man who lived a quiet retired life in this hidden oasis. He was helped by two acolytes, and there was plenty of work for them all. The elder was a lame youth who realised to the full the prestige which he had acquired in being admitted to the temple staff. He liked his present work much better than his former occupation, which was that of shepherd boy, as he was always at a disadvantage with the flock on account of his deformed foot and limping gait. The junior helper was a deaf-mute child who did all the odd jobs and searched the sands daily, basket on arm, for fragments of fuel to feed the kitchen fire. Between them they kept the temple land in good order, grew a few rows of cabbages, tended the shrines, sounded the bells, burned incense and observed all the required ceremonies, besides welcoming and caring for the pilgrims. Every guest who came brought some contribution to the store of food, and generous hospitality was the law of the house.

We once claimed that hospitality at mid-winter when the lake was a sheet of grey ice swept by bitter winds. A brigand band had commandeered our town quarters and we were left shelterless, but the guardian welcomed us as old friends and placed part of the guest-house at our disposal, for at that season pilgrims were few. In January when the blizzards blew up, or winter sand-storms blotted out the sun, the dunes were terrifying in their desolation. To be lost among them would be certain death, yet one stormy day, standing on the summit of the "thunder-sound slope," I saw a short string of camels appear between two ridges and descend toward the plain.

"Where have those camels come from?" I asked the guardian.

"They come from the charcoal-burners' camp," was the reply.

"Charcoal-burners!" I said with amazement. "Where do they get the wood for burning charcoal?"

"From dried-up tamarisk plantations," he said. "All through the winter there are people up there, but they can only stay between the eleventh and the second moons (November to February). The camels you saw had carried up blocks of ice for the men's water-supply and were coming back laden with charcoal."

I thus learnt that far back among the hills was a place where once there had been water. None now remained, but clumps of desiccated tamarisk and saksaul (*Anabasis ammondendron*) were still there. In this place a family of charcoal-burners spent four of the winter months each year. Every week the string of camels went to them laden with flour and blocks of ice, and returned to Tunhwang with a load of charcoal. At the first sign of thaw the traffic ceased, and all moved back to the city.

In early summer the borders of the lake were made even more delightful by the exquisite fragrance of the sand-jujube (*Eloeagnus latifolia*). Hidden among its silver leaves are small flowers which embalm the air with their perfume. The people of Turkestan always associate this scent with a story which is told in every home. It is related that among the prisoners of war who were carried away to Peking in the eighteenth century, from the lands beyond the Gobi Desert, was a beautiful Kashgarian girl who won the love of the Emperor Chien Lung. He lavished on her all that wealth could supply, yet still she sighed for her distant home. He built up a Kashgarian landscape in the palace grounds, and constructed a mosque within sight of her windows. In her own garden he erected a pavilion called the "Homeward-Gazing Tower" from which she might look beyond the mosque and picture far-distant Kashgar. Yet all his trouble was in vain and he could never make the exile happy. Her longings have been expressed in verse:

'Tis very like my home. From yonder tower,
Breaking the stillness of the twilight hour,
In the soft accents of my native tongue,
I hear the ballads of my country sung.
But that is all, there the resemblance ends
That only makes me grieve and crave for more;
I long for other voices, those of friends;
'Twould then be like the home I had before.
'Tis very like my home. But yet its walls
Too oft and much my other home recalls;
Filling my breast with many a vain regret,
With recollections I would fain forget.
'Twas built in kindness, yet 'tis mockery;
It makes me pine, when he would have me gay;
Why do I look? O! that my home should be
So very near and yet so far away.

What more could she need? the Emperor asked himself, and one day she told him: "I long for the fragrance of that tree whose leaves are silver and whose fruit is gold." Messengers were dispatched to Kashgaria, where they found the silver-leaved sand-jujube with its golden fruit, and when this tree was planted in her garden and the wind wafted its exquisite fragrance through her pavilion windows, her distant home seemed nearer than before, and her heart found solace in the illusion.

It is said that musical sands will give out a sound even in a laboratory far from their native dunes. It may be, yet sometimes in my London home I take up a handful of Crescent Lake sand and try to make it sing, but I listen in vain for the echo of the thunder-roll of its voice. Between the leaves of a book I have pressed a small branch of sand-jujube flowers, and whenever I catch its subtle but fading fragrance, I, like the Kashgarian exile, long for a place that seems so near and is yet so far away. Sick with longing I walk among the crowds while my spirit flees to the quiet which is found by the hidden lake among the dunes.

On Foot Across the Gobi

Slavomir Rawicz

Cavalry officer Slavomir Rawicz was captured by the Red Army in 1939 during the German-Soviet partition of Poland and sent to the Siberian Gulag along with other captive Poles, Finns, Ukranians, Czechs, Greeks, and even a few English, French, and American unfortunates who had been caught up in the fighting. A year later he and six comrades from various countries escaped from a labor camp in Yakutsk and made their way on foot nearly three thousand miles south to British India. As he recounts in his notable memoir *The Long Walk*, he later rejoined the Polish Army and fought against Germany for the rest of World War II.

Here Rawicz recounts his party's descent from the Gobi, where they had nearly met their end, to the high steppes of Tibet.

Eagles live in mountains," said the American. "Perhaps we haven't far to go to get out of the desert."

We could see a long way ahead and there were no distant mountains. "They can also fly great distances," I said.

For three or four days we were tormented with stomach pain and its attendant diarrhoea; then, as we began to long for water again, the stomach trouble passed away. As we trudged on there were days when we caught not a glimpse of a snake. Another day and we would pick up a couple basking in the sun in a morning's search. We ate them as soon as we found them. There was a red-letter day when we caught two of the kind we called Big Blacks within half-an-hour. The days dragged by. We were inspected again by both the ravens and the eagles. We were able now to make a fix on a couple of bright stars and sometimes walked long after dark. We began again to dream longing dreams of water.

I lost count of the days again. My fitful sleep was invaded by visions of reptiles so tenacious of life that though I beat at them with my club in a frenzy they still hissed at me and crawled. All my fears came bursting through in dreams. Worst of all was the picture of myself staggering on alone, shouting for the others and knowing that I should never see them again. I would wake shivering in the morning cold and be happily reassured to see Smith, Kolemenos, Zaro, Marchinkovas and Paluchowicz close about me.

Almost imperceptibly the terrain was changing. The yellow sand was deepening in colour, the grains were coarser, the smooth topped dunes taller. The sun still burned its shrivelling way across the blue, unclouded heavens but now there were days when a gentle breeze sighed out from the south and there was a hint of coolness in its caress. The nights were really cold and I had the impression that we were day by day gradually climbing out of the great heat-bowl.

It might have been a week or eight days after leaving the creek that we awoke to discover in a quickening of excitement and hope a new horizon. The day was sharply clear. Far over to the east, perhaps fifty miles away, shrouded in a blue haze like lingering tobacco smoke, a mountain range towered. Directly ahead there were also heights but they were mere foothills compared with the eastward eminences. So uninformed were we of Central Asian geography that we speculated on the possibility that the tall eastern barrier could be the Himalayas, that somehow we had by-passed them to the west, that we might even be on the threshold of India. We were to learn that the whole considerable north-to-south expanse of Tibet, ruggedly harsh and mountainous, lay between us and the Himalayas.

We plodded on for two more exhausting, heart-breaking days before we reached firm ground, a waste of lightly-sanded rocks. We lay there in the extremity of our weakness and looked back at our tracks through the sand. There were no defined footmarks, only a dragging trail such as skis make in snow. Lifeless and naked the rocky ridge sloped easily into the distance above us. In my mind was the one thought that over the hump there might be water. We rested a couple of hours before we tackled the drag upwards. We took off our moccasins and emptied them of sand. We brushed the fine dust from between our toes. Then we went up and out of the Gobi.

Over the ridge there was more desolation. By nightfall we had dropped down into a stone-strewn valley. We might have struggled on longer but Marchinkovas fell and banged his knee. In the morning he showed us a big bruise and complained of a little stiffness but was able to walk. The pain passed off as he exercised it and he experienced no more trouble from the injury. We climbed again. There was no talking because none of us could spare the breath and movement of the lips was agony. We hauled ourselves along through a faint dawn mist and did not reach this next summit for several hours. From the top there was the view again of the great range to the east, looking even more formidable than at our first sight of it. Ahead there seemed to be an unbroken succession of low ridges corrugating the country as far as we could see. Below us the floor of the valley appeared to be covered with sand and we decided to get down before dark to search for snakes.

It was the merest accident that we did not miss the water on our way down. We had all passed it when Zaro turned round and yelled the one wonderful word. It was no more than a trickle from a crack in a rock but it glinted like silver. It crept down over the curve of a big round boulder and spread thinly over a flat rock below. Kolemenos and I had been picking our way down the slope some twenty yards ahead of Zaro when his shout arrested us. We turned quickly and scrambled back. We found that the source of the little spring was a crack just wide enough to take the fingers of one hand. The water was sparkling, clean and ice-cold. We channeled the tiny stream to a point where we could lead it into our battered and much travelled metal mug, and sat down impatiently to watch it fill. The operation took fully ten minutes.

I said to Zaro, "You had passed this point. What made you turn round and find it?"

Zaro spoke quite seriously. "I think I must have smelt it. It was quite a strong impulse that made me turn my head."

The water tinkled musically into the mug until it was brimming. Carefully Zaro lifted it away and I noticed his hand was trembling a little so that some of the water spilled over. He faced Smith and with a bow and, in imitation of the Mongolian etiquette of serving the senior first, handed him the water. The mug was passed round and each man took a gulp. No nectar of the gods could have tasted so wonderful. Again and again we filled the mug and drank. And then we left it, full and running over, under the life-giving spring so that any of us could drink whenever he felt like it.

The time was around the middle of the day. We agreed readily that we should stay close to the spring for another twenty-four hours, but up here on the hillside nothing lived—and we were very hungry. I volunteered to go down into the sandy valley to search for a snake and Zaro said he would come with me. We took the two forked sticks and set off, turning at intervals to look back and fix the position of the squatting group about the spring.

The descent took us over an hour and the heat shimmered off the sandy, boulder-strewn floor of the valley. Our hopes were immediately raised by seeing a snake about a yard long slither away at our approach and disappear under a rock but we foraged around well into the afternoon after that without seeing another living thing. Then we parted and went opposite ways and I had almost decided it was time to give up the quest when I heard Zaro let out a whoop of triumph. I ran to him and found him pinning down a Big Black which was thrashing about desperately in an effort to break free. I reversed my stick and battered it to death. I put my arm about Zaro's shoulders and congratulated him. He was always our Number One snake-catcher.

Zaro wore his capture like a trophy about his neck as we toiled back up the hillside. We were soaked with sweat and exhausted by the time we reached the spring and Kolemenos took over my usual job of skinning and preparing the snake for the fire. Paluchowicz had laid a fire from our few remaining sticks on which was placed the last piece of camel dung which Zaro had gathered at the oasis. There was not enough heat to cook the meat thoroughly but we were too hungry to be squeamish. We ate and we drank as the sun went down. Only Kolemenos slept well that night; for the rest of us it was too cold for comfort.

The next morning we were on our way again. This time there were no stomach cramps, which led us to believe that we owed at least some of the previous trouble to the muddy creek. We travailed down the lone slope, across the hot valley and up the hillside facing us—a total of at least fifteen miles. From the top of the ridge we took fresh bearings. Directly ahead were some formidable heights, so we set our course over easier ground about ten degrees east of the line due south. Towards evening we were heartened by the discovery of the first vegetation we had seen since the oasis. It was a rough, spiky grass clinging hardily to dry rootholds in fissures between the rocks. We pulled up a clump, handed it round and closely examined it like men who had never seen grass before.

The wearing trek went on day after day. Our diet was still confined to an occasional snake—we lived on them altogether for upwards of three weeks from the time of our first sampling back in the desert. The nights set in with a chill which produced a frosty white rime on the stones of the upper hillsides. In vain we looked for signs of animal life, but there were birds: from time to time a pair of hovering hawks, some gossiping magpies and our old acquaintances the ravens. The wiry mountain grass grew more abundant with each passing day and its colour was greener. Then the country presented us with struggling low bushes and longrowing dwarf trees, ideal fuel for the fires which we now started to light every night. The spectre of thirst receded as we found clear-running rivulets. It was rare now that we had to go waterless for longer than a day.

There came a day when we breasted the top of a long rise and looked unbelievingly down into a wide-spreading valley which showed far below the lush green of grazing grass. Still more exciting, there were, crawling like specks five miles or more distant from and below us, a flock of about a hundred sheep. We made the descent fast, slipping and sliding in our eagerness to get down. As we got nearer we heard the bleating and calling of the sheep. We had about a quarter of a mile to go to reach the flock when we saw the two dogs, long-coated liver-and-white collie types. They came racing round the flock to take up station between us and their charges.

Zaro called out to them, "Don't worry, we won't hurt them. Where's your master?" The dogs eyed him warily.

Kolemenos growled, "I only need to get near enough to a sheep for one swing of my old axe. . . ."

"Don't get impatient, Anastazi," I told him. "It is fairly obvious the shepherd has sent his dogs over here to intercept us. Let us swing away from the flock and see if they will lead us to their master."

We turned pointedly away. The dogs watched us closely for a couple of minutes. Then, apparently satisfied, they had headed us away from the sheep, ran off at great speed together towards the opposite slope of the valley. My eyes followed the line of their run ahead of them and then I shouted and pointed. A mile or more away rose a thin wisp of smoke.

"A fire at midday can only mean cooking," said Marchinkovas hopefully.

The fire was burning in the lee of a rocky outcrop against which had been built a one-man shelter of stones laid one above the other as in an old cairn. Seated there was an old man, his two dogs, tongues lolling, beside him. He spoke to his dogs as we neared him and they got up and raced off back across the valley to the flock. Steaming over the fire was a black iron cauldron. The American went to the front and approached bowing. The old man rose smiling and returned the bow and then went on to bow to each of us in turn.

He was white-bearded. The high cheek-bones in his broad, square face showed a skin which had been weathered to the colour of old rosewood. He wore a warm goatskin cap with ear-flaps turned up over the crown in the fashion of the Mongols we had met in the north. His felt boots were well made and had stout leather soles. His unfastened three-quarter-length sheepskin coat was held to the body by a woven wool girdle and his trousers were bulkily padded, probably with lamb's-wool. He leaned his weight on a five-feet-tall wooden staff, the lower end of which was ironspiked and the upper part terminating in a flattened "V" crutch formed by the bifurcation of the original branch. In a leatherbound wooden sheath he carried a bone-handled knife which I later observed was double-edged and of good workmanship. To greet us he got up from a rug of untreated sheepskin. There was no doubt of his friendliness and his pleasure at the arrival of unexpected visitors.

He talked eagerly and it was a minute or two before he realised we did not understand a word. I spoke in Russian and he regarded me blankly. It was a great pity because he must have been looking forward to conversation and the exchange of news. I think he was trying to tell us he had seen us a long way off and had prepared food against our arrival. He motioned us to sit near the fire and resumed the stirring of the pot which our coming had interrupted. I looked into the stone shelter and saw there was just room for one man to sleep. On the floor was a sleeping mat fashioned from bast.

As he wielded his big wooden spoon he made another attempt at conversation. He spoke slowly. It was no use. For a while there was silence. Mister Smith cleared his throat. He gestured with his arm around the group of us. "We," he said slowly in Russian, "go to Lhasa." The shepherd's eyes grew intelligent. "Lhasa, Lhasa," Smith repeated, and pointed south. From inside his jacket the old fellow pulled out a prayer-wheel which looked as if it had been with him for many years. The religious signs were painted on parchment, the edges of which were worn with use. He pointed to the sun and made circles, many of them, with his outstretched arm.

"He is trying to tell us how many days it will take us to reach Lhasa," I said.

"His arm's going round like a windmill," observed Zaro. "It must be a hell of a long way from here."

Exile

Li T'ai Po and Li Yi

Chinese governments have long used the mere threat of exile to the
western deserts as a means of controlling dissent, and they have just as
often acted on the threat.

In this elegant lyric, "The Exile's Letter," the famed Chinese poet Li
T'ai Po (A.D. 701–762) recounts the pain of that banishment in the face of
memories of happier days.

To So-Kiu of Rakuyo, ancient friend, Chancellor Gen.
Now I remember that you built me a special tavern
By the south side of the bridge at Ten-shin
With yellow gold and white jewels, we paid for songs and laughter
And we were drunk for month on month, forgetting the kings and
    princes.
Intelligent men came drifting in from the sea and from the west
    border,
And with them, and with you especially
There was nothing at cross purpose,
And they made nothing of sea-crossing or of mountain-crossing,
If only they could be of that fellowship,
And we all spoke out our hearts and minds, without regret.
And then I was sent off to South Wai, smothered in laurel groves,
And you to the north of Raku-hoku,
Till we had nothing but thoughts and memories in common.
And then, when separation had come to its worst
We met, and travelled into Sen-jo,
Through all the thirty-six folds of the turning and twisting waters,
Into a valley of the thousand bright flowers,
That was the first valley;

And into ten thousand valleys full of voices and pine-winds.
And with silver harness and reins of gold,
Out came the East of Kan foreman and his company.
And there came also the "True man" of Shi-yo to meet me,
Lying on a jewelled mouth-organ.
In the storied houses of San-ka they gave us more Sennin music,
Many instruments like the sound of young phoenix broods
The foreman of Kan-chu, drunk, danced because his long sleeves
    wouldn't keep still
With that music playing,
And I, wrapped in brocade, went to sleep with my head on his lap,
And my spirit so high it was all over the heavens,
And before the end of the day we were scattered like stars, or rain.
I had to be off to So, far away over the waters,
You back to your river-bridge.

And your father, who was brave as a leopard,
Was governor in Hei Shu, and put down the barbarian rabble. And
    one May he had you send for me, despite the long distance.
And what with broken wheels and so on, I won't say it wasn't hard
    going,
Over roads twisted like sheep's guts.
And I was still going, late in the year, in the cutting wind from the
    North,
And thinking how little you cared for the cost, and you caring
    enough to pay it.
And what a reception:
Red jade cups, food well set on a blue jewelled table,
And I was drunk, and had no thought of returning.
And you would walk out with me to the western corner of the castle,
To the dynastic temple, with water about it clear as blue jade,

With boats floating, and the sound of mouth-organs and drums,
With ripples like dragon-scales, going grass green
on the water, Pleasure lasting, with courtezans, going and coming
    without hindrance,
With the willow flakes falling like snow,
And the vermilioned girls getting drunk about sunset,
And the water, a hundred feet deep, reflecting green eyebrows
—Eyebrows painted green are a fine sight in young moonlight,
Gracefully painted—
And the girls singing back at each other,
Dancing in transparent brocade,
And the wind lifting the song, and interrupting it,
Tossing it up under the clouds.
    And all this comes to an end.
    And is not again to be met with.
I went up to the court for examination,
Tried Yo Yu's luck, offered the Choyo song,
And got no promotion,
    and went back to the East Mountains
    White-headed.
And once again, later, we met at the South bridge-head.
And then the crowd broke up, you went north to San palace,
And if you ask how I regret that parting:
It is like the flowers falling at Spring's end
    Confused, whirled in a tangle.
What is the use of talking, and there is no end of talking,
There is no end of things in the heart.
I call in the boy,
Have him sit on his knees here to seal this,
And send it a thousand miles, thinking.
    Translated by Ezra Pound

Li Yi (A.D. 749–829), a scholar and court poet for Emperor Hsien-tung, was never happy with his leisurely life in the palace. He asked to be allowed to join the army instead. Hsien-tung dispatched him to the western deserts as a common soldier, and there he lived out his days homesick and forlorn, as he confesses in this lyric:

Before Hui-le Mountain, the sands drift like snow.
Above Shou-hsiang Fortress, the moon glistens like frost.
From somewhere in the desert flutes are playing,
and all night long our soldiers ache for home.

AUSTRALIA

*In the old days people knew how to dream. They did not have to
go to sleep first.*
    Friedrich Nietzche

Geographers of the ancient world had long suspected that the
unknown lower half of the globe sheltered a great "Terra Australis,"
a southern land. Dante Alighieri, with his precise knowledge of
medieval cosmography, even situated the focal point of hell there,
a vast land in which Satan, the great rebel, lay encased in ice. Later
European explorers, among them Díaz, Magellan, and Tasman,
passed right by Terra Australis in their landmark circumnaviga-
tions of the sixteenth and early seventeenth century; by the late
seventeenth century Spanish, English, and Dutch seafarers
had mapped portions of its coast, thinking them to be small
islands, and even Captain James Cook, a methodical explorer,
declared, "As to a southern continent, I do not believe any such
thing exists." Matthew Flinders eventually completed mapping
the coasts from 1801 to 1803, and it was he who gave Australia the
modern form of its long-reserved name.

The Europeans who came to Australia found a thriving
aboriginal population that had come to the long-isolated continent
some 50,000 years earlier, crossing over land bridges from New
Guinea and Indonesia during a period of worldwide glaciations.
These people had learned to live in what is in essence a vast—at
1.3 million square miles—desert fringed by the sea, living on roots,

yams, wild millet, fruit, and the occasional prey animal. They had also developed over the years an elaborate system of custom and ritual, one so sophisticated that the anthropologist Claude Lévi-Strauss has called its inventors "intellectual artistocrats" among the world's peoples. That served them little during much of the European settlement of Australia: hundreds and thousands of aborigines, perhaps even millions, were murdered by the invaders; the last indigenous Tasmanian died on May 11, 1876, his culture wiped out in his lifetime. The English writer Bruce Chatwin observed of that slaughter that "Australia is the only great colonial land mass in which the native population did not fight back. They just folded their arms and looked with a reproachful smile at their murderers, and that made the murderers jittery beyond belief."

Little explored until the last half of the nineteenth century, the arid regions that make up the Great Australian Desert are still largely unsettled; 99 percent of Australia's population still hugs 1 percent of the land, most of it bordering the ocean. The interior served first as a giant prison colony for a century and a half, then as a treasury from which to extract nickel, salt, mineral sands, bauxite, natural gas, platinum, uranium, aluminum, manganese, molybdenum, and copper. The desert also served as the proving ground for England's nuclear weapons program in the 1950s and 1960s, the subject of Michael Pattinson's 1987 film *Ground Zero*. But growing environmental and aboriginal rights movements have brought the interior more and more into world view, and Australians are increasingly coming to appreciate its fragile beauty and the necessity of protecting it from further depredations.

Where the Frost Comes From

Noongahburrah folktale

Like other aboriginal peoples, the Noongahburrah of western Australia possess a rich body of etiological—"just-so"—stories that explain why things are the way they are. This story, gathered by the folklorist and anthropologist K. Langloh Parker in *More Australian Legendary Tales*, explains the mystery of frost.

The Meamei, or Pleiades, once lived on this earth. They were seven sisters remarkable for their beauty. They had long hair to their waist, and their bodies sparkled with icicles. Their father and mother lived among the rocks away on some distant mountain, staying there always, never wandering about as their daughters did. When the sisters used to go hunting, they never joined any other tribes, though many tried from time to time to make friends with them. One large family of boys in particular thought them so beautiful that they wished them to stay with them and be their wives. These boys, the Berai-Berai, used to follow the Meamei about and, watching where they camped, used to leave offerings there for them.

The Berai-Berai had great skill in finding the nests of bees. First they would catch a bee and stick some white down or a white feather with some gum on its back between its hind legs. Then they would let it go and follow it to its nest. The honey found they would put in wirrees (bark containers) and leave at the camp of the Meamei, who ate the honey but listened not to the wooing.

But one day old Wurrunnah (fiery Ancestor) stole two of the girls, capturing them by stratagem. He tried to warm the icicles off them but succeeded only in putting out his fire.

After a term of forced captivity, the two stolen girls were translated to the sky. There they found their five sisters stationed. With them they have since remained, not shining quite so brightly as the other five, having been dulled by the warmth of Wurrunnah's fires.

When the Berai-Berai found that the Meamei had left this earth forever, they were inconsolable. Maidens of their own tribe were offered to them, but as they could not have the Meamei, they would have none. Refusing to be comforted, they would not eat and so pined away and died. The spirits were sorry for them and pleased with their constancy, so they gave them, too, a place in the sky, and there they are still. Orion's sword and belt we call them, but to the Daens (Aborigines) they are still known as the Berai-Berai, the boys.

The Daens say the Berai-Berai still hunt the bees by day and at night dance corroborrees, which the Meamei sing for them. For though the Meamei stay in their own camp at some distance from the Berai-Berai, they are not too far away for their songs to be heard. The Daens say, too, that the Meamei will shine forever as an example to all women on earth.

At one time of the year, in remembrance that they once lived on earth, the Meamei break off some ice from themselves and throw it down. When, on waking in the morning, the Daens see frost everywhere, they say: "The Meamei have not forgotten us. They have thrown some of their ice down. We will show we remember them, too."

Then they take a piece of ice and hold it to the septum of the noses of children who have not already had theirs pierced. When the septums are numb with the cold, they are pierced, and a straw or bone is placed through them. "Now," say the Daens, "these children will be able to sing as the Meamei sing."

A relation of the Meamei was looking down at the earth when the two sisters were being translated to the sky. When he saw how the old man from whom they had escaped ran about blustering and ordering them down again, he was so amused at Wurrunnah's discomfiture, and glad at their escape, that he burst out laughing and has been laughing ever since, being still known as Daendee Ghindamaylan-nah, the laughing star [Venus] to the Daens.

When thunder is heard in the winter time, the Daens say, "There are the Meamei bathing again. That is the noise they make as they jump, doubled up, into the water when playing Bubahlarmay, for whoever makes the loudest flop wins the game, which is a favorite one with the earth people, too." When the noise of the Bubahlarmay of the Meamei is heard, the Daens say, too, "Soon rain will fall, the Meamei will splash the water down. It will reach us in three days."

Aborigines

William Dampier and James Cook

The English pirate William Dampier, who explored some of the western Australian coast in 1688, was the first European to describe the continent's native peoples. He did so in decidedly unflattering terms.

The inhabitants of this country are the most miserable people in the World. The *Hodmadods* [Hottentots] of *Monomatapa*, though a nasty People, yet for Wealth are Gentlemen to these . . . and setting aside their human shape, they differ but little from Brutes. They are tall, strait-bodied, and thin, with small long Limbs. They have great Heads, round Foreheads, and great Brows. Their Eye-lids are always half-closed, to keep the Flies out of their Eyes . . . therefore they cannot see far.

They are long-visaged, and of a very unpleasant aspect; having no one graceful feature in their faces.

They have no houses, but lye in the open Air, without any covering, the Earth being their Bed, and the Heaven their Canopy. . . . The Earth affords them no food at all. There is neither Herb, Pulse, nor any sort of Grain, for them to eat, that we saw; nor any sort of Bird or Beast that they can catch, having no instruments wherewithal to do so.

I did not perceive that they worship anything.

Captain James Cook, who came to Australia a century later, offered a more balanced view.

The natives do not appear to be numberous neither do they seem to live in large bodies but dispers'd in small parties. . . . Those I saw were about as tall as Europeans, of a very dark brown color but not black nor had they wooly frizled hair, but black, and lank much like ours, No sort of cloathing or ornaments were ever seen by any one of us upon any one of them or in or about any of their hutts, from which I conclude that they never wear any. . . . However we could not know but very little of their customs as we never were able to form any connections with them, they had not so much as touch'd the things we had left in their hutts on purpose for them to take away. . . . From what I have said of the Natives of New Holland they may appear to some to be the most wretched people upon Earth, but in reality they are far more happier than we Europeans; being wholly unacquainted not only with the superfluous but the necessary Conveniences so much sought after in Europe, they are happy in not knowing the use of them. They live in a Tranquillity which is not disturb'd by the Inequality of Condition: the Earth and sea of their own accord furnishes them with all things necessary for life, they covet not magnificent Houses, Household-stuff &c., they live in a

warm and fine Climate and enjoy a very wholsome air, so that they
have very little need of Clothing and this they seem to be fully sen-
cible of, for many to whome we gave Cloth &c. to, left it carelessly
upon the Sea beach and in the woods as a thing they had no manner
of use for. In short they seem'd to set no Value upon any thing of their
own for any one article we could offer them; this in my own opinion
argues that they think themselves provided with all the necessarys
of Life and that they have no superfluities.

The Simpson Desert

Charles Sturt

Charles Sturt (1795–1869) was one of the first English explorers to
venture into the Australian interior. On his first and second expeditions he
discovered the Darling River and Lake Alexandrina on the southern coast
of New South Wales; a decade after having been appointed surveyor
general of South Australia in 1833, he set out to map the Simpson Desert.
He returned from that expedition in 1845 blind, his eyes seared by the
fiery sun on the sand. After returning to England, he dictated an account of
his voyage into the interior, from which this excerpt is taken.

On gaining the top of [a] ridge, we saw an open box-tree forest,
and a small column of smoke rising up from amongst the tress, towards which we silently bent our steps. Our approach had however
been noticed by the natives, who no doubt were at the place not a
minute before, but had now fled. We then pushed on through the
forest, the ground beneath our horses' feet being destitute of vegetation, and the soil composed of a whitish clay, so peculiar to the
flooded lands of the interior. The farther we entered the depths of

the forest, the more did the notes of birds assail our ears. Cockatoos, parrots, calodera, pigeons, crows, etc., all made that solitude ring with their wild notes, and as (with the exception of the ducks on the southern side of the Stony Desert) we had not seen any of the feathered race for many days, we were now astonished at their numbers and variety. About an hour before sunset we arrived on the banks of a large creek, with a bed of couch grass, but no water. The appearance of this creek, however, was so promising that we momentarily expected to see a pond glittering before us, but rode on until sunset ere we arrived at a place which had attracted our attention as we approached it. Somewhat to the right, but in the bed of the creek, there were two magnificent trees, the forest still extending back on either side. Beneath these trees there was a large mound of earth, that appeared to have been thrown up. On reaching the spot we discovered a well of very unusual dimensions, and as there was water in it, we halted for the night.

On a closer examination of the locality, this well appeared to be of great value to the inhabitants. It was 22 feet deep and 8 feet broad at the top. There was a landing place, but no steps down to it, and a recess had been made to hold the water, which was slightly brackish, the rim of the basin being incrusted with salt. Paths led from this spot to almost every point of the compass, and in walking along one to the left, I came on a village consisting of nineteen huts, but there were not any signs of recent occupation. Troughs and stones for grinding seed were lying about, with broken spears and shields, but it was evident that the inhabitants were now dispersed in other places, and only assembled here to collect the box-tree seeds, for small boughs of that tree were lying in heaps on the ground, and the trees themselves bore the marks of having been stripped. There were two or three huts in the village of large size, to each of which two smaller ones were attached, opening into its main apartment, but none of them had been left in such order as those I have already described.

It being the hour of sunset when we reached the well, the trees were crowded with birds of all kinds coming for water, and the reader may judge of the straits to which they were driven, when he learns that they dived down into so dark a chamber to procure the life-sustaining element it contained. The wildest birds of the forest were here obliged to yield to the wants of nature at any risk, but notwithstanding, they were exceedingly wary; and we shot only a few cockatoos. The fact of there being so large a well at this point (a work that must have required the united labour of a powerful tribe to complete), assured us that this distant part of the interior, however useless and forbidding to civilized man, was not without inhabitants, but at the same time it plainly indicated that water must be scarce. Indeed, considering that the birds of the forest had powers of flight to go where they would, I could not but regard it as a most unfavourable sign, that so many had collected here. Had this well contained a sufficiency of water, it would have been of the utmost value to us, but there was not more than enough for our wants, so that, although I should gladly have halted for a day, as our horses were both ill and tired, necessity obliged me to continue my journey, and accordingly on the 29th we resumed our progress into the interior on our original course. At about a mile we broke through the forest, and entered an open earthy plain, such as I believe man never before crossed. Subject to be laid under water by the creek we had just left, and to the effects of an almost vertical sun, its surface was absolutely so rent and torn by solar heat, that there was scarcely room for the horses to tread, and they kept constantly slipping their hind feet into chasms from eight to ten feet deep, into which the earth fell with a hollow rumbling sound, as if into a grave. The poor horse in the cart had a sad task, and it surprised me, how we all at length got safely over the plain, which was between five and six miles in breadth, but we managed it, and at that distance found ourselves on the banks of another creek, in the bed of which there was plenty of grass but no water. I was however exceedingly anxious to give the horses a day's rest; for several of them were seriously griped, and had either taken something that disagreed with them, or were beginning to suffer from constant work and irregularity of food. Mr. Browne too was unwell and Lewis complaining, so that it was advisable to indulge ourselves if possible. I therefore determined to trace the creek downwards, in the hope of finding water, and at a mile came upon a shallow pond where I gladly halted, for by this time several of the horses had swollen to great size, and were evidently in much pain. . . .

[31 Aug. 1845] Our course being one of 335° to the west of north, or nearly N.N.W., and that of the sandy ridges being 340° we necessarily crossed them at a very acute angle, and the horses suffered a good deal. In the afternoon we travelled over large bare plains, of a most difficult and distressing kind, the ground absolutely yawning underneath us, perfectly destitute of vegetation, and denuded of timber, excepting here and there, where a stunted box-tree was to be seen. While on the sand hills, the general covering of which was spinifex, there were a few hakea and low shrubs. On such ground as that whereon we were travelling, it would have been hopeless to look for water, nevertheless our search was constant, but we were obliged to halt without having found any, and to make ourselves as comfortable as we could. All the surface water left by the July rain had disappeared, and what now remained even in the creeks was muddy and thick. It was indeed at the best most disgusting beverage, nor would boiling cause any great sediment. Every here and there, as we travelled along, we passed some holes scooped out by the natives to catch rain, and in some of these there was still a muddy residuum; we moreover observed that the inhabitants of this desert made these holes in places the best adapted to their purpose, where if the slightest shower occurred, the water falling on hard clay would necessarily run into them.

The circumstances under which we halted in the evening of the 31st of August were very embarrassing. It was evident that the country into which we were now advancing was drier and more difficult than the country we had left behind. It was impossible, indeed, to hope that the animals would get on, if it should continue as we had found it thus far. There were numerous high ridges of sand to the westward, in addition to those on the plains, and so full of holes and chasms were the latter, that the horses would soon have been placed *hors de combat*, if they had continued to traverse them. Moreover, I could not but foresee that unless I used great precaution our retreat would be infallibly cut off. Whatever water we had passed, since the morning we commenced our journey over the Stony Desert, was not to be depended upon for more than four or five days, and although we might reckon with some certainty on the native well in the box-tree forest, the supply it had yielded was so very small that we could not expect to obtain more from it than would suffice ourselves and one or two of the horses. Taking all these matters into consideration, I determined on once more turning to the north for a day or two, in order that by keeping along the flats, close under the ridges, I might get firmer travelling for the cart, and in the expectation, that we should be more likely to find water in thus doing, than by crossing the succession of ridges. Accordingly, on the 1st of September, we started on a course of 6° to the west of north, or a N. 1/2 W. course, that allowing for variation, being with 1 1/2 points of a due north course. On this we went up the flat where we had slept. By keeping close to the ridges we found, as I had anticipated, firmer ground, though the center of the flat was still of the worst description. . . .

[4 Sept. 1845] The ridges had now become very long, and varied in breadth from a few hundred yards to a mile. Box-trees were scat-

tered over them, and, although generally bare, they were not altogether destitute of grass or herbage; the ridges of sand, on the
contrary, still continued unbroken, and several were covered with
spinifex; but on the whole the country appeared to be improving,
and the fall of waters being decidedly somewhat to the eastward of
south, or towards the Stony Desert, I entertained hopes that we had
crossed the lowest part of the interior, and reached the southerly
drainage. We were again fortunate in coming on another pond at 20
miles, where we halted, the country round about us wearing an im-
proved appearance. Still our situation was very precarious, and we
were risking a great deal by thus pushing forward, for although I call
the hollows (in which we found the water) ponds, they were strictly
speaking the dregs only of what had been such, and were thick,
black, and muddy; but the present aspect of the country led us to
hope for a favourable change, and on the morning of the 4th we still
held our northerly course up the flat, on which we had travelled the
greater part of the day before. As we advanced, it became more open
and grassy, and at three miles we found a small supply of very tolerable water in the bed of a shallow watercourse. We had ridden about
ten miles from the place where we had slept, and Mr. Browne and I
were talking together when Flood, who was some little distance
ahead, held up his hat and called out to us. We were quite sure from
this circumstance that he had seen something unusual, and on riding up were astonished at finding ourselves on the banks of a beautiful creek, the bed of which was full both of water and grass. The
bank on our side was twenty feet high, and shelved too rapidly to admit of our taking the horses down, but the opposite bank was comparatively low.

Ayers Rock

Baldwin Spencer and F. J. Gillen

Baldwin Spencer, a biologist and pioneering ethnologist at Melbourne University, and F. J. Gillen, a magistrate who took significant measures to protect aboriginal rights in South Australia, made several exploratory trips into the interior a century ago. In their 1912 book *Across Australia*, they write of the natural and human history of the Ayers Rock region at the continent's midpoint.

The natives had carefully avoided us, but after striking camp in the morning, preparatory to starting back to Ayers Rock, we made another attempt to come into contact with them. Fortunately, again, the faithful Lungkartitukukana was with us, and halting at the base of the hill he did his very best to bring the natives down. The contortions of his body as he gesticulated wildly, and at the same time forced out a volume of high-pitched sound, were most remarkable. We could not, of course, understand a word of what he was saying, but his intentions were clear and his efforts were finally successful. Slowly, and evidently not without fear, the blacks came down to us. We treated them to some sugar and fat, but the former, as they had not seen it before, they at first looked upon with suspicion. A savage is always thinking about magic, and to anything which he does not understand he attributes evil magic. However, when we tasted the sugar and no harm came to us, they were reassured and were soon prepared to receive any amount. We made one rather unfortunate mistake. One member of our party was anxious to give them a taste of tea, another in his desire to enter into friendly relations thought of coffee, of which we had a small supply, with the result that the two beverages were mixed in the one can. The infusion was considerably sweetened, but still the natives did not like it, though it was only when comparing notes afterwards that we understood the wry faces made by the men who, partly out of fear and partly out of their desire to please us, were too polite to refuse to drink. They must have gone about for days afterwards in fear and trembling as to the result of the white man's potent drink. To their great delight we gave a few wax matches to one or two of the older men as a mark of distinction, for in Australian tribes it is always well to pay marked attention to the older men, however decrepit they may be. The magic of the matches filled them with respect for us. We had only to rub the brown head of the little white rod on a stone, or even our own bodies, and out from it burst the fire. The matches which we gave them were promptly stowed away amongst their greasy locks and were probably of little use, as they were sure to get damp at night time when the dew fell. That they could not obtain fire from them would be easily explained by the fact that the magic of the white man was stronger than their own, and therefore the white man could obtain fire from them when they were unable to do so.

It was astonishing, when once they realised that we were friendly to them, how quickly the natives placed the most implicit trust in us; and three of the men who, only half an hour before, were in deadly fear of us, now insisted on accompanying us to Ayers Rock. Without any difficulty at all, though we were riding, they kept pace with us, sometimes running, sometimes walking, and all the time they were talking, evidently trying to point out to us the features of the land-scape which were of interest to themselves and which they naturally thought would be of interest to us—as, without doubt, would have been the case, if we could have understood what they were saying.

It was late in the afternoon when we reached our camp. To the west we could see the purple masses of Mt. Olga standing out against the orange-coloured sky. The rays of the setting sun were still shining on the precipitous sides of Ayers Rock, which once more glowed brightly, venetian-red in colour, against the cold, steel-blue of the eastern sky. Gradually the light faded away and there was left only the dim mass of the Rock with the deep chasm in its side, in which we and the natives were camped.

The natives had been lucky enough to catch two kangaroos on the way over, in addition to sundry smaller animals such as lizards. In several places we had set fire to the porcupine grass and the thin scrub, with the result that numbers of smaller animals were driven out of their shelter, to fall a prey both to the natives, who are wonderfully expert in catching them, and to the hawks, who made their appearance, in a most mysterious way, the moment the smoke of a fire was seen. The kangaroo was the common red species (*Macropus rufus*), which is the only kind, so far as we could find out, that inhabits the sterile, plain country in this part of Australia.

As soon as it was dark the natives set to work to prepare their feast, laughing gaily and chattering hard the whole time. They had a good fire, plenty of food and water, and needed nothing more to make them perfectly happy; our presence did not seem to interfere with them in the very least. Sitting round their fire, two of the men began to prepare one of the kangaroos for cooking. The first thing they did was to take the strong tendon out of each hind limb. To do this, the skin was cut through close to the foot, with the stone flake attached to the handle end of a spear-thrower. Without, at first, cutting the tendon itself, a hitch was taken round it, at its lower end, with a digging stick. Then with one foot against the animal's rump, each man pulled steadily until the upper end of the tendon gave way and he could draw it out. Then, with the loose end held in the mouth, the tendon being stretched to its full extent, the lower attachment was cut with the stone flake. After being thus carefully extracted it was rolled up and stowed away in the man's waist girdle. A tendon such as this, obtained from kangaroos and emus, is of greatest value to the savage. He uses it for such purposes as that of fixing the point on to the end of his spears and spear-throwers, binding round the splicings on the shaft of his spear or mending broken implements, in the same way as we should use string or wire. The tendon is damped so as to make it pliant, and, as it dries, of course it contracts and exerts a strong pull. Every native is provided with a sharp flint and tendon, just as every white boy has a knife and string.

As soon as the tendons had been successfully extracted, a small opening was made with the flake in the animal's body, and through this all the intestines were pulled out and cut off. The sides of the cut were fastened together with a wooden skewer, the tail cut off at the stump and the limbs dislocated. As a general rule, amongst the Arunta people at all events, as soon as ever an animal, such as a kangaroo or wallaby, is killed, its hind limbs are immediately dislocated. This is done, partly to add a feeling of security—that it cannot, even if it returns to life, run away and escape, as many of their ancestral animals are reported to have done—and partly to render its body limp and thus more easy to carry. An animal in this condition is said to be "atnuta," the nearest translation of which is our word "limp," though it also implies a condition of helplessness.

The intestines were handed to the women and children, who cooked them by means of rubbing them over and over in the hot sand and ashes of the camp fire. Two of the men had meanwhile scooped out a shallow hole with their digging sticks, just large enough to hold the body of the kangaroo, and had lighted a good-sized fire in it. After this had burned down and nothing was left save red hot ashes, the kangaroo was laid on the latter, some of which were piled over it, but not so as to cover it completely. The fur, which had been left on, was singed off or, at least, the greater part of it was, the skin serving to keep the juices within the body. After lying for an hour in the hot ashes, it was supposed to be cooked and was lifted out and placed on small leafy branches, torn from a neighbouring acacia tree. The carving was done by one man, who first of all extended the original cut so that he could take out the liver and heart, which were first eaten. Then, with the aid of a sharp digging stick, he cut the body up, very roughly indeed, into joints, using his teeth to aid him in tearing off the burnt skin and helping himself to such dainty morsels as the kidneys as he went along. There did not appear to be any special portion given to any particular individual, everyone, men, women and children, receiving a share, though of course the men were supplied before the women. The animal was, at best, only half cooked—some parts were almost raw—and those who wished their portion better cooked, simply rubbed it up and down in the hot ashes until it was done to his, or her, taste.

The sight was not at all an appetising one, and the savages looked more like wild beasts gnawing their prey than human beings; but it was intensely interesting to us, as it was the first time on which we had really come into personal contact with the absolutely wild Australian savage. We saw him, first of all, capture his prey with his sharp-pointed wooden spear. Then, quite ignorant of metal knife, he had extracted the tendons and cut its body open with a sharp stone flake and had cooked it on a fire made by rubbing two pieces of wood, a hard and a soft one, on each other. It was a truly wild scene. Our camp fires lighted up the rocks that hemmed in the chasm in which we were camped and shone upon the bodies of the natives. As we rolled our rugs round us on the hard ground and watched the stars shining down through the cleft in the great rock, we realised that we had been carried far back into the early history of mankind and that we had enjoyed an experience such as now falls to the lot of few white men. We had actually seen, living in their primitive state, entirely uncontaminated by contact with civilisation, men who had not yet passed beyond the palaeolithic stage of culture. In some parts of Australia, where food is more abundant and their sole anxiety is not that of eating it as soon as they get it, cooking arrangements are much more elaborate. A deep hole is dug, at the bottom of which hot stones are placed and these are then covered with green leaves on which the food is laid. Then comes another layer of leaves so as completely to protect the food from contact with the earth with which the hole is finally filled. Those who have tasted meat cooked in this way will realise that the savage method is not to be despised. It has the great advantage of retaining all the natural juices within the meat, more especially if the operation be conducted in circumstances which allow of a really efficient coating over the joint, such as can be provided by a layer of flour paste. A leg of mutton thus cooked is decidedly superior to the ordinary article, but perhaps the fact that one only cooks in this way out in the bush, when almost anything is palatable, makes it rather difficult to draw comparisons.

It was late at night before the natives had concluded their feast; in fact we had retired to our camp, a little way from theirs, some time before they coiled themselves around their fires and all was quiet in the dark chasm. We were up early next morning, and, soon after sunrise, started on our return journey to the George Gill Range. Our horses had had plenty to eat and drink, and we pressed on rapidly, crossing Lake Amadeus once more, until we came to the native well called Unterpata, where we hoped to find water. To our disgust we found that another dingo had fallen in since we were there before. Its body had been dragged out by some natives who had visited the well during our absence. As the horses were again thirsty, we tried to persuade them to drink some of the water, which we bailed out into a sheet of canvas, but it was so foul that only one or two of them would even taste it; the smell was quite enough for both them and us, and we carried the evil odour of that sheet of canvas with us for many days as a reminder of the native well. There was nothing for it but to take it in turns to watch the horses all night long, lest, closely hobbled though they were, they should wander away in the hope of finding water somewhere. The night hours passed by very slowly as we paced up and down, for it was cold—so cold that at daybreak our water bags were frozen solid.

After three days' ride we were back again at the George Gill Range, thankful to be camped beside a good waterpool. During the two weeks which had elapsed since we were last there, the water, to our surprise, had considerably increased in quantity, though not a drop of rain had fallen. Except during the very few days when rain is falling, running water is so extremely rarely met with in Central Australia that its occurrence excites great surprise and interest. When, with the camel team, we were camped at this spot a fortnight earlier, there was a series of disconnected, small waterpools in the bed of the creek which came down the valley. A thin stream of water now trickled in and out of them, and the lowest pool, surrounded by bulrushes, was at least three times as large as it was when we were previously camped by its side. The only possible explanation of this is that there is a constant though small supply oozing out of the hills. For the greater part of the year the evaporation is so great that the supply is hardly enough to keep the pools filled; in the cooler, winter months, when we were there, there is no evaporation for perhaps half of the twenty-four hours, or, at most, only a slight one taking place, and, in consequence of this, the supply is just sufficient to maintain a continuous flow. If the desiccation of the Central area continues, the time will come when even the present small flow of water will become less. For a time perhaps there will be a few pools which, for a little while after the rain season, will be filled with water, but the present slight flow, even during the cooler months, will cease, just as it has done already at Ayers Rock and Mt. Olga.

Native Cat Stakes Out His Territory

Pintupi folktale

The Pintupi people live west of Alice Springs in the dry lake country of northwestern Australia. In this story they show how a totemic creature, Native Cat, established a "songline"—a complex native way of naming and claiming tribal boundaries—in antiquity by chasing their forebears from his territory. Fred R. Myers relates the story in his ethnographic study *Pintupi Country, Pintupi Self.*

Native Cat's home country, men say, is Lake Macdonald (Karrku-rutintfinya). While walking near here one day, he came upon a piece of emu fat and saw the tracks of men who had dropped it. He realized that the Tingarri men had speared an emu east of the lake and cooked it at Tikartikanya. Native Cat became angry because the men had sneaked into his country unannounced and not shared the meat with him. He told his two sons at the lake to prepare themselves, for he was going to bring back these people. He started westward then, following the Tingarri men's tracks. These latter had transformed themselves into wild dogs for their return. Heading west at night, he passed the Possum people among the claypans of Yiitjurunya, the most eastward of a north–south line of fairly permanent waters in the sandhill country south of the Pollock Hills.

The possums were a revenge party chasing a man who had eloped with his mother-in-law and fled south from Warlpiri country. Gathered for a ceremony when Native Cat burst into view, they were frightened by his demeanor as he ran up a sandhill and ululated. Native Cat ran down the other side of the sandhill, racing across the claypans in the high-stepping action which men use in ceremonial performances and in displaying anger. He did not speak to the possums as he decorated himself with vegetable fluff in the design used now in ritual to represent him. At this place, a large bloodwood tree arose, marking the spot. Then Native Cat raced up another sandhill and ululated, holding a large ritual object in his hand. To this terrifying and dangerous sight, the possum men sang a verse which is included in the Tingarri song cycles now performed.

Then he headed further westward, finally sleeping near Mintjirnga. In the morning he approached Yintjintfinya, where the women of the Tingarri men were camped. He climbed a sandhill and sent up a smoke. The women saw it and tossed dirt into the air, as people do to ward off a dangerous spirit. Frightened, the women did not speak to him as he turned south for the men at Yawalyurrunya. He approached from the north as he saw smoke rising from a small hole in the ground. The Tingarri men were underground, "inside." From the desert oak on the north side of the site, he called to them. He questioned them in the ritual manner used by older men toward secluded novices. There was no answer, so he hurled a throwing stick at them, but it bounced away. He stepped back then and circled to the south side of the site. He drew on his hairstring belt, grasped another throwing stick and thrust it vertically down into the ground, twisting it back and forth, opening up a huge hole (which is now Yawalyurrunya) "like dynamite."

The first men to see him as they climbed up were those on the north side. They looked around expecting, because of the power displayed, to see many men, but there was only Native Cat. He was sitting on the edge of the sandhill to the south of the hole, crying because he was sorry for these novices whom he had blasted. Where he sat with an arm covering his face, a gnarled tree now represents him. The Tingarri men climbed up his throwing stick, just as contemporary men who care for the north side of the site climb a ladder (tjukalpa) to prepare the increase center. From the black currants (yawalyurru) the Tingarri men had with them inside the ground, it is said, come the black drippings on the walls of the sinkhole. When all the men had climbed out of the hole, they decorated themselves with ceremonial down, the process leaving loose reddish stones on the southern edge. Native Cat told them to leave the black currants behind and go to Kurlkurtanya, to wait for him in the sandstone hills to the east. He sent them away just like children. Because they left the black currants behind, their essence from The Dreaming is still at the place which men visit to make the fruit grow throughout the country.

Rain

Tingarri song

An American anthropologist once asked a Hopi Indian why all his people's songs were about water. Because it's so scarce, the Hopi replied; is that why all your songs are about love? The indigenes of the world's deserts properly hold rain as a treasure, and it marks their literature, as does this traditional Tingarri song.

Forked stick and rafters, floor posts
with a roof like a sea eagle's nest
lie by a billabong where goose eggs
give the water its huge expanse.

My people build, thinking of rain—
rain and wind from the west, clouds
slowly spreading over the billabong—
while we raise our grass huts.

Our chests heave like clouds
as we call out for the rain to fall.
Rain! dampen us with your deluge
as soon as we build our shelters.

The Music of the Desert

Bruce Chatwin

"In my childhood," Bruce Chatwin writes in his magnificent book *The Songlines*, "I never heard the word 'Australia' without calling to mind the fumes of the eucalyptus inhaler and an incessant red country populated by sheep." The adult Chatwin went to Australia as part of a study of the world's nomadic peoples; the result, a deep appreciation of native ways of knowing, is an amalgam of travelogue, ethnography, commonplace book, and philosophical treatise, a book quite unlike any other.

The Land Cruiser bumped and lurched along a double rut of dust, the bushes brushing the underside of the chassis. Alan sat in front with Timmy, with his rifle upright between his knees. Marian followed hard after, with the ladies. We crossed a sandy gully and had to change to four-wheel drive. A black horse reared up, whinnied and galloped off.

On ahead the country was open woodland. The trees made dark stripes of shadow over the grass and the ghost-gums, at this orange hour of the evening, seemed to float above the ground, like balloons that had let down their anchors.

Alan raised his hand for Arkady to stop, whipped the .22 through the window and fired into a bush. A female kangaroo and young broke cover and leaped away in great lolloping bounds, their haunches white against the grey of the scrub. Alan fired again, and again. Then he and the man in blue jumped out and sprinted after them.

"Giant red," said Arkady. "They come out for water at sunset."

"Did he hit her?"

"Don't think so," he said. "No. Look, they're coming back."

Alan's hat showed up first, above the level of the grass heads. The man in blue's shirt was ripped at the shoulder, and he was bleeding from a thorn scratch.

"Bad luck, old man," said Arkady to Alan.

Alan re-cocked the rifle and glared from the window.

The sun was touching the treetops when we came to a wind-pump and some abandoned stock-pens. There had been a settlement here in the old days. There were heaps of rotted grey timbers and the wreck of a stockman's house. The wind-pump spurted a steady stream of water into two round galvanised tanks.

A flock of galahs sat perched around the rim of the tanks, several hundred of them, pink-crested cockatoos which flew up as we approached and wheeled overhead: the undersides of their wings were the colour of wild roses.

Everyone in the party surrounded a drinking trough, splashed the dirt from their faces, and filled their water-cans.

I made a point of avoiding Marian, but she came up from behind and pinched me on the bum.

"Getting to learn the rules, I see," she grinned.

"Madwoman."

The country away to the east was a flat and treeless waste entirely lacking in cover. Alan kept raising a finger to a solitary bump on the horizon. It was almost dark by the time we reached a small rocky hill, its boulders bursting with the white plumes of spinifex in flower, and a black fuzz of leafless mallee bush.

The hill, said Arkady, was the Lizard Ancestor's resting place.

The party split into two camps, each within earshot of the other. The men settled themselves and their swags in a circle, and began talking in hushed voices. While Arkady unpacked, I went off to hack some firewood.

I had lit the fire, using bark and grass for tinder, when we heard the sound of pandemonium from the women's camp. Everyone was shrieking and howling, and against the light of their fires I could make out Mavis, hopping this way and that, and gesturing to something on the ground.

"What's up?" Arkady called to Marian.

"Snake!" she called back, cheerfully.

It was only a snake-trail in the sand, but that was snake enough to put the women into hysterics.

The men, too, began to get twitchy. Led by Big Tom, they jumped to their feet. Alan re-cocked the .22. The two others armed themselves with sticks; scrutinised the sand; spoke in hoarse, emotional whispers; and waved their arms like hammy Shakespearean actors.

"Take no notice," said Arkady. "They're only showing off. All the same, I think I'll sleep on the roof of the Land Cruiser."

"Chicken!" I said.

For myself, I rigged up a "snakeproof" groundsheet to sleep on, tying each corner to a bush, so its edges were a foot from the ground. Then I began to cook supper.

The fire was far too hot for grilling steaks without charring them: I almost charred myself as well. Alan looked on with masterful indifference. None of the others gave one word of thanks for their food, but kept passing back their plates for more. Finally, when they were satisfied, they resumed their conference.

"You know who they remind me of?" I said to Arkady. "A boardroom of bankers."

"Which is what they are," he said. "They're deciding how little to give us."

The steak was charred and tough, and after Hanlon's lunch we had very little appetite. We cleared up and went to join the old men's circle. The firelight lapped their faces. The moon came up. We could just discern the profile of the hill.

We sat in silence until Arkady, judging the moment, turned to Alan and asked quietly, in English, "So what's the story of this place, old man?"

Alan gazed into the fire without twitching. The skin stretched taut over his cheekbones and shone. Then, almost imperceptibly, he tilted his head towards the man in blue, who got to his feet and began to mime (with words of pidgin thrown in) the travels of the Lizard Ancestor.

It was a song of how the lizard and his lovely young wife had walked from northern Australia to the Southern Sea, and of how a southerner had seduced the wife and sent him home with a substitute.

I don't know what species of lizard he was supposed to be: whether he was a "jew-lizard" or a "road-runner" or one of those rumpled, angry-looking lizards with ruffs around their necks. All I do know is that the man in blue made the most lifelike lizard you could ever hope to imagine.

He was male and female, seducer and seduced. He was glutton, he was cuckold, he was weary traveller. He would claw his lizard-feet sideways, then freeze and cock his head. He would lift his lower lid to cover the iris, and flick out his lizard-tongue. He puffed his neck into goitres of rage; and at last, when it was time for him to die, he writhed and wriggled, his movements growing fainter and fainter like the Dying Swan's.

Then his jaw locked, and that was the end.

The man in blue waved towards the hill and, with the triumphant cadence of someone who has told the best of all possible stories, shouted: "That . . . that is where he is!"

The performance had lasted not more than three minutes.

The death of the lizard touched us and made us sad. But Big Tom and Tommy had been in stitches since the wife-swapping episode and went on hooting and cackling long after the man in blue sat down. Even the resigned and beautiful face of old Alan composed itself into a smile. Then one by one they yawned, and spread out their swags, and curled up and went to sleep.

"They must have liked you," Arkady said. "It was their way of saying thanks for the food." We lit a hurricane lamp and sat on a couple of camping-chairs, away from the fire. What we had witnessed, he said, was not of course the *real* Lizard song, but a "false front," or sketch performed for strangers. The real song would have named each waterhole the Lizard Man drank from, each tree he cut a spear from, each cave he slept in, covering the whole long distance of the way. He had understood the pidgin far better than I. This is the version I then jotted down:

The Lizard and his wife set off to walk to the Southern Sea. The wife was young and beautiful and had far lighter skin than her husband. They crossed swamps and rivers until they stopped at a hill—the hill at Middle Bore—and there they slept the night. In the morning they passed the camp of some Dingoes, where a mother was suckling a brood of pups. "Ha!" said the Lizard. "I'll remember those pups and eat them later."

The couple walked on, past Oodnadatta, past Lake Eyre, and came to the sea at Port Augusta. A sharp wind was blowing off the sea, and the Lizard felt cold and began to shiver. He saw, on a headland nearby, the campfire of some Southerners and said to his wife, "Go over to those people and borrow a firestick."

She went. But one of the Southerners, lusting after her lighter skin, made love to her—and she agreed to stay with him. He made his own wife paler by smearing her from head to foot with yellow ochre and sent her, with the firestick, to the solitary traveller. Only when the ochre rubbed off did the Lizard realise his loss. He stamped his feet. He puffed himself up in fury, but, being a stranger in a distant country he was powerless to take revenge. Miserably, he turned for home with his uglier, substitute wife. On the way he stopped to kill and eat the Dingo puppies but these gave him indigestion and made him sick. On reaching the hill at Middle Bore, he lay down and died . . .

And that, as the man in blue told us, was where he was.

Arkady and I sat mulling over this story of an antipodean Helen. The distance from here to Port Augusta, as the crow flew, was roughly 1,100 miles, about twice the distance—so we calculated—from Troy to Ithaca. We tried to imagine an Odyssey with a verse for every twist and turn of the hero's ten-year voyage.

I looked at the Milky Way and said, "You might as well count the stars."

Most tribes, Arkady went on, spoke the language of their immediate neighbour, so the difficulties of communication across a frontier did not exist. The mystery was how a man of Tribe A, living up one end of a Songline, could hear a few bars sung by Tribe Q and, without knowing a word of Q's language, would know exactly what land was being sung.

"Christ!" I said. "Are you telling me that Old Alan here would know the songs for a country a thousand miles away?"

"Most likely."

"Without ever having been there?"

"Yes." One or two ethnomusicologists, he said, had been working on the problem. In the meantime, the best thing was to imagine a little experiment of our own.

Supposing we found, somewhere near Port Augusta, a songman

who knew the Lizard song? Suppose we got him to sing his verses into a tape-recorder and then played the tape to Alan in Kaititj country? The chances were he'd recognise the melody at once—just as we would the "Moonlight" Sonata—but the meaning of the words would escape him. All the same, he'd listen very attentively to the melodic structure. He'd perhaps even ask us to replay a few bars. Then, suddenly, he'd find himself in sync and be able to sing his own words over the "nonsense."

"His own words for country round Port Augusta?"

"Yes," said Arkady.

"Is that what really happens?"

"It is."

"How the hell's it done?"

No one, he said, could be sure. There were people who argued for telepathy. Aboriginals themselves told stories of their songmen whizzing up and down the line in trance. But there was another, more astonishing possibility.

Regardless of the words, it seems the melodic contour of the song describes the nature of the land over which the song passes. So, if the Lizard Man were dragging his heels across the saltpans of Lake Eyre, you could expect a succession of long flats, like Chopin's "Funeral March." If he were skipping up and down the MacDonnell escarpments, you'd have a series of arpeggios and glissandos, like Liszt's "Hungarian Rhapsodies."

Certain phrases, certain combinations of musical notes, are thought to describe the action of the Ancestor's *feet*. One phrase would say, "Salt-pan"; another "Creek-bed," "Spinifex," "Sandhill," "Mulga-scrub," "Rock-face" and so forth. An expert songman, by listening to their order of succession, would count how many times his hero crossed a river, or scaled a ridge—and be able to calculate where, and how far along, a Songline he was.

"He'd be able," said Arkady, "to hear a few bars and say, 'This is Middle Bore' or 'That is Oodnadatta'—where the Ancestor did X or Y or Z."

"So a musical phrase," I said, "is a map reference?"

"Music," said Arkady, "is a memory bank for finding one's way about the world."

"I shall need some time to digest that."

"You've got all night," he smiled. "With the snakes!"

ANTARCTICA

*Antisthenes says that in a certain faraway land the cold is so
intense that words freeze as soon as they are uttered, and after
some time then thaw and become audible, so that words spoken
in winter go unheard until the next summer.*

  Plutarch, *Moralia*

Estimated to be 13,209,000 square miles in area (the geodetic
survey is still incomplete as of late 1994), the vast continent of
Antarctica receives the least precipitation of any region on the
earth. Some scientists maintain that a desert must also contain
soils and vegetation, but most agree that the continent is, in fact,
the planet's largest arid region.

  Greek geographers and astronomers had posited the existence
of a southern pole as long ago as the fifth century B.C., and certain
Polynesian legends suggest that Rarotongan longboats had reached
the continent's encircling ring of pack ice in the seventh century
A.D. Proof positive of the Antarctic came to us only slowly over the
last three centuries, however. The French sailor Bouret de Lozier
came close to the Antarctic Circle in 1738, and he wrote that some
supreme mystery surely lay on the other side. Thirty-five years
later, on January 17, 1773, Captain James Cook did cross that
imaginary line and came to within 1,500 miles of the South Pole,
but great icebergs blocked his progression. Cook noted the area's
abundant sea life while rightly concluding that agricultural
societies could never take root there. Cook's published reports

inspired Samuel Taylor Coleridge's great poem "The Rime of the Ancient Mariner" (1798):

And now there came both mist and snow
And it grew wondrous cold:
And ice, mast-high, came floating by,
As green as emerald.

Cook's journals also found a wide readership among other oceangoers, and the southern ocean soon teemed with whalers and sealers from the United States, Russia, western Europe, and Australia, reaping vast harvests in hitherto unknown seas.

The English sailor Edward Bransfield has been credited with the first sighting of the Antarctic mainland, on January 30, 1820. The first person to gain landfall was the American sealer John Davis, arriving on February 7, 1821; after Davis came a succession of explorers, notably the Scottish cartographer James Clark Ross, who mapped much of the continent in the winter of 1841. The end of the nineteenth and beginning of the twentieth centuries saw fresh interest in the region, as the world's great powers sought to seize portions of the continent for its untold mineral wealth. A series of international accords reserved Antarctica from military occupation by any power, but many nations, from Argentina to Japan (where half the meat consumed comes from whales), Norway to the United States, still look jealously past penguins and nematodes to the continent's vast stores of precious metals, natural gas, and oil.

World's End

Edgar Allan Poe

Edgar Allan Poe (1809–1849) disguised his only published novel, *The Narrative of Arthur Gordon Pym of Nantucket* (1837), as a memoir entrusted to him by a mysterious stranger whom he met in Richmond, Virginia. In fact, the novel—which one critic of the day lambasted as "a rapid succession of improbabilities"—is a strange mix of proto-science fiction, travel account, and horror story that draws heavily on two books Poe knew well, Benjamin Morrell's *Narrative of Four Voyages to the South Seas and Pacific* (1832) and Jeremiah Reynolds's *Address on the Subject of a Surveying and Exploring Expedition to the Pacific Ocean and South Seas* (1836). He may also have been thinking of other false memoirs like *Robinson Crusoe* and *Gulliver's Travels* as he concocted this strange, unfinished story of a whaler's tragic descent into the depths of Antarctica.

We now found ourselves in the wide and desolate Antarctic Ocean, in a latitude exceeding eighty-four degrees, in a frail canoe, and with no provision but the three turtles. The long Polar winter, too, could not be considered as far distant, and it became necessary that we should deliberate well upon the course to be pursued. There were six or seven islands in sight belonging to the same group, and distant from each other about five or six leagues; but upon neither of these had we any intention to venture. In coming from the northward in the *Jane Guy* we had been gradually leaving behind us the severest regions of ice—this, however little it may be in accordance with the generally received notions respecting the Antarctic, was a fact experience would not permit us to deny. To attempt, therefore, getting back, would be folly—especially at so late a period of the season. Only one course seemed to be left open for hope. We resolved to steer boldly to the southward, where there was at least a probability of discovering other lands, and more than a probability of finding a still milder climate.

So far we had found the Antarctic, like the Arctic Ocean, peculiarly free from violent storms or immoderately rough water; but our canoe was, at best, of frail structure, although large, and we set busily to work with a view of rendering her as safe as the limited means in our possession would admit. The body of the boat was of no better material than bark—the bark of a tree unknown. The ribs were of a tough osier, well adapted to the purpose for which it was used. We had fifty feet room from stem to stern, from four to six in breadth, and in depth throughout four feet and a half—the boats thus differing vastly in shape from those of any other inhabitants of the Southern Ocean with whom civilized nations are acquainted. We never did believe them the workmanship of the ignorant islanders who owned them; and some days after this period discovered, by questioning our captive, that they were in fact made by the natives of a group to the southwest of the country where we found them, having fallen accidentally into the hands of our barbarians. What we could do for the security of our boat was very little indeed. Several wide rents were discovered near both ends, and these we contrived to patch up with pieces of woollen jacket. With the help of the superfluous paddles, of which there were a great many, we erected a kind of framework about the bow, so as to break the force of any seas which might threaten to fill us in that quarter. We also set up two paddle blades for masts, placing them opposite each other, one by each gunwale, thus saving the necessity of a yard. To these masts we attached a sail made of our shirts—doing this with some difficulty, as here we could get no assistance from our prisoner whatever, although he had been willing enough to labor in all the other operations. The sight of the linen seemed to affect him in a very singular manner. He could not be prevailed upon to touch it or go near it, shuddering when we attempted to force him, and shrieking out, *Tekeli-li.*

Having completed our arrangements in regard to the security of the canoe, we now set sail to the south-southeast for the present, with the view of weathering the most southerly of the group in sight. This being done, we turned the bow full to the southward. The weather could by no means be considered disagreeable. We had a prevailing and very gentle wind from the northward, a smooth sea, and continual daylight. No ice whatever was to be seen; *nor did I ever see one particle of this after leaving the parallel of Bennett's Islet.* Indeed, the temperature of the water was here far too warm for its existence in any quantity. Having killed the largest of our tortoises, and obtained from him not only food but a copious supply of water, we continued on our course, without any incident of moment, for perhaps seven or eight days, during which period we must have proceeded a vast distance to the southward, as the wind blew constantly with us, and a very strong current set continually in the direction we were pursuing.

MARCH 1. Many unusual phenomena now indicated that we were entering upon a region of novelty and wonder. A high range of light gray vapor appeared constantly in the southern horizon, flaring up occasionally in lofty streaks, now darting from east to west, now from west to east, and again presenting a level and uniform summit—in short, having all the wild variations of the Aurora Borealis. The average height of this vapor, as apparent from our station, was about twenty-five degrees. The temperature of the sea seemed to be increasing momentarily, and there was a very perceptible alteration in its color.

MARCH 2. Today, by repeated questioning of our captive, we came to the knowledge of many particulars in regard to the island of the massacre, its inhabitants, and customs—but with these how can

I now detain the reader? I may say, however, that we learned there were eight islands in the group—that they were governed by a common king, named *Tsalemon* or *Psalemoun*, who resided in one of the smallest of the islands—that the black skins forming the dress of the warriors came from an animal of huge size to be found only in a valley near the court of the king—that the inhabitants of the group fabricated no other boats than the flat-bottomed rafts—the four canoes being all of the kind in their possession, and these having been obtained, by mere accident, from some large island in the southwest—that his own name was Nu-Nu—that he had no knowledge of Bennett's Islet—and that the appellation of the island we had left was *Tsalal*. The commencement of the words *Tsalemon* and *Tsalal* was given with a prolonged hissing sound, which we found it impossible to imitate, even after repeated endeavors, and which was precisely the same with the note of the black bittern we had eaten upon the summit of the hill.

MARCH 3. The heat of the water was now truly remarkable, and its color was undergoing a rapid change, being no longer transparent, but of a milky consistency and hue. In our immediate vicinity it was usually smooth, never so rough as to endanger the canoe—but we were frequently surprised at perceiving, to our right and left, at different distances, sudden and extensive agitations of the surface— these, we at length noticed, were always preceded by wild flickerings in the region of the vapor to the southward.

MARCH 4. Today, with the view of widening our sail, the breeze from the northward dying away perceptibly, I took from my coat pocket a white handkerchief. Nu-Nu was seated at my elbow, and the linen accidentally flaring in his face, he became violently affected with convulsions. These were succeeded by drowsiness and stupor, and low murmurings of *Tekeli-li! Tekeli-li!*

MARCH 5. The wind had entirely ceased, but it was evident that we were still hurrying on to the southward, under the influence of a powerful current. And now, indeed, it would seem reasonable that we should experience some alarm at the turn events were taking—but we felt none. The countenance of Peters indicated nothing of this nature, although it wore at times an expression I could not fathom. The Polar winter appeared to be coming on—but coming without its terrors. I felt a numbness of body and mind—a dreaminess of sensation—but this was all.

MARCH 6. The gray vapor had now arisen many more degrees above the horizon, and was gradually losing its grayness of tint. The heat of the water was extreme, even unpleasant to the touch, and its milky hue was more evident than ever. Today a violent agitation of the water occurred very close to the canoe. It was attended, as usual, with a wild flaring up of the vapor at its summit, and a momentary division at its base. A fine white powder, resembling ashes—but certainly not such—fell over the canoe and over a large surface of the water, as the flickering died away among the vapor and the commotion subsided in the sea. Nu-Nu now threw himself on his face in the bottom of the boat, and no persuasions could induce him to arise.

MARCH 7. This day we questioned Nu-Nu concerning the motives of his countrymen in destroying our companions: but he appeared to be too utterly overcome by terror to afford us any rational reply. He still obstinately lay in the bottom of the boat; and, upon our reiterating the questions as to the motive, made use only of idiotic gesticulations, such as raising with his forefinger the upper lip, and displaying the teeth which lay beneath it. These were black. We had never before seen the teeth of an inhabitant of Tsalal.

MARCH 8. Today there floated by us one of the white animals whose appearance upon the beach at Tsalal had occasioned so wild a commotion among the savages. I would have picked it up, but there came over me a sudden listlessness, and I forbore. The heat of the water still increased, and the hand could no longer be endured within it. Peters spoke little, and I knew not what to think of his apathy. Nu-Nu breathed, and no more.

MARCH 9. The white ashy material fell now continually around us, and in vast quantities. The range of vapor to the southward had arisen prodigiously in the horizon, and began to assume more distinctness of form. I can liken it to nothing but a limitless cataract, rolling silently into the sea from some immense and far-distant rampart in the heaven. The gigantic curtain ranged along the whole extent of the southern horizon. It emitted no sound.

MARCH 21. A sullen darkness now hovered above us—but from out the milky depths of the ocean a luminous glare arose, and stole up along the bulwarks of the boat. We were nearly overwhelmed by the white ashy shower which settled upon us and upon the canoe, but melted into the water as it fell. The summit of the cataract was utterly lost in the dimness and the distance. Yet we were evidently approaching it with a hideous velocity. At intervals there were visible in it wide, yawning, but momentary rents, and from out these rents, within which was a chaos of flitting and indistinct images, there came rushing and mighty, but soundless, winds, tearing up the enkindled ocean in their course.

MARCH 22. The darkness had materially increased, relieved only by the glare of the water thrown back from the white curtain before us. Many gigantic and pallidly white birds flew continuously now from beyond the veil, and their scream was the eternal *Tekeli-li!* as they retreated from our vision. Hereupon Nu-Nu stirred in the bottom of the boat; but upon touching him, we found his spirit departed. And now we rushed into the embraces of the cataract, where a chasm threw itself open to receive us. But there arose in our pathway a shrouded human figure, very far larger in its proportions than any dweller among men. And the hue of the skin of the figure was of the perfect whiteness of the snow.

Death in the Polar Desert

William Bowers and Robert Scott

In the early years of the twentieth century, explorers from many nations vied to be the first to reach the South Pole and claim the Antarctic continent for their countries. The foremost rivals were the Norwegian Roald Amundsen and the Briton Robert Scott, who set out late in 1911 in a race across the ice shelf. Amundsen's team took along ample provisions, including extra dogs for their sleds, so that when an animal died it could be fed to its fellows. Scott, by contrast, carried inadequate supplies on his human-drawn sledges, a strange oversight for someone as skilled in arctic exploration as he. His party—made up of Scott, Dr. Edward Wilson, Edward Evans, and William Bowers—crossed from Ross Sea over Mt. Discovery and arrived at the South Pole on January 17, 1912, only to discover that Amundsen had reached the spot thirty-four days before. Bowers's diary describes the difficult trip across the ice.

DECEMBER 26 [1911]. We have seen many new ranges of mountains extending to the S.E. of the Dominion Range. They are very distant, however, and must evidently be the top of those bounding the Barrier. They could only be seen from the tops of the ridges as waves up which we are continually mounting. Our height yesterday morning by hypsometer was 8,000 feet. That is our last hypsometer record, as I had the misfortune to break the thermometer. The hypsometer was one of my chief delights, and nobody could have been more disgusted than myself at its breaking. However, we have the aneroid to check the height. We are going gradually up and up. As one would expect, a considerable amount of lassitude was felt over breakfast after our feed last night. The last thing on earth I wanted to do was to ship the harness round my poor tummy when we started. As usual a stiff breeze from the south and a temperature of

273

$-7°$ blew in our faces. Strange to say, however, we don't get frost-bitten. I suppose it is the open-air life.

I could not tell if I had a frost-bite on my face now, as it is all scales, so are my lips and nose. A considerable amount of red hair is endeavouring to cover up matters. We crossed several ridges and after the effects of overfeeding had worn off did a pretty good march of thirteen miles.

DECEMBER 27. There is something the matter with our sledge or our team, as we have an awful slog to keep up with the others. I asked Dr. Bill and he said their sledge ran very easily. Ours is nothing but a desperate drag with constant rallies to keep up. We certainly manage to do so; but I am sure we cannot keep this up for long. We are all pretty well done up to-night after doing 13.3 miles.

Our salvation is on the summits of the ridges, where hard névé and sastrugi obtain, and we skip over this slippery stuff and make up lost ground easily. In soft snow the other team draw steadily ahead, and it is fairly heartbreaking to know you are putting your life out hour after hour while they go along with little apparent effort.

DECEMBER 28. The last few days have been absolutely cloudless, with unbroken sunshine for twenty-four hours. It sounds very nice, but the temperature never comes above zero and what Shackleton called "the pitiless increasing wind" of the great plateau continues to blow at all times from the south. It never ceases, and all night it whistles round the tents, all day it blows in our faces. Sometimes it is S.S.E., or S.E. to S., and sometimes even S. to W., but always southerly, chiefly accompanied by low drift which at night forms quite a deposit round the sledges. We expected this wind, so we must not growl at getting it. It will be great fun sailing the sledges back before it. As far as weather is concerned we have had remarkably fine days up here on this limitless snow plain. I should like to know what there is beneath us—mountains and valleys simply levelled off to the top with ice? We constantly come across disturbances which I can only imagine are caused by the peaks of ice-covered mountains, and no doubt some of the ice-falls and crevasses are accountable to the same source. Our coming west has not cleared them, as we have seen more disturbances to the west, many miles away. However, they are getting less and less, and are now nothing but featureless rises with apparently no crevasses. Our first two hours' pulling to-day. . . .

DECEMBER 29. A nasty head wind all day and low drift which accumulates in patches and makes it the deuce of a job to get along. We have got to put in long days to do the distance.

Bitterly disappointed on finding that the Norwegians had beaten them to their goal, Scott's party set out for base camp during a period of abnormally cold temperatures and several days-long blizzards. None survived the return trip, and the frozen team was not found until April 11 at their last camp on the windswept Ross Ice Shelf. The rescue party found an open letter Scott had written on March 20.

MESSAGE TO THE PUBLIC

The causes of the disaster are not due to faulty organization, but to misfortune in all risks which had to be undertaken.

1. The loss of pony transport in March 1911 obliged me to start later than I had intended, and obliged the limits of stuff transported to be narrowed.
2. The weather throughout the outward journey, and especially the long gale in 33° S., stopped us.
3. The soft snow in lower reaches of glacier again reduced pace.

We fought these untoward events with a will and conquered, but it cut into our provision reserve.

Every detail of our food supplies, clothing and depots made on the interior ice-sheet and over that long stretch of 700 miles to the Pole and back, worked out to perfection. The advance party would have returned to the glacier in fine form and with surplus of food, but for the astonishing failure of the man whom we had least expected to fail. Edgar Evans was thought the strongest man of the party.

The Beardmore Glacier is not difficult in fine weather, but on our return we did not get a single completely fine day; this with a sick companion enormously increased our anxieties.

As I have said elsewhere, we got into frightfully rough ice and Edgar Evans received a concussion of the brain—he died a natural death, but left us a shaken party with the season unduly advanced.

But all the facts above enumerated were as nothing to the surprise which awaited us on the Barrier. I maintain that our arrangements for returning were quite adequate, and that no one in the world would have expected the temperatures and surfaces which we encountered at this time of the year. On the summit in lat. 85°–86° we had – 20°, – 30°. On the Barrier in lat. 82°, 10,000 feet lower, we had – 30° in the day, – 47° at night pretty regularly, with continuous head-wind during our day marches. It is clear that these circumstances come on very suddenly, and our wreck is certainly due to this sudden advent of severe weather, which does not seem to have any satisfactory cause. I do not think human beings ever came through such a month as we have come through, and we should have got through in spite of the weather but for the sickening of a second companion, Captain Oates, and a shortage of fuel in our depots for which I cannot account, and finally, but for the storm which has fallen on us within 11 miles of the depot at which we hoped to secure our final supplies. Surely misfortune could scarcely have exceeded this last blow. We arrived within 11 miles of our old One Ton Camp with fuel for one last meal and food for two days. For four days we have been unable to leave the tent—the gale howling about us. We are weak, writing is difficult, but for my own sake I do not regret this journey, which has shown that Englishmen can endure hardships, help one another, and meet death with as great a fortitude as ever in the past. We took risks, we knew we took them; things have come out against us, and therefore we have no cause for complaint, but bow to the will of Providence, determined still to do our best to the last. But if we have been willing to give our lives to this enterprise, which is for the honour of our country, I appeal to our countrymen to see that those who depend on us are properly cared for.

Had we lived, I should have had a tale to tell of the hardihood, endurance, and courage of my companions which would have stirred the heart of every Englishman. These rough notes and our dead bodies must tell the tale, but surely, surely a great rich country like ours will see that those who are dependent on us are properly provided for. —R. SCOTT

Scott also left behind two undated letters addressed to Dr. Wilson's widow and to his good friend J. M. Barrie, the author of the famous stage play *Peter Pan*.

My dear Mrs. Wilson:

If this letter reaches you Bill and I will have gone out together. We are very near it now and I should like you to know how splendid he was at the end—everlastingly cheerful and ready to sacrifice himself for others, never a word of blame to me for leading him into this mess. He is not suffering, luckily, at least only minor discomforts.

His eyes have a comfortable blue look of hope and his mind is peaceful with the satisfaction of his faith in regarding himself as part of that great scheme of the Almighty. I can do no more to comfort you than to tell you that he died as he lived, a brave, true man— the best of comrades and staunchest of friends.

My whole heart goes out to you in pity,

Yours, R. SCOTT

My dear Barrie,

We are pegging out in a very comfortless spot. Hoping this letter may be found and sent to you, I write a word of farewell. . . . More practically I want you to help my widow and my boy—your godson. We are showing that Englishmen can still die with a bold spirit, fighting it out to the end. It will be known that we have accomplished our object in reaching the Pole, and that we have done everything possible, even to sacrificing ourselves in order to save sick companions. I think this makes an example for Englishmen of the future, and that the country ought to help those who are left behind to mourn us. I leave my poor girl and your godson, Wilson leaves a widow, and Edgar Evans also a widow in humble circumstances. Do what you can to get their claims recognized. . . . I may not have proved a great explorer, but we have done the greatest march ever made and come very near to great success. Good-bye, my dear friend,

Yours ever, R. SCOTT

Cold

Richard Byrd

American naval officer Richard Byrd spent the winter of 1934 in a weather station 160 miles south of the naval base at Little America, with an often-malfunctioning radio his only contact with other people. As the days went by, he found himself growing weak and ill, and only after weeks had passed did he realize that a faulty heater was filling his underground bunker with carbon monoxide fumes. Without the heater he would die; with it, he ran about the same chances of survival. Keeping a door flung open for ventilation during most weather, he endured, a tribulation he describes in his 1938 memoir *Alone*.

July 1. It is getting cold again—65° below zero today by the minimum thermometer. I have a feeling that it is going to be a very cold month, to make up for June. It was a great piece of luck that June was relatively so warm. I could not have survived otherwise. Now, when the stove is going, I keep the door cracked as wide as I can stand it; and, when it has been out long enough for the fumes to dissipate, I stuff rags (worn-out shirts and underwear, to be exact) up the engine ventilator in the tunnel and into the intake ventilator, so that the tunnel and shack won't get too cold. As a matter of fact, I do without the stove anywhere from twelve to fourteen hours a day. Believe me, it is a strain on the fortitude. Last night I froze an ear in the sleeping bag.

I'm worried about drift. Ever since I've been unable to attend to it, the drift has been deepening over the roof. This morning, when I went topside for the observations, I noticed how high the ridges were over the Escape Tunnel and the tunnels west of the shack. However, I may be able to do something about this before long. Advancing the radio schedules to the afternoon has been an immense help in bringing me back to my feet. With more time to prepare, the drain on me is not quite so heavy. Today's schedule, though tiring, did not knock me out as the others did. There was no news to speak of from Little America. Hutcheson said that Charlie and John Dyer were out skiing, and that "Doc" Poulter was with the meteor observers. Lord, how I envy them the multitudinous diversions of Little America; even, I suppose, as they must on their side envy the people home with whom they chat on the radio. . . .

I sent a message approving the meteor journey, subject to its being made with full regard for its hazards.

July 2. I've begun to read again—two chapters from *The House of Exile*, which I hope to continue with tonight. It's the best thing imaginable for me—takes me out of myself for a blessed hour or two. And tonight, also, I played the phonograph after supper—"In a

Monastery Garden," "Die Fledermaus," "Tales from the Vienna Woods," and "The Swan." As I listened the hope swept over me that I have a good chance to pull through, unless another serious setback comes. Although still stupidly weak, I have made real progress the past week. The knowledge is exhilarating. . . .

JULY 3. Cold spell still holding—62° below zero today. The ice is a foot higher on the walls. I have at last managed to get rid of a good deal of the frozen slop which for the most part I've been dumping into the tunnel—just outside the door. Sitting on the rim of the hatch, I've been hauling the stuff topside with a bucket and line, and dumping it a little to leeward. Of course, this meant half a dozen trips up and down the ladder to fill the bucket; and I thought how wonderful it would be if I had a Man Friday topside and had only to shout: "Take a strain, Friday, it's full." As it is, I have to sit down and rest after every trip. However, the job was well worth doing. The tunnels are much tidier.

JULY 4. I was greatly encouraged over finding myself able to level some of the drifts. Yet, I had to drive myself, for the temperature was in the minus 50's; and, animal-like, I seem to shrink instinctively from anything that hurts. It's odd that I should have changed so much. The cold never used to bother me. I rather liked it for its cleansing, antiseptic action. But now I seem to have very little resistance. This afternoon, for example, I froze my nose rather severely; and, in the minute or two I had my hands out of my gloves to attend to it, I nipped five fingers. It has been good for me to be outside. I suppose that I was in the air for nearly two hours altogether, though not more than half an hour at a time. The night is still very dark, but at noon the colors on the northern horizon had the hint of sunrise. The sun is now twelve days nearer . . . I have always valued life, but never to the degree I do now. It is not within the power of words to describe what it means to have life pulsing through me again. I've been thinking of all the new things I'm going to do and the old things I'm going to do differently, if and when I ever get out of here. I hope that I won't be like the monk in the rhyme which goes something like this:

The monk when sick a monk would be,
But the monk when well, the devil a monk was he. . . .

These were days of great beauty, shadowless days. Scarcely a cloud marred the sky. Looking upwards, I seemed to be able to see into depths which at home could scarcely be penetrated by a telescope. Once more I paced my walk, never far nor for long, but enough to take confidence from repossessing the wheeling constellations, the stars, and the opulent inventions of the aurora australis. In the steepening cold the aurora flowered to perfection. For hours on end the Barrier was bathed in the cold white incandescence of its excitation. At times the sky was coursed by a great luminous stream, a hundred times broader than the Mississippi; at other times it was made up of scattered petals of pale light which I liked to think of as wind flowers. And the glow in the ventilator was like the reflection from a forest fire.

Times when the temperature was in the minus fifties or sixties, a wind would come rustling out of the cold, edged with a breath so sharp that it fairly sliced the skin from the face. Turn, twist, and wriggle as I might, I could never elude its numbing clasp. Maybe my toes would first turn cold and then dead. While I was dancing up and down to flex them and restore the circulation, my nose would freeze; and, by the time I had attended to that, my hand would be frozen. The wrists, the throat where the helmet chafed, the back of the neck, and the ankles pulsed and crawled with alternating fire and ice. Freezing to death must be a queer business. Sometimes you feel simply great. The numbness gives way to an utter absence of feeling.

You are as lost to pain as a man under opium. But at other times, in the enfolding cold, your anguish is the anguish of a man drowning slowly in fiery chemicals.

The Barrier shrank from the cold. One could almost feel the crustal agony. The snow quakes came with greater violence. Sometimes the sound was like thunder, with one clap breaking upon the other. The shack quivered to the worse concussions, and a few were severe enough to awaken me from sound sleep. I rather had the idea that I was in the equivalent of an earthquake epicenter zone, for the succession of shocks, increasing as the months wore on, meant nothing less than that crevasses were opening up all around Advance Base. Perhaps they were portents. Like the Barrier crust, my reviving security was based upon a doubtful equilibrium—one strong blow could break it in two.

The blow did in fact fall on Thursday the 5th. That day the gasoline-driven radio generator went out of commission. I had everything in readiness for the schedules, even the engine running. Casually I flipped the switch to test the voltage. Zero, read the dial. A loose connection, probably. But no. When, in tracking down the fault, I arrived at the generator, I found that it was not turning on the shaft. This is bad, very bad, I said to myself; I'd sooner lose an arm than have anything go wrong with this.

Giving up all intention of meeting the schedule, I fell to on the machine. By supper time I had it apart. The fault was fatal. The lug on the generator drive shaft had sheared off. No improvisation of mine would do, although I tried everything that my imagination suggested. Except for a pause to eat or rest, I worked steadily into the night. When midnight came, the table was cluttered with parts and the bunk with tools, but I was no nearer to a solution than at noon. The only possible repair was a new shaft; and where in God's name was I to get that? Bent over with weariness and despair, I concluded finally that my world was falling to pieces. There remained the emergency hand-powered set, but I doubted that I was strong enough to work it. Ordinarily two men were required to operate these sets, one cranking to supply power to the transmitter, and the other keying. I, who did not possess the strength of half a well man, would have to go it alone. The pity was that the failure had to come at such a critical hour when the tractor trip was hanging fire. Nor was this all. My imagination was racing. I thought of Dyer calling KFY for hours and becoming worried, perhaps alarmed. No, the failure could not have come at a worse time. All that I had suffered in June to maintain communication was undone by the failure of an inconspicuous bit of steel.

Friday I awakened feeling miserable and uncertain. I unpacked the emergency equipment. Having tested the receiver several weeks before, I knew that it was all right. The transmitter was the doubtful part. It was housed in a steel box about seven inches square which was fixed to a steel tripod, of which one leg had a seat for the operator. Two short crank handles were fitted into the sides of the box; turning these generated "juice." With the help of the instruction book, I finally succeeded in making the right connections. A copper hand switch, clamped to the antenna lead, enabled me to throw either the transmitter or receiver into the antenna. Rigged up and standing hard by my radio table, the set looked workmanlike and simple. But I had a premonition of what it would do to me.

I glanced at my wrist watch. It was nearly 1 o'clock. I had been working with hardly a stop for four hours. I had, of course, missed the 9:30 emergency schedule; but Dyer had said he would also listen in at 2 o'clock in the event of my losing a regular broadcast period. Lunch was a hurried affair of hot milk, soup, and crackers. At 2 o'clock I made the first attempt with the new setup. I threw the antenna switch on the transmitter side, and planted Strumpell's *Practice of Medicine* on the key to hold it down, so that Little America would hear a continuous signal if they were listening. Then, straddling the seat, I started to crank with both hands. The strain was even greater than I had supposed. Just what the magnetic resistance load to overcome was, I do not know; but to me it was a long, uphill push. As soon as the thing was turning fast, I knocked the book off the key, and with left hand still winding, I tried to spell out KFY-KFZ. Have you ever tried that parlor trick of rubbing your stomach around and around with one hand, while with the other hand you pat the top of your head straight up and down? Well, this was like that; except that the organization of my movements was infinitely complicated by my weakness and my unsure handling of the Morse code.

I called for five minutes, then switched to the receiver. My fingers were trembling as I tuned in on the wave length Dyer had assigned for this set. I heard only the scraping of static. I tried the two other frequencies which Dyer had marked as alternatives. Nothing there, either. Then I went up and down the dial. Complete silence. Either my transmitter wasn't on the air, or I hadn't tuned the receiver properly, or Little America wasn't listening in. I could have wept from disappointment. After resting ten minutes or so in the bunk, I called again, although it was evident that my strength would soon be exhausted at this rate. When I switched to the receiver, I was almost too tired to care. Then Dyer's voice welled for a second out of the silence. I lost it right away. Desperately I experimented with the tuning dial, trying to find the hairline paystreak.

"Go ahead, KFY. We heard you. Go ahead, go ahead, please. We heard you." It was Dyer. How wonderful, how perfectly wonderful, I thought.

I switched to the transmitter, and told Dyer in a few words that my engine was "shot" and that I was having a hard time with the emergency set.

"We're sorry to hear that," Dyer said, "and we'll try to keep our messages down." Murphy came on and read the dispatch he proposed to send to the U.S. in connection with the meteor trip. What he said about me was no longer important. When he finished I simply said, in effect: "OK. Radio uncertain from now on. Don't be alarmed by missed schedules."

Then, speaking slowly and softly, Charlie had this to say: "As you know, the journey to Advance Base may be hard, and it certainly is chancy. We consider it so here. Therefore, the possibilities are being examined; and the preparations are being made with the utmost care. If I were you, I wouldn't count overmuch on the possibility of the tractors before the end of July. There is a good chance it may be considerably later."

For an instant I was taken aback. The thought struck me that they knew the trip was dangerous but were still going ahead with it. Had I somehow given myself away? My heart sank at the thought of having done such a stupid thing. I interrupted with a sharp protest that, if they thought the trip dangerous, they should give it up. There were other things I wanted to say, but I simply couldn't turn the handle any more. I keyed KK, the signal to go ahead, and waited.

In spite of the atrocious sending, they evidently understood, because Murphy, still in the same even tone, said he was sorry I had interpreted his statement that way. He went on: "All I meant to imply was this: that, appreciating how long the last three and a half months must have been, I can also appreciate how disappointing it might be if, after all this talk, the arrival of the tractor were a long time delayed." He talked a long time; but I didn't hear much of it, because my heart was thumping and my head had turned dizzy, and also because the signal, for an unaccountable reason, was fading in and out.

Poulter then gave a quick résumé of the preparations. Much of this, too, I missed; but I did hear him ask if I had any suggestions as to the men who should go.

"No," was my answer.

Beside the key was a long message I had written the morning before, relating to various safety precautions—the need for a big fuel reserve for the tractor, face masks for the men, fur gauntlets, and a suggestion that two complete sets of rations and camping gear be carried, one on the sledges towed behind and one in the tractor cabin, as protection in case one or the other fell down a crevasse. When Poulter finished, I sent what I could of this message before my arms gave out. "Have very thorough drill on trail; also more flags," I concluded, and keyed the signal to repeat it back. If they replied, I did not hear them. Then I spelled the sentence again, and signed off, cursing my weakness as I sagged over the generator head. But, even so, I drew comfort from the fact that Little America, so far as I could tell, had not suspected anything.

The temperature was 60° below zero, but sweat was pouring down my chest. I turned off the stove and stumbled to the sleeping bag. It was the third serious relapse; and, coming on top of five weeks of depleting illness, it very nearly did me in. If it had not been for the week's supply of fuel, plus the three weeks' supply of food, which I had stored squirrel-wise near at hand, I doubt whether I could have lived the period out. Once again I was reduced to doing what had to be done in slow-motion steps, which were ghastly caricatures of my ambitions. The pain came back, as did the vomiting and sleeplessness.

JULY 7. Everything—myself included—is saturated with cold. For two solid weeks the red thermograph trace has been wandering through the minus 40's, 50's, and 60's. A moment ago, when I turned the flashlight on the inside thermograph, the pen was edging past minus 65°. The ice over the skylight is fanning out to meet the ice on the walls, which has risen level with my eyes. I hope fervently that the cold will let up, for I simply must have more warmth, even at the expense of less ventilation and more fumes.

I am still in wretched condition. My brain seems unspeakably tired and confused. Last night was agony. This morning was one of my worst. The gloom, the cold, and the evenness of the Barrier are a drag on the spirits; my poise and equanimity are almost gone. This new setback reminds me of the one that followed that attack of typhoid fever which I contracted in England during the midshipman cruise. For weeks I ran a high temperature. Then it subsided to normal. The day I was slated to receive solid food (and I was famished) I suffered another relapse; so I had the whole siege to endure again. And now, as then, I am facing another illness with a weakened body and mind.

Today I missed another radio schedule with L.A. I called and listened for at least half an hour, which was as long as I could stand. No luck. Then, on the chance that they could hear me, I broadcast blind: "Can't hear anything. Receiver out of order. OK here. OK, OK, OK." The whole business was disheartening, and I was teetering on the thin edge of oblivion.

Wafted in by the prevailing southerlies, the cold clamped down on the Barrier. From that day to and through July 17th the minimum daily temperature was never higher than 54° below zero; much of the time it was in the minus 60's, and on the 14th reached −71°. Frost collected inside the instrument shelter like moisture on the outside of a mint julep. The air at times was alive with ice crystals, precipitated in a dry, burningly cold rain. In a sense, I could almost see the cold fall; for, whenever I opened the trapdoor, a thick fog formed as the super-chilled air from the Barrier met the warmer air in the tunnels and the shack. Even when the stove burned fifteen and sixteen hours a day, it did not throw off enough heat to melt the ice crawling up the wall, an inch a day. The ceiling was half covered with crystals that seldom thawed. And meanwhile the glacial film mounted on the walls until at last it met the ceiling on every side except the west, where the heat from the stove stayed the creeping advance. In spite of the fire risk, I left a lantern burning under the register night after night to keep the batteries from freezing.

All this time I lived on the food which was stored under the bunk and on the shelves. It was an uninspired diet—Klim, Eskimo biscuits, tomatoes, canned peas, turnip tops, rice, corn meal, lima beans, chocolate, jelly, preserved figs, and I still had some of my mother's wonderful ham. While these dreary things contained adequate nourishment, I did not concentrate on them for this reason alone. It was simply impossible for me, during this bad time, to prepare anything more complicated. Even after the canned stuff had stood for hours near the stove, I often had to break it out with a hammer and chisel. My fingers were burned raw again from touching cold metal; no matter how much food I forced into my stomach or how much clothing I wore, it seemed impossible to revive the heat-generating apparatus of the body. One night, when I felt up to taking a bath (the first in a week), I was horrified to find how close I was to emaciation. My ribs showed through the flesh, and the skin sagged loosely on my arms. I weighed 180 pounds when I went to Advance Base. I doubt if I weighed more than 125 pounds in July.

Admiralty Bay

David Campbell

Antarctica is the last place most people think of as a vacation destination. For David Campbell, a professor of biology at Grinnell College, there is no finer place for a summer's sojourn, and he has returned there several times as a guest of international scientists. This excerpt, describing one of the better venues, comes from his 1992 book *The Crystal Desert*.

During the austral summer of 1987 I was invited to the Brazilian station to conduct marine biological research. By then it had grown to fifty-one prefabricated tractor-trailer containers linked by narrow corridors much like railroad cars, giving it a boxy, unfinished appearance. Huge rubber bladders of fuel wallowed on the beach, oozing oil into the bay.

The industrial age had come to Admiralty Bay. The tranquility that I so vividly remembered from five years before was gone. A diesel generator, which ran twenty-four hours a day, shredded the silence, and I had to walk beyond the old Argentine station, 200 meters south, to be free of the noise. The generator was the metabolic heart of the station, an artificial sun that kept the personnel warm, incinerated their garbage, and provided the power to link them with the outside world.

"Polar exploration is at once the cleanest and most isolated way of having a bad time which has been devised," wrote Apsley Cherry-Garrard more than a half-century ago. But we had fun. Visitors affectionately nicknamed the Brazilian station "Little Copacabana." Its spirit was buoyant and welcoming. Just inside the door, one stripped off boots and woolen clothing in an arid, hot foyer and hung one's clothing on the wall. The halls are lined with hooks, each designating someone's little vertical territory: a pair of boots, a red parka, gloves and a hat. Three hooks were reserved for visitors. As in any Brazilian household, the kitchen was the center of social activity. Coconut snacks and sugary *cafezinho*, served in demitasses, were always available on a wide counter covered by a plastic tablecloth printed with Santa Clauses. The automatic dough-kneading machine plodded like a metronome, filling the air with yeast smells. A traditional Saturday feast of *feijoada completa*, a Cariocan dish of black beans, sausage, and pig's ears, was simmering on the stove. Behind the kitchen was the radio room, where a squawking box linked the station with the disembodied voices of lovers, children, and bureaucrats in the crowded parts of the world. In the central dining room and lounge, on a cluster of sofas, a group of scientists watched a video of *Back to the Future*, and in another corner, someone was playing a kung-fu game on a Brazilian clone of the Apple II computer. The electronic imitation of karate kicks became a constant acoustical backdrop at the station during my visit.

The walls were paved with the emblems of ships that had visited the station, the banners of Rotary and Lions clubs, portraits of station members over the years. On the western wall was an oil portrait of Comandante Ferraz, one of the first Brazilians to travel to Antarctica, after whom the station was named. In the far corner was the bar, which also served as a post office (you canceled your own letters and they were picked up every two months). It was stacked neatly with crystal brandy snifters to be used only for special events, which, because of the Brazilian *joie de vivre*, occurred often. The bar also stored the accordion, drums, and tambourines. Parties often lasted all night, and Carnival lasted three days. Behind the bar was mounted a fossil leaf of a southern beech tree, 16 million years old, found at Point Hennequin across the bay. One eastern window of the lounge had been shattered by a tempest-flung rock, and the shards had been colored with cellophane and rearranged in the form of a *papagayo*, the cloth and bamboo parrot kite of Copacabana Beach.

Beyond the lounge was a warren of sleeping modules, each equipped with a set of bunk beds, a small table, and a double-paned window. A central module contained the toilets and showers, men's on the north, women's on the south. The water was heated to scalding by the exhaust of the generator. Only the commander, Queiroz, who by tradition was a navy captain, had a private module and bath. Next to his module was the gym, the only structure that was not modular, with tall windows overlooking the expanse of black beach. It was cluttered with mountaineering equipment, skis, barbells, and weights. At its center was a snooker table, plenty of chalk and cues, and a slate blackboard with a system of numbered beads for keeping score. The clack of billiard balls was another pervading sound of the station.

During the summer Little Copacabana was a favorite stop for the tourist ships, which would disgorge legions of passengers, all clad in red parkas so that their leaders could keep track of them. Most visits lasted only an hour or two, and the tourists didn't learn, or see, much. After the obligatory pose for a portrait with Cousteau's whale skeleton, they shuffled into the station to buy stamps, postcards, key rings, and other mementos utterly irrelevant to Antarctica. Some offered to barter T-shirts and other wampum with the station personnel, as if they were primitive tribesmen. Snuffling and sneezing, the tourists usually left colds in their wake. Regardless, the hospitable Brazilians had a limitless tolerance for these intrusions. Often they would organize a soccer game with the ship's crew and break out the *cachaça* and the accordion.

The tourists were innocuous and friendly, but the visitors who made us truly uneasy were those from Greenpeace, which had a ship patrolling the area. Ready with criticism and armed with video cameras, Greenpeace has brought to world attention many environmental problems in Antarctic stations and has advocated the concept of an Antarctic world park. "If they come, don't offer them any information," cautioned Queiroz. "Let them ask first." When Greenpeace visited Comardante Ferraz in April 1987, the Brazilians, true to their nature, threw them a party. Greenpeace reported that "the Brazilian station is one of the tidiest seen. . . . It is obvious that they not only took good care of their base, but also the surrounding environment."

The hospital, aquarium, and biology laboratories were separate from the living modules, under a gloomy metal roof that protected them from drifting snow. The base physician, deputy commander, and postal clerk was Dutra, an urbane doctor from Rio de Janeiro, who kept the operating room scrubbed and instrument-ready for sudden emergencies.

I spent much of each day, and the long bright night, in the three biology modules. We had to wear warm parkas while working in the aquarium module, which was kept at near-freezing in order not to poach the heat-sensitive organisms that we were studying. On some nights, while manipulating the cold steel knobs of the microscope, I would wear gloves. On very windy days the module would shake so much that it was impossible to use the microscope. It was a damp, cold, noisy place, filled with the gurgle of filters and the hiss of water jets, which were continually charged with seawater pumped through a black PVC pipe that snaked over the rock beach from the bay. The water supply had to be constantly monitored to keep it from freezing. If the catch had been good that week, the nets and baited traps not snarled by drifting ice or, worse yet, lost, the aquariums were populated with all manner of marine organisms from the bay: brown antifreeze fish, big-mouthed, nacreous icefish, starfish, sea anemones, isopods, amphipods, sea spiders, and krill. A few of the krill were forced to swim against an artificial current in a physiological chamber, their oxygen consumption measured by instruments that periodically tested the water. This corner belonged to Phan, a Vietnamese-Brazilian physiologist. The Brazilian station lacked the trawl nets and swift boats necessary to capture krill on the open sea. But Phan had devised a system of high-powered lights that attracted krill (and myriad other organisms) close to shore in front of the station, where they could be conveniently caught in hand nets. At the opposite corner of the laboratory were the glass aquariums used for behavioral studies. This was Claude's corner. He spent long hours staring into the aquariums to observe the feeding strategies and food preferences of captive amphipods, trying to imagine what they would be doing on the unseen bottom of the bay.

The two other labs were under a sheltering canopy and therefore slightly warmer, but you still needed to wear a heavy coat inside. These contained more microscopes, dissecting tables, cupboards of chemicals, scales, plates of agar, and sinks with hot and cold running fresh water. On the days the nets were brought in, the labs reeked of formaldehyde. Renato, the veterinarian, worked here. It was Renato who had invited me to work at the station as part of a team trying to figure out the life cycles of parasites that live in seals, fish, and crustaceans.

The station had a homey ambiance the summer I was there. But we were probably just lucky. Crews for Antarctic stations are like classrooms full of students: each has its own, unpredictable collective personality. But the psychological stress of prolonged confinement, with minimal privacy, in modules crowded in a hostile environment, often gets to even the strongest individuals. Antarctic workers frequently develop a dazed, almost autistic condition known as "big eye." Therefore the screening of candidates for the stations is serious business, particularly for the personnel who will endure the long, dark winter. At one of the Soviet Antarctic stations a worker killed another with an axe in a dispute over a chess game. During the autumn of 1983, the staff doctor at the Argentine station Almirante Brown, on the edge of Paradise Harbor, 400 kilometers south of King George Island, forced his own rescue by burning the base down.

Candidates for the Brazilian Antarctic program were evaluated according to fifteen criteria, including "resistance to long periods of confinement, resistance to frustration, capacity for prolonged sexual abstinence and capacity to sustain long separation from one's family." How the evaluator could possibly ascertain this information was beyond me. In addition to the eight support personnel from the navy, all men, Ferraz Base had twenty-one scientists, five of whom were women. In many ways the station personnel become a surrogate family and, like all families, they may be supportive or abusive. The Brazilians were wonderfully supportive, and we hugged and cried at the end of the summer in one *grande tristeza* of homesickness that lingers even now, two years after.

It was sometimes easy to forget, in that snug station on the edge of a blue bay, that we were living in an alien environment, beyond the edge of the habitable earth. Only the generator and a few membranes of metal and cloth prevented us from freezing to death. But the station, although necessary for our survival in Antarctica, was an upstart intruder in a timeless, frozen place. We were scientists who had come to study more enduring things: fossils and glaciers, the ebb and flow of seasons, wind and albatrosses, metropolises of penguins, and the crowded, unseen Antarctic underwater realm, which brims with life as no other sea on Earth. We were pilgrims in the last new land on Earth.

SOURCES

Aarons, John, and Claudio Vita-Finzi. *The Useless Land: A Winter in the Atacama Desert*. London: Hale, 1962.

Abbey, Edward. *Desert Solitaire*. New York: Lippincott, 1968.

————. *The Journey Home*. New York: Dutton, 1977.

Aebi, Ernst. *Seasons of Sand*. New York: Simon & Schuster, 1994.

Ahlwardt, Wilhelm. *Divans of the Six Ancient Arabian Poets*. Osnabrück, Germany: Biblio Verlag, 1972.

Allchin, Bridget, Andrew Goudie, and Karunarkara Hegde. *The Prehistory and Palaeogeography of the Great Indian Desert*. New York: Academic, 1978.

Allen, William, and T. R. H. Thomson. *The Narrative of the Expedition to the River Niger in 1841*. London: Bentley, 1848.

Altmann, Alexander. *Biblical Motifs: Origins and Transformations*. Cambridge, MA: Harvard University Press, 1966.

Attar, Farid Ud-Din. *The Conference of the Birds*. Translated by Afkham Darbandi and Dick Davis. Harmondsworth, England: Penguin, 1984.

Austin, Mary. *The Land of Little Rain*. New York: Allen & Unwin, 1926.

Bagnold, Ralph A. *The Physics of Blown Sand and Desert Dunes*. London: Methuen, 1941.

————. *Sand, Wind & War: Memoirs of a Desert Explorer.* Tucson: University of Arizona Press, 1991.

Bahamonde Silva, Mario. *Antología del Cuento Nortino.* Antofagasta: Universidad de Chile, 1966.

Bailey, Clinton. *Bedouin Poetry from Sinai and Negev.* New York: Oxford University Press, 1991.

Bailey, F. M. *Mission to Tashkent.* London: Cape, 1946.

Bancroft, Herbert Eugene. *Font's Diary of the Second Anza Expedition.* Berkeley: University of California Press, 1931.

Bancroft, John M., ed. *The Deserts in Literature.* Special issue of the *Arid Lands Newsletter* (Office of Arid Lands Studies, University of Arizona), Spring–Summer 1994.

Barfield, Lawrence. "Recent Discoveries in the Atacama Desert and the Bolivian Altiplano." *American Antiquity* 27 (1961): 93–100.

Barth, Henry [Heinrich]. *Travels and Discoveries in North and Central Africa.* London: Collins, 1859.

Bateson, Mary Catherine. *Structural Continuity in Poetry: A Linguistic Study of Five Pre-Islamic Odes.* The Hague: Mouton, 1970.

Baughman, T. G. *Before the Heroes Came: Antarctica in the 1890s.* Lincoln: University of Nebraska Press, 1994.

Bell, Gertrude. *The Desert and the Sown.* London: Constable, 1907.

Blackburn, Julia. *Daisy Bates in the Desert.* New York: Pantheon, 1994.

Bleek, W. H. I., and L. C. I. Lloyd. *Specimens of Bushmen Folklore.* London: Murray, 1911.

Borges, Jorge Luis. *Labyrinths.* New York: New Directions, 1961.

Bridges, E. Lucas. *Uttermost Part of the Earth: Indians of Tierra del Fuego.* New York: Dutton, 1949.

Briggs, Lloyd Cabot. *Tribes of the Sahara.* Cambridge, MA: Harvard University Press, 1967.

Brooks, George R., ed. *The Southwest Expedition of Jedediah S. Smith, 1826–1827.* Lincoln: University of Nebraska Press, 1977.

Burnes, Alexander. *Travels into Bokhara.* London: Murray, 1835.

Burton, Richard Francis. *Personal Narrative of a Pilgrimage to Al-Medinah and Meccah.* London: Tylston and Edwards, 1893.

Butor, Michel. *The Spirit of Mediterranean Places.* Translated by Lydia Davis. Marlboro, VT: Marlboro Press, 1986.

Byrd, Richard. *Alone.* Garden City, NY: International Collectors Library, 1938.

Byron, Robert. *The Road to Oxiana.* London: Macmillan, 1937.

Cable, Mildred. *The Gobi Desert.* London: Hodder and Stoughton, 1942.

Campbell, David. *The Crystal Desert: Summers in Antarctica.* Boston: Houghton Mifflin, 1992.

Carruthers, Douglas. *Beyond the Caspian: A Naturalist in Central Asia.* Edinburgh: Oliver and Boyd, 1949.

Carter, Paul. *The Road to Botany Bay: An Essay in Spatial Geography.* London: Faber and Faber, 1987.

Casson, Lionel. *Travel in the Ancient World.* London: Allen & Unwin, 1974.

Castro, Josué de. *Death in the Northeast.* New York: Vintage, 1959.

Chatwin, Bruce. *The Songlines.* New York: Viking, 1987.

Cherry-Garrard, Apsley. *The Worst Journey in the World.* New York: Dial Press, 1930.

Christie, Ella R. *Through Khiva to Golden Samarkand.* London: Seeley, Service, 1925.

Cocker, Mark. *Loneliness and Time: The Story of British Travel Writing.* New York: Pantheon, 1992.

Cressey, George B. *Crossroads: Land and Life in Southwest Asia.* Chicago: Lippincott, 1960.

Curtis, William Elerey. *Turkostan: The Heart of Asia.* New York: Hodder and Stoughton/Doran, 1911.

————. *Between the Andes and the Ocean*. Chicago: Stone, 1890.

Curzon, George N. *The Pamirs and the Source of the Oxus*. London: Royal Geographical Society, 1896.

da Cunha, Euclides. *Rebellion in the Backlands*. Translated by Samuel Putnam. Chicago: University of Chicago Press, 1944.

Dalrymple, William. *In Xanadu*. London: Collins, 1989.

Darwin, Charles. *The Voyage of the Beagle*. Harmondsworth, England: Penguin, 1955.

Dawood, N. J., ed. *Tales from the Thousand and One Nights*. Harmondsworth, England: Penguin, 1954.

Desmond, Adrian, and James Moore. *Darwin: The Life of a Tormented Evolutionist*. New York: Warner, 1992.

Doughty, Charles M. *Travels in Arabia Deserta*. Cambridge, England: Cambridge University Press, 1886.

Edwards, Amelia. *A Thousand Miles up the Nile*. London: Routledge, 1891.

Eiseley, Loren. *All the Strange Hours*. New York: Scribner's, 1975.

Eliade, Mircea. *Australian Religions*. Ithaca, NY: Cornell University Press, 1973.

————. *Shamanism: Archaic Techniques of Ecstasy*. Princeton, NJ: Bollingen/Princeton University Press, 1964.

Elkin, A. P. *Aboriginal Men of High Degree*. St. Lucia: University of Queensland Press, 1945.

Etherton, P. T. *Across the Great Deserts*. London: Lutterworth Press, 1948.

Evenari, Michael, Leslie Shanan, and Naphtali Tadmor. *The Negev: The Challenge of a Desert*. Cambridge, MA: Harvard University Press, 1971.

Fernández-Armesto, Felipe, ed. *Times Atlas of World Exploration*. New York: HarperCollins, 1991.

Fitzpatrick, Kathleen, ed. *Australian Explorers*. London: Oxford University Press, 1958.

Flood, Josephine. *Archaeology of the Dreamtime*. Honolulu: University of Hawaii Press, 1983.

Forrest, John. *Explorations in Australia*. London: Sampson Low, Marston, Low & Searle, 1875.

Fowler, Barbara Hughes. *Love Lyrics of Ancient Egypt*. Chapel Hill: University of North Carolina Press, 1994.

Frazer, James. *The New Golden Bough*. Theodor H. Gaster, ed. New York: New American Library, 1964.

Frobenius, Leo. *African Genesis*. London: Faber and Faber, 1928.

Froth, Zahra, and H. V. F. Winstone. *Explorers of Arabia from the Renaissance to the End of the Victorian Era*. London: Allen & Unwin, 1978.

García Lorca, Federico. *Poema del Cante Jondo*. Madrid: Catédra, 1978.

Gardi, René. *Blue Veils—Red Tents*. London: Harrap, 1970.

George, Uwe. *In the Deserts of This Earth*. New York: Harcourt Brace Jovanovich, 1977.

Ghosh, Amitav. *In an Antique Land*. New York: Knopf, 1993.

Gillen, F. J. *Gillen's Diary*. Adelaide: Libraries Board of South Australia, 1968.

Glacken, Clarence J. *Traces on the Rhodian Shore: Nature and Culture in Western Thought from Ancient Times to the End of the Eighteenth Century*. Berkeley: University of California Press, 1967.

Glazebrook, Philip. *Journey to Khiva*. London: Harvill, 1992.

Glueck, Nelson. *Rivers in the Desert: A History of the Negev*. New York: Farrar, Straus & Cudahy, 1959.

Goldstein, Melvyn C., and Cynthia M. Beall. *The Changing World of Mongolia's Nomads*. Berkeley and Los Angeles: University of California Press, 1994.

Gramont, Sanche de. *The Strong Brown God: The Story of the River Niger*. Boston: Houghton Mifflin, 1975.

Graves, Robert. *The White Goddess*. New York: Farrar, Straus & Giroux, 1966.

Griaule, Marcel, and Germaine Dieterlen. *Le Renard Pâle*. Paris: Institut d'Ethnologie, 1954.

Grousset, René. *The Empire of the Steppes: A History of Central Asia*. New Brunswick, NJ: Rutgers University Press, 1970.

Haklyut, Richard. *Voyages and Discoveries*. Jack Beeching, ed. Harmondsworth, England: Penguin, 1972.

Harding, Jeremy. "Polisario." *Granta* 26 (Spring 1989): 19–40.

Hazleton, Lesley. *Where Mountains Roar: A Personal Report from the Sinai and Negev Desert*. New York: Holt, Rinehart and Winston, 1980.

Herbert, Frank. *Dune*. Radnor, PA: Chilton, 1965.

Herodotus. *The History*. A. D. Godley, ed. London: Heinemann, 1931.

Hibbert, Christopher. *Africa Explored*. Harmondsworth, England: Penguin, 1982.

Hill, Ernestine. *The Great Australian Loneliness*. Sydney: Angus & Robertson, 1940.

Hillel, Daniel. *Negev: Land, Water, and Life in a Desert Environment*. New York: Praeger, 1982.

Hills, E. S., ed. *Arid Lands: A Geographical Appraisal*. London: Methuen, 1966.

Hingston, R. W. G. *Nature at the Desert's Edge: Studies and Observations in the Bagdad Oasis*. London: Witherby, 1925.

Hodson, Peregrine. *Under a Sickle Moon: A Journey Through Afghanistan*. London: Hutchison, 1986.

Holditch, Colonel Sir Thomas. *The Gates of India: An Historical Narrative*. London: Macmillan, 1910.

Hourani, Albert. *A History of the Arab Peoples*. Cambridge, MA: Harvard University Press, 1991.

Hudson, W. H. *Idle Days in Patagonia*. New York: Dutton, 1917.

Hughes, Robert. *The Fatal Shore: The Epic of Australia's Founding.* New York: Knopf, 1987.

Hugot, H. J. "The Origins of Agriculture: Sahara." *Current Anthropology* 9 (1968): 483–88.

Ignatieff, Michael. "An Interview with Bruce Chatwin." *Granta* 21 (Spring 1987): 21–37.

Ives, Ronald. *Land of Lava, Ash, and Sand: The Pinacate Region of Northwestern Mexico.* Tucson: Arizona Historical Society, 1989.

Jabés, Edmond. *From the Desert to the Book.* Barrytown, NY: Station Hill Press, 1980.

Jaeger, Edmund C. *The North American Deserts.* Stanford, CA: Stanford University Press, 1957.

Jafri, Sardar, and Qurratulain Hyder. *Ghalib and His Poetry.* Bombay: Popular Prakashan, 1970.

Kazantzakis, Nikos. *Journeying.* San Francisco: Ellis/Creative Arts, 1984.

Keay, John. *When Men and Mountains Meet: The Explorers of the Western Himalayas, 1820–75.* London: Murray, 1977.

Khazanov, Anatoly M. *Nomads and the Outside World.* Translated by Julia Crookenden. Cambridge, MA: Cambridge University Press, 1984.

Kinahan, John. *Pastoral Nomads of the Namib Desert.* Windhoek: Namibia Archaeological Trust/New Namibia Books, 1991.

Kramer, Samuel Noah, ed. *Mythologies of the Ancient World.* New York: Doubleday, 1961.

Lattimore, Owen. *Inner Asian Frontiers of China.* New York: American Geographical Society, 1940.

Lawlor, Robert. *Voices of the First Day: Awakening the Aboriginal Dreamtime.* Rochester, VT: Inner Traditions, 1991.

Lawrence, T. E. *Seven Pillars of Wisdom.* London: n.p., 1926.

Leopold, A. Starker. *The Desert.* New York: Time-Life, 1961.

Limerick, Patricia Nelson. *Desert Passages: Six American Encounters with the Southwestern Deserts, 1840–1910*. Albuquerque: University of New Mexico Press, 1984.

Lines, William J. *Taming the Great South Land: A History of the Conquest of Nature in Australia*. Berkeley and Los Angeles: University of California Press, 1991.

Llagostera Martinez, Agustín. *Formaciones pescadoras prehispánicas en la costa del Desierto de Atacama*. México, DF: Centro de Investigaciones y Estudios Superiores en Antropología Social, 1984.

Lopez, Barry. *Desert Notes*. Kansas City: Andrews and McMeel, 1976.

Loti, Pierre. *The Desert*. Translated by Jay Paul Minn. Salt Lake City: University of Utah Press, 1993.

Lumholtz, Carl. *New Trails in Mexico*. New York: Scribner's, 1912.

MacLeod, Anne Campbell. *Letters from India*. London: Macmillan, 1911.

Mandeville, John. *The Travels*. Translated by C. W. R. D. Moseley. Harmondsworth, England: Penguin, 1983.

Martin, Henno. *The Sheltering Desert*. Edinburgh: Nelson, 1958.

Marx, Emanuel. *Bedouin of the Negev*. New York: Praeger, 1967.

May, Earl Chapin. *2000 Miles Through Chile*. New York: Century, 1924.

McLean, Fitzroy. *To the Back of Beyond: An Illustrated Companion to Central Asia and Mongolia*. Boston: Little, Brown, 1975.

Meighan, Clement, and D. L. True, eds. *Prehistoric Trails of Atacama: Archaeology of Northern Chile*. Monumenta Archaeologica 7. Los Angeles: UCLA Institute of Archaeology, 1980.

Merwin, W. S. *Travels*. New York: Pantheon, 1994.

Moorhouse, Geoffrey. *The Fearful Void*. Philadelphia: Lippincott, 1974.

———. *India Britannica*. London: Harvill, 1983.

———. *To the Frontier*. London: Hodder and Stoughton, 1984.

Morris, Yaakov. *Masters of the Desert: 6000 Years in the Negev*. New York: Putnam's, 1961.

Mowaljarlai, David, and Jutta Malnic. *Yorro Yorro: Aboriginal Creation and the Renewal of Nature*. Rochester, VT: Inner Traditions, 1994.

Mu'allaqat. *The Seven Odes: The First Chapter in Arabic Literature*. Translated by A. J. Arberry. London: Allen & Unwin, 1957.

Mudie, Ian. *The Heroic Journey of John McDouall Stuart*. Sydney: Angus & Robertson, 1968.

Muir, John. *Steep Trails*. San Francisco: Sierra Club Books, 1994.

Müller, Mark. *Namibia*. Volketswil, Switzerland: Living Colours, 1994.

Myers, Fred R. *Pintupi Country, Pintupi Self.* Washington, DC: Smithsonian Institution Press, 1986.

Negev, Abraham. *Cities of the Desert*. Tel Aviv: Lewin-Epstein, 1966.

Nelson, Bryan. *Azraq: Desert Oasis*. London: Allen Lane, 1973.

Neruda, Pablo. *Confieso que he vivido: Memorias*. México, DF: Editorial Joaquín Mortiz, 1974.

Newby, Eric. *On the Shores of the Mediterranean*. Boston: Little, Brown, 1984.

Onians, Richard Broxton. *The Origins of European Thought*. Cambridge, England: Cambridge University Press, 1951.

Ovid. *Transformationi*. Rome: Brettschneiders, 1921.

Owens, Mark and Delia. *Cry of the Kalahari*. Boston: Houghton Mifflin, 1984.

Oz, Amos. *In the Land of Israel*. San Diego: Harcourt Brace Jovanovich, 1983.

Palmer, Edward Henry. *The Desert of the Exodus*. Philadelphia: Chambers, 1899.

Parker, K. Langloh. *More Australian Legendary Tales*. London: Nutt, 1898.

Patnaik, Naveen. *A Desert Kingdom: The Rajputs of Bikaner*. New York: Vendome Press, 1990.

Peterson, Roger Tory. *Wild America*. Boston: Houghton Mifflin, 1955.

Petrov, M. P. *The Deserts of Central Asia*. Leningrad: Science Publishing, 1967.

Pfefferkorn, Ignaz. *Sonora: A Description of the Province*. Translated by Theodore Treutlein. Albuquerque: University of New Mexico Press, 1944.

Philby, H. St J. B. *The Empty Quarter*. New York: Holt, 1933.

Pianka, Eric R. *The Lizard Man Speaks*. Austin: University of Texas Press, 1994.

Platonov, Andrei. *The Fierce and Beautiful World*. Translated by Joseph Barnes. New York: Dutton, 1971.

Pliny the Elder. *Naturalis Historiae*. M. St Clare Byrne, ed. London: Etchells, 1926.

Poe, Edgar Allan. *The Narrative of Arthur Gordon Pym of Nantucket*. New York: Harper, 1837.

Polis, Gary A., ed. *The Ecology of Desert Communities*. Tucson: University of Arizona Press, 1991.

Polo, Marco. *The Travels*. New York: Orion Press, n.d.

Pond, Alonzo W. *The Desert World*. New York: Nelson, 1962.

Porch, Douglas. *The Conquest of the Sahara*. New York: Knopf, 1984.

Pumpelly, Raphael. *Explorations in Turkestan*. Washington, DC: Carnegie Institution, 1908.

Pyne, Stephen J. *Burning Bush: A Fire History of Australia*. New York: Holt, 1991.

———. *The Ice*. Ames: University of Iowa Press, 1986.

Ramos, Graciliano. *Barren Lives*. Translated by Ralph Edward Dimmick. Austin: University of Texas Press, 1965.

Ratcliffe, Francis. *Flying Fox and Drifting Sand*. Sydney: Angus & Robertson, 1942.

Rawicz, Slavomir. *The Long Walk*. London: Constable, 1956.

Roosevelt, Theodore and Kermit Roosevelt. *East of the Sun and West of the Moon*. New York: Scribner's, 1901.

Rothenberg, Jerome, and Harris Lenowitz, eds. *Exiled in the Word: Poems & Visions of the Jewish People from Tribal Times to Present*. Port Townsend, WA: Copper Canyon Press, 1989.

Rudolph, William E. *Vanishing Trails of Atacama*. New York: American Geographical Society, 1963.

Saint-Exupéry, Antoine de. *Courrier Sud* (Southern Mail). Paris: Gallimard, 1929.

Schoff, Wilfred H., ed. *The Periplus of Hanno*. Philadelphia: Commercial Museum, 1913.

———. *The Periplus of the Erythraean Sea*. London: Longmans, Green, 1912.

Seabrook, William B. *Adventures in Arabia*. New York: Harcourt, Brace, 1927.

Selous, Frederick Courteney. *African Nature Notes and Reminiscences*. London: Macmillan, 1908.

Severin, Tim. *In Search of Genghis Khan*. New York: Macmillan, 1991.

Sheard, Lauri E. *An Australian Youth among Desert Aborigines*. Adelaide: Libraries Board of South Australia, 1964.

Simpson, George Gaylord. *Attending Marvels: A Patagonian Journal*. New York: Harcourt, Brace, 1934.

Spencer, Baldwin, and F. J. Gillen. *Across Australia*. London: Macmillan, 1912.

———. *The Arunta: A Study of a Stone Age People*. London: Macmillan, 1927.

———. *The Native Tribes of Central Australia*. London: Macmillan, 1899.

———. *The Northern Tribes of Central Australia*. London: Macmillan, 1904.

St George, George. *Soviet Deserts and Mountains*. Amsterdam: Time-Life, 1974.

Stark, Freya. *Beyond Euphrates*. London: Murray, 1951.

———. *The Coast of Incense*. London: Murray, 1953.

———. *Dust in the Lion's Paw*. London: Murray, 1961.

———. *The Southern Gates of Arabia*. London: Murray, 1936.

Stein, M. Aurel. *Ruins of Desert Cathay*. London: Macmillan, 1912.

Steinbeck, John. *Log from the Sea of Cortez*. New York: Viking, 1962.

Stobridge, Idah Meacham. *In Miner's Mirage-Land*. Los Angeles: Baumgardt, 1904.

Strabo. *The Geography*. H. C. Hamilton, ed. London: Bohn, 1857.

Strehlow, Theodor Georg Heinrich. *Aranda Traditions*. Melbourne: Melbourne University Press, 1947.

Stroud, Mike. *Shadows on the Wasteland*. New York: Overlook, 1994.

Swift, Jeremy. *The Sahara*. Amsterdam: Time-Life, 1975.

Teichman, Eric. *Journey to Turkistan*. London: Hodder and Stoughton, 1937.

Thesiger, Wilfred. *Arabian Sands*. New York: Dutton, 1959.

Thubron, Colin. *Behind the Wall: A Journey Through China*. London: Heinemann, 1987.

———. *Journey into Cyprus*. London: Heinemann, 1975.

———. *Mirror to Damascus*. London: Heinemann, 1967.

Tschiffeley, A. F. *Southern Cross to Pole Star*. New York: Simon & Schuster, 1933.

Turnbridge, Dorothy. *Flinders Range Dreaming*. Canberra: Aboriginal Studies Press, 1988.

Twain, Mark. *Roughing It*. London: Routledge, 1872.

Underhill, Ruth. *Singing for Power: The Song Magic of the Papago Indians*. Berkeley: University of California Press, 1962.

Vámbéry, Arminius. *Travels in Central Asia*. New York: Harper, 1865.

Van der Post, Laurens. *The Heart of the Hunter*. New York: Morrow, 1961.

———. *The Lost World of the Kalahari*. London: Hogarth Press, 1958.

———. *Venture to the Interior*. New York: Morrow, 1951.

Westermarck, Edward. *Ritual and Belief in Morocco*. London: Macmillan, 1926.

Wharton, Edith. *In Morocco*. London: Cape, 1920.

Wilson, Edward O. *On Human Nature*. Cambridge, MA: Harvard University Press, 1978.

Wolpert, Stanley. *A New History of India*. 3d ed. New York: Oxford University Press, 1989.

Younghusband, Francis. *Among the Celestials*. London: Murray, 1898.